REBELLION IN WICKLOW

... uniting the Catholics and the Dissenters.

For a fair and open war I was prepared;
if that has degenerated into a system of
assassination, massacre and plunder
I do ... most sincerely lament it.

Theobald Wolfe Tone's trial speech, Dublin, 10 November 1798

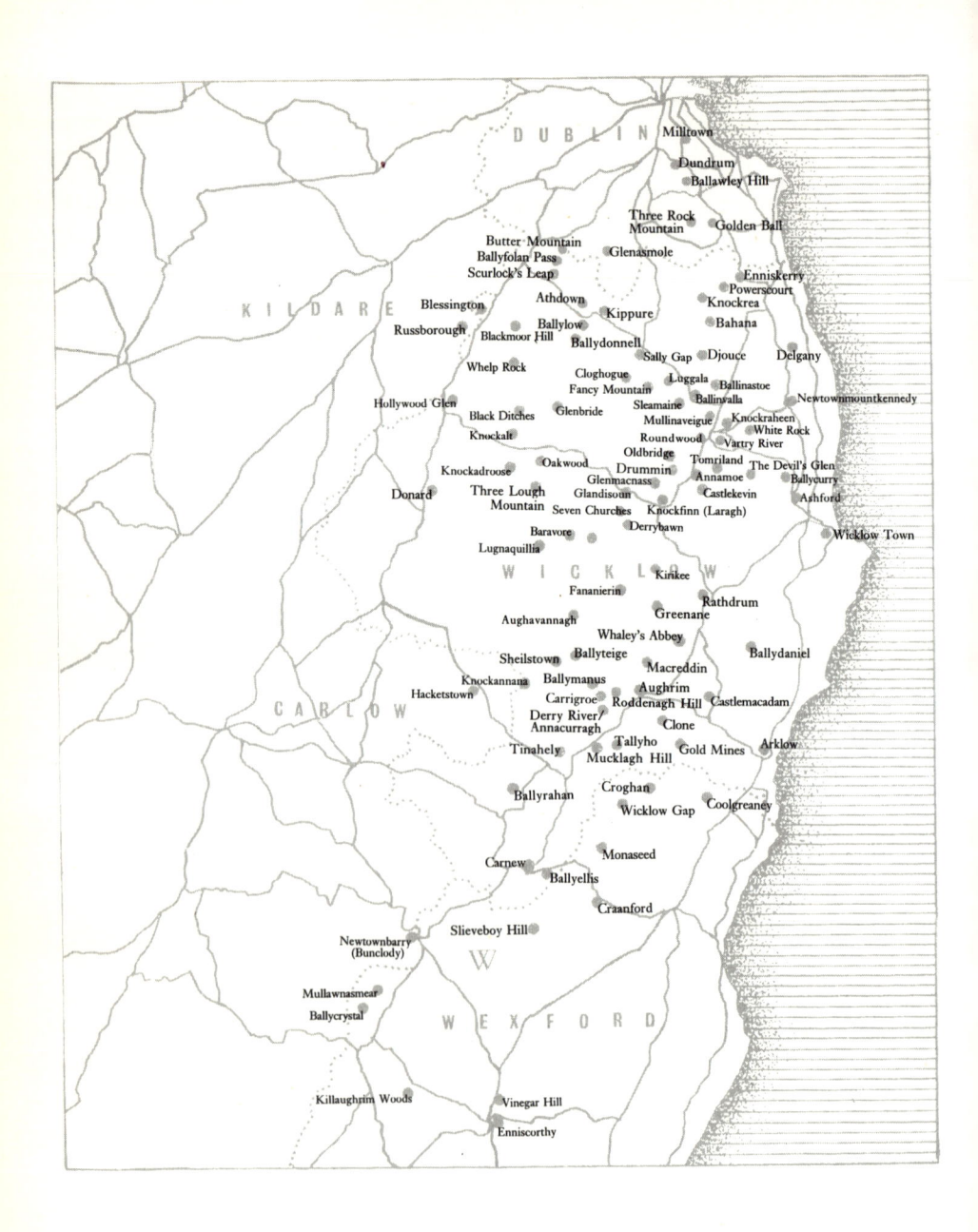

Map of South Dublin, Wicklow and North Wexford

REBELLION IN WICKLOW

General Joseph Holt's personal account of 1798

EDITED BY
PETER O'SHAUGHNESSY

FOUR COURTS PRESS

Set in 10.5 on 12.5 point Ehrhardt for
FOUR COURTS PRESS
Fumbally Lane, Dublin 8, Ireland
e-mail: info@four-courts-press.ie
and in North America for
FOUR COURTS PRESS
c/o ISBS, 5804 N.E. Hassalo Street, Portland, OR 97213.

© Peter O'Shaughnessy 1998
Holt manuscript © State Library of New South Wales 1998

A catalogue record for this title
is available from the British Library.

ISBN 1-85182-366-2

All rights reserved. No part of this publication
may be reproduced, stored in or introduced into
a retrieval system, or transmitted, in any form or by
any means (electronic, mechanical, photocopying,
recording or otherwise), without the prior
written permission of both the copyright
owner and publisher of this book.

Printed in Ireland
by ColourBooks, Dublin

FOREWORD

It comes as a shock that the much-quoted remark from Holt's memoirs about 'private wrongs and individual oppression' being the basis of the 1798 rebellion is not in the original manuscript at all but is an interpolation in 1838 by its editor, Thomas Crofton Croker. Peter O'Shaughnessy made it clear in *A Rum Story (Joseph Holt in New South Wales)* in 1988 how extensive the additions and omissions were. That book also provided a substantial account of Holt's Irish career and of the Irish sections of his writing. Because it was embedded in a book dealing with his Australian career, it never got in Ireland the attention that its importance deserved. However, Peter O'Shaughnessy generously made his transcripts available to others, and his work has been a catalyst therefore in the fuller story that is now beginning to emerge. The 1838 edition is itself a rather scarce one, and the accessibility of a new and complete edition of Holt's Irish account is essential to the task of completing the story of the year in Wicklow.

The publication of Holt's book in 1838 was part of a new beginning in writing on the great rebellion of 1798. Maxwell's *O'Hara* and Banim's *Croppy* in the 1820s treated the themes in fictional form; old participants like Teeling in 1828 and 1832 and Cloney in 1832 set the pattern in more direct accounts. All this writing was prompted by current political preoccupations more than by the past itself. Crofton Croker was influenced by Co. Cork politics and had already displayed, largely irrelevantly in the context of what he was actually publishing in the 1820s, an interest in the rebellion. His editing was an effort to sanitise Holt as a sort of edifying antidote, by a rebel who surrendered, to writing which, Banim apart, was unapologetic about the events of the year. More wisely, Isaac Butt in the *Dublin University Magazine* saw the dangers of any writing, with its silences and nuances, by a former rebel, and the *Magazine* was to rail throughout the 1840s against the flood of new writing on 1798.

Holt's account even in its sanitised form, as Butt had instantly seen, left much unsaid and raised questions. Peter O'Shaughnessy intersperses the memoirs with commentaries which help the reader, and the footnotes, embodying much research and local knowledge, further lighten his task. He stresses Holt's braggart tendencies and touch of megalomania. We have then to read the account with care, and the line between belief in what Holt says and rejection is a difficult one. What were his motivations as a United Irishman, and given the fact that he was a United Irishman earlier than he admits, how and why did he become one? Was Holt not only to contemporaries but even to himself the social equal of Hugo, the former high sheriff of Wicklow, that his account at times seems to imply? While we can accept his courage and abilities (and other testimony bears them out), how do we measure his reticence to say much about the rebellion from 30 May to mid-June, and his economy for later months in giving credit to, even to mentioning, not only McMahon for instance but more relevantly, because controversy in 1838 hinged on it, Michael Dwyer? Was sectarian tension quite as clear cut as Holt suggested to government when he was negotiating terms for himself after his surrender, or years later in writing an account which he intended to publish? All these questions require careful thought, and may not lend themselves to final or clear cut answers.

Holt's account because of its reticence, silences, and self-justification, has its limitations. Nevertheless, it is a valuable account especially for the months in Wicklow after the embers of rebellion in the central plain had died, and its detail and tone are often convincing (just as his Australian sections command respect in Australian history). Holt was already an object of some controversy because of rumours of informing on surrender, and in fact he appears to have given information, drawing a distinction which for guerrilla war may seem somewhat unreal, between informing on criminally motivated activity and on other actions. This issue was discussed at some length in Peter O'Shaughnessy's *Rum Story*, and is touched on briefly in the commentaries and footnotes. Inevitably, given long memories, such a sensitive question was still alive when on returning to Ireland in 1814 he opened a tavern in the Liberties: to some, on his own words, he was a croppy, to others an Orangemen. The same question surfaced in 1838, when the book put him literally before the nation, and rejection of the book by Isaac Butt in the conservative pages of the *Dublin University Magazine* and a revival of old rebel controversy in Wicklow repeated the former pattern of divide. Miles Byrne's own memoirs in 1863 have a special interest for attempts to assess Holt. Byrne, who had known Holt and served with him, was aware of the renewed controversy publication prompted, and his account was directed to carefully identifying the contributions of both Holt and Dwyer; without getting involved in taking sides in partisan fashion.

Inevitably, in Wicklow controversy centred on many things: the absence in the memoirs of a wider background notably of events in Newtownmountkennedy (though that was of itself not a defect as Holt confined his attention to this own circumstances, and only Crofton Croker's editorial work seemed to make Holt insensitive to the issues), and their lack of generosity to other participants, including Dwyer, whose role, though at the time smaller than Holt's, was real and who held out for several more years. In fact, it seems that it was this controversy at large that drew Luke Cullen into the collection of the surviving lore. Just as we must ask whether Holt was fair in withholding credit or recognition, the question remains whether Cullen's informants, and indeed Cullen himself, were fair. Luke Cullen's account has its own *parti pris* compared with the more judicious approach of Miles Byrne. But such questions are the very stuff of the ambiguous science of history. Indeed, the legends which have grown around Thomas Hugo, Holt's *bête noir*, equally pose the question whether, however highhanded his actions in the loyalist panic of April and May 1798, he was the monster, political and sexual, that local folklore paints. Such legends are usually not factual, but accretions to account for the prominent place, in hate or affection as the case may be, that figures of social consequence assumed in larger-than-life fashion in popular recollections.

Holt's account is an important one. Its detail itself bears out that (and it is often illuminating on aspects of local life, quite apart from the politics of the period), and it gains in significance as publication in 1838 prompted the quest for information by Luke Cullen who had just returned from a life of seafaring, and whose background in Bray was his conduit into the debate. Thus, the status of Holt's memoirs rests not only on the man's own standing but on the fact that their publication led to the compilation of the other main source for Wicklow's history in 1798. Luke Cullen's information was available to R.R. Madden, who made little use of it. It is among the many lesser ironies of history that Cullen's labours long languished in obscurity, just as for a century and a half Holt was accessible only in an edition which alike distorted the man and the events around him.

L.M. CULLEN

Trinity College, Dublin
February 1998

CONTENTS

Foreword by Professor L.M. Cullen	5
Preface	11
Calendar of Events	12
Songs	13
Editor's Introduction	15
THE LIFE AND ADVENTURES OF JOSEPH HOLT *prior to his transportation*, annotated	19
Editor's Postscript	137
Appendices	
1 Some opinions regarding Joseph Holt	139
2 Unrest in Wicklow in the months before the Rebellion	147
3 The battle of Ballyellis	149
4 Croppy Biddy Dolan	151
5 Informers' reports	154
6 Documents concerning Holt's surrender	158
7 Thomas Hugo	166
8 Holt witnesses an 'exemplary' flogging in New South Wales	168
Source References	171
Maps	2, 10
Index	172

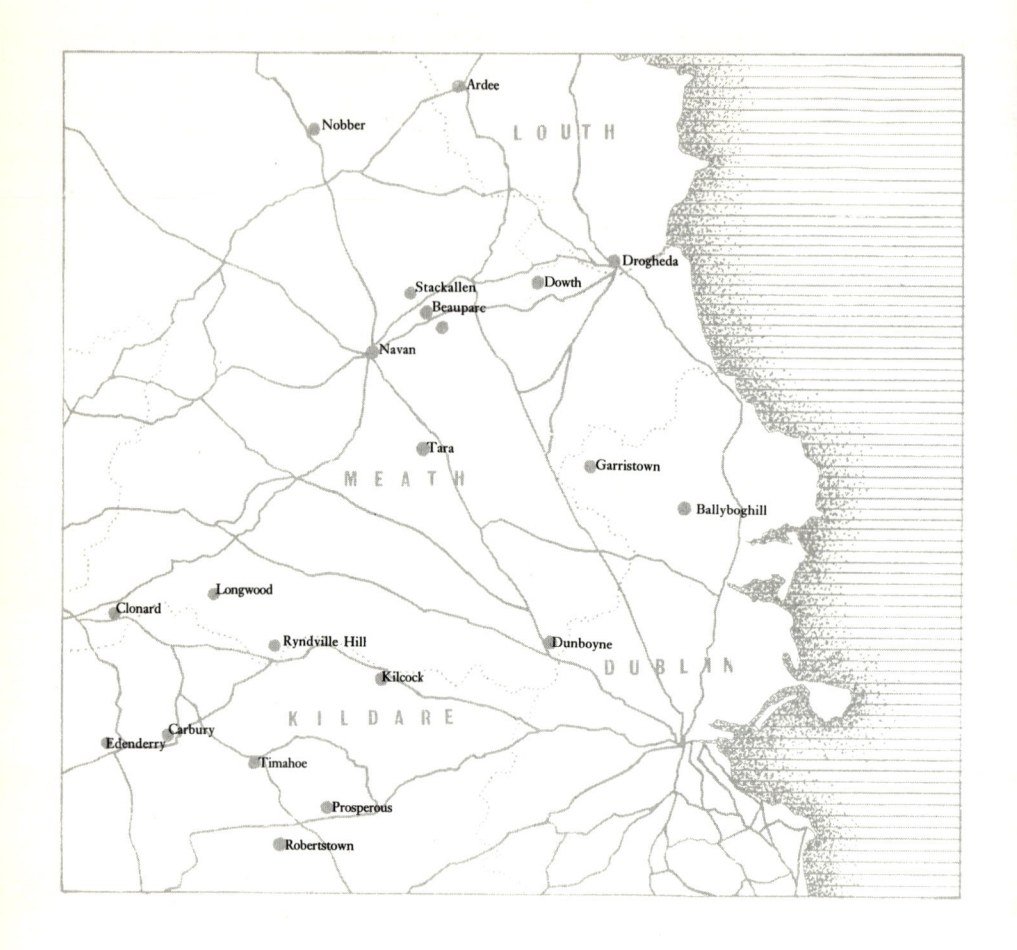

Map of part of Leinster

PREFACE

My grateful acknowledgements are, first of all, due to the late Sheila Holt, of Roundwood, and to Sean and Annie Holt, of Aughrim, whose encouragement in 1987 first set me on the trail of the story of the life of Joseph Holt.

During my researches in the Roundwood district over a period of ten years, Sean and Mary Malone and family, of Ballinacorbeg, have shown me such warmth and hospitality that they have become firm friends: to Mary Malone I owe thanks for introducing me to various people in the district who would help in my researches. Among members of the Roundwood Historical Society to whom I owe thanks for their encouragement and assistance are Ian Cantwell, Imelda Duffy, Sean Kavanagh, Kathleen Donohoe, Martin Timmons, Joe Timmons and Frank McGillick. Thanks also to the Reverend G. Baynham, of Castlemacadam (formerly vicar of Avoca), who was good enough to allow me to examine the baptismal register of the parish; to the late seanchaí and local historian, Billy Byrne of Glenmalure, who led me to the site of Pierce Harney's cottage and had lively tales to tell; to the late Professor Tom O'Neill, who made many suggestions which helped to elucidate the manuscript; to the late Robert Childers, who escorted me around the estate at Drummin and had much interesting information about Thomas Hugo; and to Shane Bisgood who, for a time, was manager of the estates at Drummin and Luggala.

Professor Kevin Whelan was unstintingly generous in referring me to documents which unlocked valuable clues to Holt's background, and especially to evidence of Holt's enlistment as a United Irishman. Ruan O'Donnell, who has become a recognised authority on Joseph Holt, shared with me research into newspapers and periodicals published at the time of the Rebellion, and some papers in the State Papers Office (as it then was). Above all, I owe him thanks for many details about United Irish military personnel and military engagements.

To Bernadette Hayden I offer warm thanks both for her hospitality and for her permission to reproduce the portrait of Joseph Holt in her possession. Among others in Ireland who provided me with valuable information are Joe Hayes, formerly Chief Librarian of Wicklow County Library at Greystones, Seamus Ó Saothraí and David O'Shea. Martin Beckett and Jennifer Broomhead, of the State Library of New South Wales, have always responded readily to my requests for information. I thank them for their indispensable assistance and co-operation.

Grateful acknowledgements are due to the National Archives, the National Library, Trinity College Library, and the Royal Irish Academy for permission to publish extracts from documents held by them; and, most especially, to the State Library of New South Wales for permission to publish the Holt manuscript.

Finally, thanks to my grandson, Daniel O'Shaughnessy, whose assistance in deciphering the Holt manuscript was invaluable.

CALENDAR OF EVENTS

1759(?)			Birth of Joseph Holt at Ballydonnell.
1780			Joseph Holt marries Hester Long, of Roundwood.
1780–98			Holt a farmer, overseer for the construction of roads and bridges, inspector of cloths at Rathdrum, a 'Tory' hunter.
1798	Mar.	12	Arrest of Dublin United Irish leaders.
		30	Imposition of martial law.
	May	10	Joseph Holt's house burnt down.
		23	Rebellion breaks out in Leinster. Centres on Wexford.
		25	First battle of Hacketstown.
		30	Wexford town captured by rebels.
		30	Battle of Newtownmountkennedy.
	June	2	Irish prisoners, held in Carnew guardhouse, executed.
		5	Rebels defeated at Corbet Hill in the battle of New Ross.
		6	United Irish outbreak in Ulster.
		9	Rebels defeated at the battle of Arklow.
		21	Rebels defeated at Vinegar Hill, Enniscorthy.
		25	Second battle of Hacketstown.
		29	Rebel victory at Ballyellis (Carnew).
	July	11	Rebels routed at Clonard (Midlands campaign).
	Aug.	21	French expeditionary force lands at Killala Bay, Co. Mayo.
		27	'Castlebar Races'; declaration of Connaught Republic.
	Sept.	8	General Humbert surrenders at Ballinamuck, Co. Longford.
	Oct.	12	French naval forces defeated off Co. Donegal.
	Nov.	3	Theobald Wolfe Tone, under arrest, brought ashore at Buncrana.
		10	Joseph Holt surrenders to Lord Powerscourt.
		11	Holt held in Dublin Castle. Trial of Theobald Wolfe Tone.
		19	Death of Theobald Wolfe Tone, after attempted suicide.
1799	Jan.	1	Holt put aboard prison hulk in Dublin Bay for Passage West and Cork.
	Aug.	24	Holt, his wife and two of their children sail in the *Minerva* for New South Wales, arriving 10 January 1800.
1812	Dec.	4	Holt, with his wife and son, Joseph, sail from New South Wales.
1814	Feb.	22	Holt lands at Liverpool. On 5 April he returns to Ireland.
c.1818			Holt settles in Kingstown (Dun Laoghaire) and writes his 'History'.
1826	May	16	Holt dies.

SONGS

All have heard sure of Vinegar Hill,
Likewise of the Battle of Tara,
And of General Holt and his men,
With the drums they call tanta ra-ra-ra-ra.

Protections for Ever *
(to the tune of 'Magic Grapes')

You rebels bold attend to me,
I'll lead you on to glory;
You never can mistake the way,
It's as plain as the nose before you.
To rob all night, and drink all day
You need not dread detection,
For when you're tired, you've nothing to do
But come in and get a protection.

      So now my heroes, fight away
      No matter what befalls us;
      We're always sure of a friend in court
      Success to Molly Wallis.

There was Holt so brave, on Wicklow Hill
He staid, while he had good weather;
And there he used to rob and kill
And did not care a feather;
But when the air was getting cold
He feared he'd get infection,
So gave himself up to a Lord so bold
Came in, and got a 'protection'.

---

*Royal Irish Academy MS 23 G 33(e)

Not him alone, but many more
Have got the like indulgence,
For royal mercy ne'er before
Has shone with such effulgence.
Some say this was the surest way
To gain the people's affection,
And faith on them a trick we'll play
As soon as we get protection.

So now I've plainly shown to you
A trade you cannot fail in
Ev'n though you're taken and sent abroad
It's a pleasant thing to be sailing.
At the yeos we'll laugh, we fear them not,
For they'd meet with dire correction
If they dare to lay a hand upon
A man that has got a protection.

Brave General Holt,
As wild as a colt,
Tis he is no dolt,
On the side of a mountain
He levels his gun,
And the *Delzos* run
Like a bit of fun
Beyond the powers of counting.

> At his pop-pop-pop
> He makes them to hop
> And they never stop
> To take a look behind 'em,
> Though brave Holt may not
> Be upon the spot
> Yet tis he has got
> The credit – if you mind 'em.

EDITOR'S INTRODUCTION

In 1965, after four years working in England and Ireland, I returned to Australia with my one-man show *Diary of a Madman*. This proved such a success at the Perth Festival that, finding myself on a winning run, I decided to settle in Australia again. Having been invited to tour another one-man show, I decided, in a surge of nationalist sentiment, to perform an anthology, compiled from ballads, poems, official documents, short stories and yarns, in which I would give audiences a two-hour tour through their own early history. To the surprise, I think, of the Arts Council and the Australian Elizabethan Theatre Trust the programme proved popular.

My research led me to a book published by Collins and compiled by the historian Tom Inglis Moore. Entitled *A Book of Australia*, it included the blood-curdling and passionately indignant description of a public flogging witnessed by Joseph Holt in New South Wales, which I always included in my recital (see Appendix 8). Years later, during my many stays in Ireland the name of Joseph Holt cropped up often enough in my reading to arouse my curiosity. In 1985 I returned to Australia to be Visiting Fellow for the year at University House, in the Australian National University in Canberra. Having easy access to the Chifley Library, I decided to browse in the Australian history shelves and see if I could unearth the Holt memoirs. When I did, I turned to the description of the flogging and was at once struck by the disparity between Thomas Crofton Croker's version and the much more arresting account in Holt's own words as transcribed by Tom Inglis Moore. Thus was I led to the Mitchell Library in Macquarie Street Sydney and the original manuscript.

Later, it was Dr Kevin Whelan who guided me to two tell-tale documents which proved that Holt had been enlisted as a United Irishman before his house was burnt.

THE TEXT

In 1818, Joseph Holt, articulate, if semi-literate, began to write, and partly dictate his 'History', as he called it, probably referring to copious notes he had made during his trials and adventures. Some sections, particularly those telling of his harrowing life in New South Wales, are lively and vivid enough to suggest that they were committed to paper shortly after the event.

The spelling of the 'History' is erratic, there are no paragraph divisions and, apart from random commas, there is no punctuation. I have assorted the text into paragraphs and punctuated it, but left the spelling intact. Where place names have been misspelt I have, when the name first occurs in the text, appended the correctly spelt name in square brackets

In reading the reports of Holt given by the informants of Brother Luke Cullen, one is left in no doubt that Holt had the gift of the gab to the point of garrulousness. Reading Holt's manuscript one sometimes has the impression that an uneducated farmer is *talking* – with great verve; perhaps, when 'the General' was in full spate, the scratching quills of the copyists were hard put to keep pace with his lively tongue; certain errors in the text make it clear that the copyist failed to *hear* the General accurately: how else would one explain Carbury Hill being written as Corebuey Hill (p. 49) other than that the speaker had slurred the word Carbury. On the other hand, when Mullawnasmear is rendered as Mullanasmareen (p. 22) it seems likely that a copyist has failed to read the original 'rough copy' accurately.

There are five different hands decipherable from the manuscript. The text transcribed on pages 19 and 20 of this book are written by A in a cramped, jerky hand whose configuration of the letters bears some resemblance to that of Joseph Holt; it may have been copied by a member of his family after discovering that he first few pages had begun to disintegrate through want of a folder. Page 21 and most of page 22 are written by B in a firm, clear hand. Five lines down in the last paragraph at 'putting on his small clothes', a third scribe, C, takes over. He writes with a meticulous, elegant, flowing hand suggesting that he may have been a professional copyist with experience as law clerk, and so responsible for the many pedantically prefaced 'saids', 'sds', 'aforementioneds', and 'abovementioneds' which punctuate the text, until the last paragraph but three on page 73 when, after the words 'survives near Rathdrum', a fourth scribe, D, takes over. He also may have been a professional copyist, one not bound by the conventions of legal terminology. On page 113, in the second paragraph, after 'will be after my departure,' Scribe C resumes and is responsible for the remainder of the text here published.

Holt's own hand is not evident in the Irish section of his 'History' here published, but it can be identified in the New South Wales section by comparing passages in the manuscript with some of the documents written by Holt after his surrender, for example, the letter to Matthew Doyle (see Appendix 7).

THOMAS CROFTON CROKER'S 'MEMOIRS OF JOSEPH HOLT'

Sir William Betham (Ulster King of Arms and an antiquary) who, like Joseph Holt, is buried in Carrickbrennan cemetery, Monkstown, Co. Dublin, knew Holt and spoke well of him. When Holt's younger son, Joseph, emigrated to New South Wales, shortly after his father's death, he left the manuscript of the memoirs with Betham, who was a close friend of Thomas Crofton Croker, to whom he passed on the manuscript. Croker, born in Buckingham Square, Cork, in 1798, was for thirty years a senior clerk at the Admiralty. He was also an antiquary and a distinguished collector of Irish folk tales, some of them later translated into German by the brothers Grimm. In 1838, Croker published the *Memoirs of Joseph Holt* in a much 'edited', sometimes bowdlerised, sometimes 'improved and enlarged' text.

Passages of Croker's own invention, or interpolation, as opposed to revisions, amount to a hundred and sixty, while there are more than eighty passages where names and expressions of opinion are 'censored' or cut from the manuscript text. In the manuscript Holt is often intent on representing himself as a reluctant rebel and sometimes feels called on to affirm his loyalty to 'His Majestie'. In Croker these sentiments are amplified. Croker's Holt is, for instance, made to say that he was 'forced into an association which I detested'; and the government and 'the Castle' are exculpated from all blame for the Rebellion. In the passage transcribed in page 87 of the present edition, Holt gives an intelligent summary of the causes of the Rebellion. Croker builds on this and puts the following words into his hero's mouth:

> If the laws were fairly and honestly administered, the people would have little reason to complain. It was private wrongs and individual oppression quite unconnected with the government which gave bloody and inveterate character to the rebellion in the county of Wicklow.

But even Croker's literary skill could not succeed in laundering Holt or making him acceptable to the Dublin literati, or at Trinity College. The review (written by the young Isaac Butt, of all people) published in the *Dublin University Magazine* in the same year (1838) as the publication of Croker's version of the Holt manuscript, dismissed the work with contempt (see Appendix 1.5 below).

When Lord Strangford indignantly denied the authenticity of an interview Holt claimed to have had with him at Rio de Janeiro (see *A Rum Story*) Croker seems to have developed cold feet: perhaps he felt the security of his long tenure as a clerk at the Admiralty in Westminster was under threat. In a deferential, even abject, letter to Strangford, he wrote:

> I trust your Lordship will perceive that I have most cautiously avoided identifying myself or my opinions in any particular, with my hero. My notes are merely quotations from contemporary authorities, for early in my editorship I made the discovery that Holt was not to be trusted, and this involved me in considerable difficulties as to how decently I could accept the task I had undertaken.

It was Sir William Betham who had 'saddled' Croker with this assignment. Betham may even have committed himself contractually to a publisher, thought better of it and persuaded Croker to take over. Whatever the case, it is intriguing to read of the strong implication that Croker was given access to State papers which, under the statutes, would still have been withheld from publication. No doubt those papers would have included some of the letters written by Holt and reports of the 'Information' he had given.

However, although Croker was flagrantly dishonest in disavowing the extent of his 'editorial' interference, one might enter a plea on behalf of Croker and indeed of Betham. The latter had known Holt personally, and both men were probably persuaded that Holt had told the truth about how he came to be enlisted. After all, many men had actually been driven into the ranks of the United Irishmen by force of circumstance rather than by conviction.

THE LIFE AND ADVENTURES OF JOSEPH HOLT

Joseph Holt's background

Joseph Holt is buried in Carrickbrennan cemetery, Monkstown, Co. Dublin. The inscription on the tombstone reads: 'Joseph Holt, late of Kingstown, who departed this life 6th May 1826 aged 64 years. Also his wife Esther, who died the 24th June 1827 aged 70. Erected by their son Joshua of Sidney [sic], also their daughter Marianne, relict of Mr William Shaw.'

If the inscription were accurate this would mean that Holt was born in 1761 or 1762. However, the register of births held in the Church of Ireland rectory at Castlemacadam, Co. Wicklow, records the date of baptism as 22 July 1759. In The Life of Michael Dwyer, *Charles Dickson says that 'in 1798, Holt was 42', which would put his year of birth in 1756, or 1755. Dickson's authority for this would probably have been the last lines of the Holt manuscript which, according to Thomas Crofton Croker, had been written by Holt's son, Joshua: 'Joseph Holt Departed 16th May, 1826 Aged 70 years'.*

Although occasionally families might allow some time to pass before baptism and official registration, it seems reasonable to assume that Holt was born in 1759 (see note 222).

Holt omits to mention that, in his early years he had been employed by Thomas Fleming, chief magistrate and, at one time, lord mayor of Dublin. The Courier *of 11 October 1798 stated that Fleming had dismissed him 'in consequence of some very wanton cruelty, exercised on one of the alderman's horses'.*

Known by the title of Genneral Holt in the Irish Rebellion of 98 – who was born in Bally Danniel [Ballydaniel][1] in the Parish of Castle McCadam [Castlemacadam], Cy [County] of Wicklow, younger son of John Holt of sd parish.

My father[2] had five sons more, namely John, Thomas, William,[3] Joshua and Johnathan, and one daughter, named Mary. My father held a very comfortable farm of land, at a very low rent, wich still remains in the possesion of my eldess brother's family to this day. My father gave them all trades in the building way, but me, but I was more inclined for agriculture than building, so I went to a friend of my father, a Mr John Low, a steward and gardinner to Mr Sweeny in the County of Dublin near Bray, and their continued five year and three months.

---

1 Ballydaniel (now known as Ballydonnell) is near Redcross. Holt later lived at Ballymoneen, above Castlemacadam.   2 Holt's father, John, died on 3 March 1785, and is buried in the old churchyard at Castlemacadam.   3 Of John Holt's other sons, William and Jonathan were enlisted as United Irishmen, the former having been involved in recruiting for the movement as early as mid June 1797. Thomas too was probably sympathetic to the United Irishmen; some years after the Rebellion his movements were watched closely by Dublin Castle agents.

Then I went to ventur[e] to the North of Ireland to improve my business. I stoped there a little time and, at my return, walking from the Phinix [Phoenix] Park,[4] I was acosted by a Gentle Man of the name of Phits Gerrald [Fitzgerald] – Captain of the 32nd Regiment of Foot destined for the East India Company. He and I had a conversation together and he said he would wish of all things he had the like of me in his Compa[n]y and he would a point me, on the first commencement, Pay Master Sergent; so I complyed and remained till I recruted of 32 men for sd regiment in the course of twenty-one days, but being requested home by my parents, I declined to go a broad and left the regiment.

I remaind with my parents till the year 1780, two years after, at wich time[5] I got marryide to Mrs Long's[6] daughter of Round Wood, County of Wicklow, a widdow who held a very comfortable farm of land under Andrew Price, Esqr.[7] I their remaind as farmer and agent over publick works in the Barney [barony] of Ballen Cur [Ballinacor][8] and parish of Dirrilosroy (Dirrelossary). I also held a commission under Sir John Blackiere [Blacquière],[9] Knight of the Bath and Chief County Keeper and Billet Master, and held that commission till the year 1793.

Being joined by Mr Brian Byrne and Mr Martin Byrne I saled [sealed][10] the woolen old drapery of the County Wicklow and Wexford and part of the County Dublin.

Holt's career prior to enlistment as a United Irishman

Holt's part-time occupation as a barony sub-constable enforcing the law must have earned him a qualified respect as well as a great deal of unpopularity for being a 'Tory' hunter – the word 'Tory' deriving from the Irish tuirseach, *one who tracks down criminals.*

According to Luke Cullen, the great collector of '98 reminiscences, Tory hunting was thought to be 'the expiring spark of priest hunting'. Whereas the Avoca district in which Holt was born had been heavily 'planted' after the Cromwellian war and was predominantly Protestant, in Roundwood Catholics were in the majority; so that being a Protestant might have added to Holt's unpopularity in the district of Roundwood.

For much of his life Holt would be dogged by the suspicion that, at heart, his

---

4 Holt's commission under Sir John Blacquière (see below) may have brought him to the Phoenix Park on the occasion, for Sir John was bailiff of the park and lived in a lodge there.   5 It is possible, but I think unlikely, that 'at which time' should read as 'at Tigh Linn'. If so, the marriage may have been celebrated at an earlier church built on the site of the present Church of Ireland at Nuns Cross, about two miles to the east of Tigh Linn, the youth hostel.   6 Mrs Long's maiden name had been Manning; her family was reputed to have Orange connections.   7 Price was a sheriff and Grand Jury member in 1790. He joined John Verner's Orange Lodge on 7 March 1798. Price was also one of the two local magistrates. Major Hardy looked on him as a 'dove'. In a letter dated 27 May 1797 Hardy wrote that Price was ailing and 'in action' and therefore not able to carry out all the duties expected of a magistrate in such troubled times.   8 More precisely, Ballinacorbeg. Ballinacor is south west of Rathdrum.   9 See note 4.   10 Assessed its quality.

sympathies lay with 'the Government' (which indeed they often did). This is why, at the outset of his 'History', he is at pains to define the parameters of his work as an officer of the law, and to stress his honourable principles: only too ready to hunt and capture a criminal, he scorns the idea of ensnaring a man by subterfuge. In his own eyes, he is 'to disobeyers of justice a terror' while, at the same time, amusing himself 'with the same gratification as should glow in breast of a sportsman in pursuit of animals of chace, and without fee or reward' (see note 252). As to the latter, he contradicts this later by saying the work 'brot me at least fifty pounds a year'.

Having often been called on to testify in court proceedings, Holt acquired some familiarity with legal terminology. This could explain why, in his 'History', he (if not one of his copyists) is apt to make use of terms such as 'the aforementioned', or 'the aforesaid'.

In the year 1794 there was a large banditti assembled in Dublin and came up in the neighbourhood of Roundwood in the County of Wicklow, robbed Luke Toole of Annamow [Annamoe], Laughlin Byrne of Ashtown, Christopher Limes of Nucraheen [Knockraheen], Mr Thomas Bell, near Delganee [Delgany] and several others.

Now, my gentle reader, I am going to give you and account of some of my passages in early days.[11] In August, 1794, when returning from Monnostown [Moneystown], a small village about two miles from Roundwood, I saw Andrew Price, Esqr., Francis Earley [Eardley], Esqr. in company with two men. Higginbottom [Higginbotham] (one of the two) addressed me, saying, 'Did you see Pat Rogers today?' I answered, 'No.'

'If ye set[12] him for me, I will give you one hundred pounds.'

I looked at him with scorn and asked him did Rogers deserve to be taken. He answered, 'Yes.'

I replyed, 'I will apprehend him,' and fulfilled my promise; but I told him that I should never become a setter. Mr Price answered, 'Sir, you are mistaken in Mr Holt. He will do the duty of a man.'

This Higginbottom asked me was I able to take him. I answered, 'Him and another like him.'

I soon gave them my direction and proceeded in search of Rogers, and after a chace of 500[13] miles, at the hour of twelve a night I took him in a place called

---

11 Holt is bent on establishing with the reader his credentials as an upholder of law and order. His days as a 'Tory' hunter (which he goes on to describe) were blemished by two charges of pilfering brought by men he had arrested. On one occasion, Holt's absence from court was excused by a note from Andrew Price saying that Holt was ill. The magistrates dismissed both charges as malicious.   12 A 'setter' gained the confidence of his prey by seeming to befriend him.   13 This may be a clerical error: the actual distance, as the crow flies, might have been about 50 miles; on the other hand, the chase might have involved a circuit of 500 miles.

Mullanasmareen [Mullawnasmear][14] in the corner of a field in the County of Wexford. Having received information of the road which the rober went, and having communicated the matter to Mr Price, who immediately wrote to Mr Thomas Bradnor, of Tomarcork.[15] I proceeded on my journey accompanied by two men, who were appointed by Mr Bradnor to assist me.

We rode on, till half after ten at night we came near new town Barry [Bunclody].[16] I bid the two men show me the first sheebeen house, where drams was sold. They showed me a house belonging to Mr Bulger. We dismounted, went in and called for a half a pint of whiskey and asked Mr Bulger if he had seen a young man on such a day in his house. He said he had, and that he was inquiring his way to Mullanasmareen. Said I, 'You are very right, that is my friend, he is a shoemaker by trade. He and I were in a dreadfull fight. I have reconciled the parties and am going to bring him home.'

'Very well, sir, I am glad to direct you the right way. You will find him at the Widow Hughses,[17] or at Tom Nails [Neill's] near Ballycrystal.

We drank the second half pint, being cheerful after hearing this good information. After we paid the landlord, we proceeded on our journey towards the house of Mrs Hughs. I told my companions to let me know when I was within a half a mile of the house. They did. I dismounted, and having a dark lanthorn and wax candle, I went into a house and light it, placed it in my lanthorn and put it in my pack.[18]

In a few minutes after, we reached the house of Mrs Hughs. I leapt from my horse and forced the door; and having turned my lanthorn, I pulled out a double barrel pistol with my other hand. I asked if they had a female lodger in the house. They said, no. The whole family was very much alarmed. I searched the entire house to no purpose. To hinder suspicion, I said that the servant maid had robbed my wife and that I had got information she was in that neighbourhood.

When [we] left the place, the girl of the house crossed the fields and repaired to the house of Tom Nale. I watched her running. She soon gave the alarm, and I saw a door open suddenly. I left my comrades and horse in the field, and, seeing light on a precipice and a man running out naked, immediately supposed him to be my object and pursued him to the summit of the hill. I saw the robber putting on his small clothes. I advanced and told him he was my prisoner. He said he was very glad that a man from his own neighbourhood should have him at his jurisdiction. He according submitted, but instantly took the advantage of me and brought me to the ground. Finding myself in that situation, I redoubled my efforts and sprung off my

---

14 The actual name has little phonetical concordance with what is written on the manuscript: this reinforces the proposition that the 'scribe' was probably copying from an earlier draft which was hard to decipher.   15 Two miles north of Carnew, and the site of a barracks (now demolished).
16 In Co. Wexford. In the 1930s a local plebiscite resulted in the decision to revert to the Irish name.   17 Although I was told that the Hughes family had long since left the district, I found that a field in Ballycrystal, quite destitute of habitation, is, to this day, known as 'Hughes's field'.   18 The pack attached to the saddle of his horse.

back and cast him under me. During this time he caught my sword. It happened to be by the blade. I instantly took off my garters, compelling him (by force) to dwell on the ground till I tyed him. When I had the game securd, my comrades comes up, asking me how I escaped or got rid of them. I answered them that I was a true sportsman that never mist the game.

This country is very mountanious. Its inhabitants are quite wild and wicked. I cried out to Devinan and Dobbs to tell the gentlemen that I had Rogers taken, merely as a prevention of any applying to take the prisoner. These words struck them with such terror[19] that I commanded several of them to fetch me to Justice James, of Ballycrystal,[20] leaving my pistols in a corner of the field till morning, as in the conflict they dropt from me. Some of these affrighted people says. 'Sir, Mr James [is] a very wicked man, he will probably fire on us when [we] call him.' I answered, 'I shall compel him to wait on me and company.'

In a very short time I entered the court, or lawn, of Mr James and most vehemently called. He instanly raised his room window, asking, 'Who comes there?' I answered my name was Holt and that I had in custody, 'Patk. Rogers, the noted robber', and called to him for protection. He immediatly ran downstairs. We all went into his house. He asked me several questions concerning Rogers, and, when I related to him a[ll] the detail of the particulars, he asked Rogers what induced him to come into that neighbourhood. He answered he came on a visit. Mr James answered him, 'Holt fortunately came to pay you a visit.

At this time it was about two oclock in the morning. I told Mr James that I had dropt my pistols in the field. Mr James sent a man with me to look for them and found them in the place expeced. During my absence Mr James took care of the prisoner Rogers. At my return, it was about five oclock in the morning, so I took leave of Mr James and proceeded on my journey.

I soon reached Newtownbarry. I went into a tavern. The news immediatly transpired through the town that Rogers, the noted criminal, was taken. In a short time three magistrates entered the tavern room. They wer accompanied by Henry Gowan, brother of Hunter Gowan.[21] Their curiosity led them to see the prisoner and, after some conversation, they told me that they would take the prisoner and commit him to Wexford Goal. I told him that he was taken and that by a man who was able so to do, and that I would not give up my prisoner as I considered that they gave me an insult, and desired that they might quit the room, and told them if they refused they

---

19 Perhaps because, lacking an official order, they and Holt might be judged to have taken the law into their own hands.   20 Ballycrystal House, the residence of Mr James, was about two miles to the east. It no longer stands.   21 John Hunter Gowan, of Mount Nebo, Co. Wexford, was the leader of a cavalry corps, known as 'the black mob' , and was described by Miles Byrne (in his Memoirs) as having the 'ferocious propensity of murdering his Catholic neighbours'. When the going got too hot, Gowan moved from the Gorey district, his 'home' hunting-ground, to Wicklow where he liked to go hunting with his hounds. On one such occasion he crossed the path of the elder Garret Byrne, of Ballymanus who, outraged at the presumption and effrontery of this 'upstart', laid into Gowan with his whip.

should receive the contents of my pistol. The aforesad Henry Gown told them that I spoke according to law as no person was liable to enter a room where a prisoner was in custody without leave from the person who detained him, then immediately quit the room and Rogers, the prisoner, said that hede loes his life before I should be offended. This expression caused a compasionate feeling to arise in my breast for him. I instantly ordered him the best breakfast the house could afford. This unfortunate man had sprained his leg in the engagement with me, so that I had no reason to fear of his effecting an escape.

I called after the aforesd magistrates for their assistance to put me out of their county. I told them I was well known in the County of Wicklow. I gave them little or no satisfaction who I was, as I was under no controul nor had I even a warrant against the prisoner. Though I shewed the leg was sprained, nevertheless the gentlemen caused him to be tyed under the horse's belly. A vast number came to the bounds of the County and parted me there. Then I liberated the prisoner from his cords. We proceeded to the house of Major Chamney, of Ballyrahin [Ballyrahan],[22] a worthy gentlemen who received me in the warmest terms of gratitude. When I entered the Major's yard he ran out and asked who was the man that had taken Rogers. I stept up and answered that it was I. He then asked my name, and from whence. I answed, 'Holt, from Round wood, and a near neighbour to the prisoner.' He said that I had given proof of being bapti'ed truly, 'as I see you are Holt[23] by nature'.

He ordered me to walk in. I answed, 'Sir, as soon as I see the prisoner sitting down in safety, I shall obey your order.' Then I sat down an got some refreshment. The Major asked me what magistrate gave me the warrant. I answered I never had any such thing. He imidiately sent for Henry Moreton, Esqr.,[24] who was a Justice of the Peace, and, on my proving (before him) that the prisoner was a Patrick Rogers who was so notorious in reprobacy as to be gazetted 1 [sic]. After said declaration Mr Moreton wrote his committual. During this time Major Chamney sent for two constables, by name Francis Rice and William Hendrick. I was made special in the committual.

We set forward for Tinehely [Tinahely], a market town. I entered the house of Ralph Tounrel and engaged a room. I ordered a bed for the prisoner. Those two constables, I heard them say, 'If he makes his escape we are not accountable, as Holt

---

22 The house still stands, a few miles south of Tinahely; opposite the gate is a Croppy monument. Chamney commanded the Coolattin Yeomanry and would be later killed during the siege at Ballyrahan House, in 1798, which followed the battle of Ballyellis, just to the east of Carnew. He is supposed to have offended Lord Fitzwilliam because he had seduced one of his own servants.   23 'Holt' taken to mean tenacious, reliable, presumably.   24 James Moreton, captain of Tinahely Yeomanry Infantry, would also figure in the siege at Ballyrahan House. His own house stood only a few hundred yards to the north, towards Tinahely. During the siege the lamps from Moreton's house shone across the fields, thus lighting up the movements of the rebels who were attempting to storm Ballyrahan House.

holds the committual.' I came in and says to Hendrick, 'You must go and sleep with Rogers, and Rice shall watch you both when both lying down.' I called the host and handcuffed them both. I said to Hendrick, 'I hope you won't endeavour to escape.' So I went to bead, it being the fourth night since I had slept.

I arose next morning early. I being only twenty-two miles from the town of Wicklow and six days from home, I hurried myself to get rid of my first criminal. On the way Rogers got very solid and serious. I asked him several questions, to which he answered, and from his information it enabled me to make out where more of his accomplices dwelt.

When I left him in the goal of Wicklow, I proceeded in pursuit of sd offenders for the space of 3 months, which served to amuse me with the same gratification as should glow in the breast of a true sportsman in pursuit of animals of chace, and without fee or reward.

Gentle Reader, was I to specify the particulas of each criminal person whom I was instrumental to bring to condign punishment in fine it would tire even Fabian[25] to relate each case, but I now refer ye to Captain Thomas Archer of Mount John to identify my fortunate exertions in taking robbers, pickpockets, coiners and other disobeyers of the law. I had such an element in punishing criminals as induced me to go to Dublin, where I apprehended a Martin Sinnot, a celebrated coiner, in New St., a John Morgan, a Thomas Keenan. In fine, my name was to the disobeyers of justice a terror.

I still continued as Alinnger [alnager].[26]

Why did Holt join the United Irishmen?

Holt's account in this section of his enlistment by force of circumstance as a United Irishman is, to say the least, disingenuous and acquires another intriguing dimension if the reader fills in the interstices:

After leaving the 32nd Regiment of Foot and returning to Roundwood, he had joined the Volunteer Corps in Arklow, having thus acquired a thorough training as a soldier to complement his subsequent experience as a 'Tory' hunter. In 1793 the Volunteer Corps had been disbanded due to fears that, far from offering protection against a possible French invasion, it might be nurturing 'seditious' elements. In the previous section Holt has left us in no doubt about his penchant for armed combat. How, in 1797, a year before the outbreak of the Rebellion, might he have viewed the Society of United Irishmen? In Co. Wicklow, the Ascendancy landlords were relatively benign and 'liberal', the climate permissive and, after April 1797, there had been such an acceleration in recruitment to the United Irish cause in the county that, by May 1798, it had the largest pro rata enrolment in Leinster: approximately 14,000 men. At first, with no evidence of it having a threatening

---

25 'Holt probably alludes to "Fabian's Chronicles". Semi-literate Irishmen invariably seize upon all occasions to exhibit the full extent of their knowledge, and the result is a national reputation for oratory' (Croker).   **26** Inspector who tested the quality and determined the grade of a cloth.

military arm, there had been no stigma attached to enrolment: many men, having also joined the local Yeomanry, were doubly enlisted. Until the autumn of 1797, although public meetings had been banned since 1794, it was not illegal to enrol: after the proscription by the viceroy, Lord Camden, Garret Byrne, one of those doubly enlisted, chose to resign from the yeomanry.

Against the tolerance of the landlord grandees of Co. Wicklow, and the liberality of its MPs, one might weigh the attitudes of the most powerful 'middle men' of Wicklow, one of whom was Holt's near neighbour, Thomas Hugo of Drummin (high sheriff of Wicklow, in 1796) and commander of the Yeomanry at Annamoe; the other, Thomas King, the powerful Rathdrum magistrate and commander of the local yeomanry, 'the Cronebane Men'. These two men were 'hawks', ever alert to hints of 'sedition' and proclaiming their loyalty to the crown with provocative stridency. In this they would have had the support of Dublin Castle and, in particular, that of Major Joseph Hardy, commander of the militia in Wicklow and North Wexford.

These are important factors to bear in mind when it comes to assessing the background to Holt's future career: an early enlistment would not necessarily have carried with it a commitment to military service; two of his brothers were enlisted, as also were his friends, Thomas Brady and Matthew Doyle – the latter a zealous proselytiser for the movement. Nor, although Dublin Castle bruited such a rumour about, did the United Irishmen have any Catholic bias prior to the outbreak of the Rebellion.

Might it not then be expected that Holt, with his appetite for 'the chase', would have doubly enlisted? Roundwood, one mile to the south of his home in Mullinaveigue, did not have a corps of Yeomanry, while Annamoe, five miles to the south, did – commanded by Thomas Hugo who, according to one of Luke Cullen's informants, had once been on friendly terms with Holt and had since (on Holt's testimony, which he is most unlikely to have fabricated in its entirety) become his sworn enemy. Moreover, the two men, probably both of the same social stratum, might often have come into contact with one another in Rathdrum, Holt, in his capacity as seal master, on occasions perhaps being called on to 'touch the forelock' to the squireen who, in 1796, had become high sheriff and, in the following year, was tipped to be appointed as a magistrate. At once then we have compelling reasons for Holt not being enlisted in the Yeomanry, and some persuasive reasons for him being inclined to take the United Irish oath, especially since, being fiercely ambitious, he would have been alive to the portents of a successful United Irish insurrection. But even then, surely it would have gone against the grain of this barony sub-constable?

Let us turn to two stories relayed by Luke Cullen about the circumstances of Holt's enlistment: one version is that on a day when a fair was due to be held in Rathdrum, an exasperated mob, their blood running high, turned on the sub-constable in Mullinaveigue, where Holt lived, and threatened his life; having escaped their clutches, Holt at once went to his friend, James Kavanagh, the most prominent United Irishman in Roundwood and proprietor of an inn and general store there, and, on bended knees, pleaded to be sworn in as a United Irishman.

Another story goes that Kavanagh, aware of Holt's brash ways and loose tongue, at first hesitated to swear in his friend, but eventually complied. Kavanagh's misgivings proved only too well founded, however, when Holt tried to enlist the aid of one of Thomas Hugo's stewards in procuring ashplants to make pike handles. The steward 'blabbed' to his master. After this, we might imagine, Hugo seized on this pretext to take his personal revenge on the creditor who persisted in harassing him.

Both stories may be founded on truth, nor would they be essentially incompatible with Holt's own version. It is not unlikely that Hugo's high-handed refusal to honour his debt to him was the last straw for Holt; and that, after the confrontation with that mob, he was faced with a stark choice: How, held at bay by that mob, could he turn to Hugo of all people for support? With the mob at his back, he would therefore fight Hugo: thus would this become Holt's personal war, not a war against the Establishment.

An alternative, or, if you like, a variant of, and sequel to, these stories is soundly based on fact, and 'Information'. This had been given to Lord Powerscourt by Daniel Nailor, who bore a grudge against Holt for initiating a prosecution against him for recovery of money owed to Edward Brady. Powerscourt informed Hardy, who later burned down Holt's house; in spite of himself, Hardy protests in a letter, since in general he had resolved on restraining his men from indiscriminate burning; what snapped Hardy's restraint was the discovery that Holt, abusing his vocation as billet master, had subverted some of the Antrim Militia whose lodging he had arranged: 'This irritated me so much,' wrote Hardy, 'that I burned his house.'

Although in what follows immediately in this section of his 'History', Holt fails to mention his presence, later in the text he does implicate Thomas King in the burning.

When had Holt enlisted? It could have been as early as mid 1797: a document cited by Sir Richard Musgrave in Memoirs of the Different Rebellions in Ireland, *lists Holt as holding the rank of captain in that year. Later in his 'History', describing his meeting with Lord Powerscourt, Holt says that, in November, it had been eight months since his enlistment, that is, he implies that he may have become committed to action early in March 1798, a critical month.*

On 29 March, Lord Camden had proclaimed martial law, and this had been taken by General Lake as licence to let loose a savage persecution of many Catholic farmers and others suspected of being United Irishmen. Major Hardy (Acting Brigadier-General Hardy, to be precise) had done little to check the activities of the yeomanry and militia, who had often run riot and burnt down houses, sometimes merely because they bore a personal grudge against their victims. This bloody mayhem actually boosted recruitment by driving hesitant farmers into the arms of the United Irish forces for protection. On the very day Hardy personally attended at the burning of Holt's house, 10 May, he had set three thousand troops at large to scour the countryside for arms. His claim that Holt's case had been exceptional can be assessed in this context.

The Rebellion broke out on 23 May. Against all expectations it soon centred on Wexford, where United Irish enrolment had been relatively low. Marianne Elliott has written that, since in Wexford and elsewhere, the insurrection was sparked off by local grievances and vicious sectarianism, it was not therefore a United Irish rebellion at all. That view is, in some respects, consistent with Holt's account of how he was drawn into the insurrection against his will. Against that simplistic bit of casuistry we might set the 'moral' pressures which may have been brought to bear on him by his family and friends; and perhaps above all, Holt's overweening personal ambition.

Finally, we might measure the degree of his reluctance to join the Rebellion in the light of our knowledge that he was listed as a United Irish captain in that document cited by Musgrave, which was probably drawn up no later that mid 1797.

On 30 May an attack was made on Newtownmountkennedy, but only one of the three columns assigned to the operation actually took part. The rebels were routed and Major Hardy licensed, or turned a blind eye to, the massacre of at least twenty-two civilians in the town. Sir Richard Musgrave reported that Holt did lead a contingent of six hundred men toward the town but that it arrived too late to take part in the action. Holt's forces had probably been thrown into disarray as a result of Hugo's burning of the village of Cloghogue, which he carried out as a reprisal for the attack on his house at Drummin.

After some time Francis Sing [Synge], Esqr.[27] (a gentlemen of fame for taking care of road, bridges, pipes, gullets, &c.) placed me as overseer over 84 perches of that road leading from Dublin to Roundwood.[28] My performance pleased him so well that he continued me for many years in sd employment.

Mr Thomas Hugo, of Drummeen [Drummin], spoke to me to measur a piece of that road leading from Newtounmountkenedy [Newtownmountkennedy] to Roundwood, in the parish of Newcastle. I measured 184 perches from a thornbush on John Hodges' field to the corner of Pat Keenan's house. I next estimated for arched cop-

---

27 Owner of Roundwood Park estate and, with Andrew Price, one of the two local magistrates. The tolerance and liberality of these two magistrates appears to have perturbed Hardy, who had proposed that Thomas Hugo be appointed to the magistracy. Hugo's appointment may well have been a decisive factor in Holt's decision to throw in his lot with the United Irishmen and take 'to the field' in active command; for henceforth Hugo (his rival?) would have the whip hand.   28 One perch equals five and a half yards. Thus the stretch of road covered might have been 462 yards, about a quarter of a mile. With the passing of the Road Act of 1760, all public works, such as this, had to be approved by the Grand Jury. Since Andrew Price was a member, it may have been that he brought some influence to bear in furthering the career of his up-and-coming tenant.

ing on Vartry Bridge,[29] under pining butments and paving arches. The whole entire work amounted to £89. 12s. 6d. – which was presented at March assizes, agreed to and paid to Abraham Crichley [Critchley], then county treasurer. Mr Thos Hugo was overseer with me.

I carried on sd work, and agreeable to estimation, and paid the men whom I employed every Saturday night. Mr Hugo neither supported me with money nor attention.

Pardon me, good reader, the labyrinth I must lead you through to explain that sd Mr Hugo's tyranny to me caused me to wade through most innumerable and painful sorrows. After the assizes Mr Hugo received the aforementioned sum from the treasurer; when I went for the money I was told by treasurer that Mr Hugo received it from him. I said I was very sorry that he done so as Mr Hugo didn't give me any money to pay the executors of sd work, and of cource that I now want the money to discharge the debts sd work involved me in.

On my return from Mr Critchly's I called to Mr Hugos, ask him for the sd money, which he promised to give me in a few days. I repeated my visits for nine different times. At length, being provoked, I told him that I would take as speedy steps for recovery of sd money as the law directs.

I went once more to the treasurer, leting him know Mr Hugo's conduct, saying I would immediatly have the advice of Counsellor Guinness of Messrs [Mercer?] Street, No. 9, that hede direct me what to do. I mounted my horse and rode of. I was hailed by the treasurer's brother[30] who advised the treasurer to pay me and deal with Hugo himself. He accordingly did. He (Mr Hugo) swore that hede be revenged of me and made good his most ungrateful and wicked designs.

Gentle and Impartial reader, on reading (perusing) my publication you shall see how the spirit of resentment roused me to obtain satisfaction on sd cruel & inhumane tyrant, Hugo. He was the first man who commenced burning houses in that part of the county of Wicklow. One morning he consumed 14 of his poor tenants' houses & came (to) the house of a Patrick Merigan [Merrigan],[31] asking him if he had his rent. Merigan said he would have it in the course of a week, that he had a piece of flannel and that as soon as he sold he would pay him. 'I shall give you a receipt in full,' says Hugo, taking out a pistol and shooting him dead on the spot. You must know that this poor man was called from his bed, which prevented his disconsolate wife having the trouble of striping him, being naked.

---

29 In 1863 this section of the Vartry river would be submerged with the creation of the Vartry reservoir, since then a source of Dublin's water supply.   30 James Critchley, who had a reputation for cruelty and ordered the beheading of two men in Glenmalure, using a large boulder as a 'block'. From time to time the boulder was said to 'weep' blood.   31 According to one of Luke Cullen's informants, Patrick Merrigan had been sworn in as a United Irishmen. If so, Hugo might have claimed 'justification'. Thomas Hugo *was* one of the most ruthless, probably *the* most ruthless, of those landlords in Wicklow who terrorised tenants by burning down their houses (see pp 167–8 below).

You shall now see that I was at this period employ in various stations where strict honesty and faithfulness was required. I was care keeper, wood ranger, sale [seal] master in Ballycurry for Mrs Tottenham,[32] with an unblemished carecter. I also was receiver and care keeper for Mr Miles and Bryan Byrne, of Ballynabarney, & Kurakee [Kirakee], and in the various situations of life that I filled enabled me to support my family in a decent manner. I was likewise billet master for all moving militias and army that passed through that part of the country.

In the year 1798 a part of the militia of the County Antrim came in that part of the country where I then lived.[33] I gave them billets on the different houses where I thought they would be best used and be most useful. I gave a billet on my own house to a serjaunt and his wife, having a spare bed and room.[34]

I had three presentments passed at March assizes to repair that season, so I got my work done early in Spring to be ready. I little thought of the following enterprizes to have to undertake: On the tenth day of May I was finishing cuting my turf.[35] On the morning of sd day, about half after five, Thos Hugo and some of the Fermangh [Fermanagh] Militia[36] came in my yard enquiring for me. Mrs Holt told them where I was. They went away and returned about twelve oclock and made a slight enquiry for me and was told as before. At two oclock I came to dinner and was siting in the parlour when the serjaunt's wife entered, saying, 'God help you, poor man, yr life is in danger.' I aroe up and asked her the reason. She said, 'Your house is condemned and I am ordered out of it.'

So I went out. I went to the door and saw a vast number of military men in company with Thos Hugo & from knowing Hugo's heart to me, conveyed to my senses his inhumane designs, which fortunately gave me notice to effect an escape. After some time, despairing of finding me, they disappeared. I returned to my af-

---

32 She lived at her estate in Woodstock. The Tottenhams possessed many estates, one of them abutting onto the Devil's Glen. Mrs La Touche, who later would play such an important part in Holt's surrender, was a daughter of Mrs Tottenham. 33 At Mullinaveigue, about one mile to the north of Roundwood. 34 In a deposition given at Dublin Castle after his surrender, Holt claimed that 28 men of the Antrim Militia deserted to him (see Appendix 6.1). It is only too likely that, at this stage, he had already enlisted some of them, as Major Hardy claimed. Having first emphasised his customary restraint, 'this irritated me so much,' wrote Hardy, 'that I burned his house.' 35 Holt's obituarist, writing in the *Courier* newspaper, stated that Holt had told him that, at this time, he had been absent in Carnew (see Appendix 1.1). In his Journal, Hardy's entry for 10 May says that on this day he 'commenced a general search for arms in one day through the whole of Wicklow, with about 3,000 troops'. This puts the burning of Holt's house into context. 36 During the following two years Thomas Hugo may have cultivated close relations with officers of the Fermanagh Militia. In 1800, his daughter Elizabeth – whom, according to Luke Cullen, he had once hoped to match in marriage with the dashing Billy Byrne (hanged at Wicklow town in 1799) – married Captain John Armstrong of the Fermanagh Militia. Cullen says that Hugo had once borrowed money from Byrne; if so, it is plausible that, at this time, he may have been hard pressed financially. The villain would prosper: with his memorial to the Church of Ireland archbishop of Dublin in 1800, soliciting permission for the marriage to be celebrated, Thomas Hugo tendered the astonishingly munificent donation of £1,000.

flicted wife, afflicted with anxiety of mind and said that Hugo was determined to purputrate his most ungrateful and undeserved promise.[37]

I instantly to[ok] my cane-sword,[38] a case of pistols, got some money from my wife, and took my leave of her, my son and daughter. I crossed Vartry River and went on to White Rock, formerly occupied by a Mr Edwards and at that time by Mr James McClutchy [McClatchy], sub-sherriff of the County of Wicklow. I sat down to meditate what step had I better take.

About 7 oclock, same evening, like Lott's wife I looked back – and my house in flames! I then roused spirits and vowed revenge of the wicked puputrator, as you shall hear I made good in some time after.[39] Good reader, promises made in wrath are often attended with difficulty and sorrow.

I then proceeded on towards the Devil's Glen, thinking on my wife and children whose lives were dearer to me than my own. My wife came to me, letting me know that this inhumane tyrant said that burning my house was little gratification to him, as he hadn't me to partake of the flames.

The soldiers [had] broken open my desk and made themselves master of all I was worth in cash,[40] loaded themselves with beef, bacon, hams &c. My wife and children, being destitute of shelter, was abandoned to travel about exposed to the efforts of the wicked and merciless.[41]

Gentle Reader, I omitted to remark to you that a man – name of Daniel Nailor who lived at Mullen reamon [Mullenraymond],[42] a miller whom I mad[e] pay the sum of seven pounds to Edward Brady of Balinacor [Ballinacorbeg] (by virtue of a decree I sold his mare), sd Nailor vowed that hede have his revenge of me. He

---

37 Of revenge. A reminder that Hugo had previously warned Holt.   **38** Hollow walking-stick, which could serve as a scabbard, or sheath, for the sword. Holt has inadvertently let slip circumstantial evidence of his enlistment prior to the burning: under martial law, which was in force at this time, he would not have been permitted to have weapons.   **39** On 16 June *Saunders News-Letter* reported that Hugo's house and outlying buildings, had been burned to the ground, this being the second attack on the house in two weeks. Although Holt probably led the expedition, in his 'History' he does not fulfil his promise to tell the reader what form his revenge took. He may have been deterred by the thought that, although twenty years had elapsed since the burning and his enemy, Thomas Hugo, had died in 1809, Hugo's son, Captain Thomas Hugo, was still living and might have brought charges against him had Holt admitted complicity. According to Tom King, Holt undoubtedly did take part in the burning. On 28 March 1799, Neil Devitt was tried and found guilty of taking part in the burning. His punishment was to be deported to serve in the army of the King of Prussia. The same issue of *Saunders News-Letter* reported the burning of the houses of John Critchley, of Laragh, Abraham Critchley of Derrybawn and William Weekes, of Annamoe. At least five houses were burnt out in Tomriland, five in Ballinastoe and three in Castlekevin.   **40** In Holt's obituary in the *Courier* it seems to be implied that certain compromising letters were found in Holt's house.   **41** Later in Holt's 'History' we learn that, in July, his wife, Hester, and his two children, were staying with Holt's brother at Ballinascorney, near Bohernabreena. Subsequently, Hester would come to stay at the Mill House, in the north-eastern corner of Andrew Price's estate and probably was given some protection by her landlord. Perhaps Price was absent at the time of the burning and Major Hardy, Hugo and Thomas King took advantage of his absence.   **42** Hollybrook, just outside of Bray.

attended accordingly at the burning of my house. At this time the country was under martial law, so that any miscreant who swore disaffection against any individual was liable to die and no further investigation.[43]

I continued on my journey towards the Devil's Glen where I met with a few pursecuted creatures similar to myself. We betook ourselves to a cave where we passed the night. Next morning, being the 11th of May, an old man, name of Edward Saul, came to look for me, carrying with him some refreshment. Many words passed betwixt us concerning the terifick appearance the present times made.

I cannot help to remark that at least ⅓ of the people of sd Glen was Protestants,[44] but, an short, I discovered it was hard to be sure who had escaped the oath of a United Irish man, though I realy think it must be nothing less then diabolical influence should imbibe such an idea in the heart of man; but I hope from the aforesaid barbarous treatment I have received will form an apology for my iritation in endeavouring to obtain satisfaction of that most cruel Hugo. Gentle reader, I write from no disgust or bigotry to any sect of people, nor will I spare explaining the facts and cruelties that I saw by each sect. I write from my own knowledge and not from verbal information.[45]

Night approaching, I betook to my cell, which was a hole in a rock in the Devil's Glen. A young man, name of John Arundle [Arnold],[46] stayed with me all night. The 12th inst. in the morning I was cordially visited by my old friend, Edward Saul, bringing me support as the day before. When refreshed, I walked out, wishing to hear from the distressed people of the sd Glen, but to my sorrow couldn't hear a sentence from my wife and children.

I being at the time loaded with sorrow mixed with the spirit of revenge, I says, 'Come, Arundle, come as far as Bolinalea [Ballinalea] (a small village about 1 mile

---

[43] This is no special pleading but an accurate report on the terrorist tactics authorised by General Lake.   [44] The proportions Holt cites may be correct but we ought not assume that he had made a count of heads, or even that the figures are based on personal observation. After his return from New South Wales Holt is likely to have read all, or part of, the Histories written by people such as Musgrave, Taylor and Teeling, and based his figures an their accounts. Nevertheless, it is a significant indication that, at this stage, Holt did not feel, as he would later, 'exceptional' because of his Protestantism.   [45] Here the reader might take pause: given that Holt has concealed his enlistment as a United Irishman prior to the burning of his farm, and saddled the villainous Hugo with all responsibility for his being thrust into allegiance to a cause whose principles he claims to be anathema to him, has not the writer forfeited the right to credibility in what follows? I don't think so. While the burning of Holt's form was certainly not the occasion for his enlistment, his feud – and perhaps rivalry – with Hugo may have swung the balance and landed him in the United Irish camp, where no doubt this 'Tory' hunter would have been warmly welcomed by two of his brothers and by his friends, Thomas Brady and Matthew Doyle. In truth then, Hugo may have been critical in Holt's enlistment. In some circumstances, Holt may have been on the same social footing as the squireen: they had rubbed shoulders at Rathdrum, where Hugo may have come to be exalted above him – in the post of high sheriff no less. Holt had watched his enemy's star rising. Now Hugo was a magistrate. For Holt that might have been the last straw, enough for him to go over to the other side.   [46] From Ballycurry, which adjoins the Devil's Glen.

distant) and we will get some whiskey.' He readily complyed, and so we went. We crossed Ashford bridge & came to the house of Thos Kavanagh.

Mrs Kavanagh knew me very well (she yet servives) – and gave me refreshment, saying, 'My dr Holt, I am sorry for your misfortunes. I would with a good heart give you support for a year, could I convey it to you with safety.' I drank freely for some minutes, which only served to agravate my mind, by bringing to more lively recolection the state of my distressed family.

Mr Kavanagh runs rapidly to the room, saying, 'You will be taken, for here comes Marks and Chapman.' I asked her was there only two? She answed, 'No.' I replyed, 'I shall take them.'

I took out my pistol, and walked towards them, saying, 'Do ye want me?'

They answered, 'No, sir.'

I replyed, 'You lye, you damned cowards. I'd soon send ye to Eternity.'

Arundle and I passed safe into sd Glen.

At this time the drink began to opperate on me, which kindled my effection, and I set out in quest of my agrieved family, first borrowing a musquet from one of my persecuted comrades and a few rounds of ball cartridge, prepared my pistol and set forward to Millinavigue [Mullinaveigue], by [but] could get no tidings of my care.[47]

There were several of the militia stationed at Justice Price's. I[t] happened at the time I arived at the ruins of my dwelling that four of the sd militia was passing from Roundwood to Mr Price's. I was so exasperated from my former treatment that, (knowing at this time) all of their army was my sworn enemies, I fired on them, which made them expedite their motion to Mr Price's. The[y] got under arms instantly, saying Holt was coming 'with at least a hundred men.'[48]

I charged my peice and walked towards a neighbour's house. Sd person told me my family were well, and said the army had consumed every thing in my house, taking with them money and, in fine, everything they wished to be encumbered with.

I then walked back to aforementioned Glen, remained there for three weeks, each day hearing more news of the confused state of the country. At this time there were about 60 men in sd Glen, in the like forlorn and wretched state as myself.[49]

47 Irish expression for 'my children', or family.   **48** Another significant slip of Holt's. If he had not already been enlisted and held office as a captain, it is not credible that, in such a short time, he would have been able to muster a hundred men. And who more likely to know that he held rank than members of the Antrim Militia?   **49** The preface to this section describes the various engagements which Holt has thought it politic to overleap. Although it is possible that he has compounded an early visit to the Devil's Glen with another in late May, I fancy that the '60 men' in 'the like forlorn wretched state' were rebels wounded in the battle of Newtownmountkennedy on 30 May. Mrs Ann Tottenham believed the number of rebel refugees in the glen were 'in vast numbers' (Musgrave, *Rebellions*). Archibald McLaren, of the Dumbartons, believed that 'eighty skulking rebels had been killed' in the glen, 'around which a cordon had been established'. On 30 May, Major Hardy did indeed burn out the glen. Charred stumps testified to this for some years afterwards. Sir Francis Hutchinson's plantation on the south side was completely destroyed, while the Tottenham estate, on the Ballycurry side, escaped.

I called a council of advice. I rimarked to them that I saw several men whom I conceived to be spies, from which I said it was safer to remove. They were all residents and seemed not willing to quit. I mustered up my little affairs and stepped on towards my old ruins and got to the Grouce [Grouse] House, over Legallaw [Luggala] Mountain. Being weary, I lay down on my grassy bed and slept for some time soundly. Next morning, looking towards the Glen, and saw it in a conflagration.

I gave God thanks for the present escape.

Holt's activities in May and early June 1798

Holt wishes to skip over a multitude of events by telling the reader, at the start of this section, that he 'proceeded promiscuously towards the mountains'. 'Promiscuously'? A tell-tale word: since those events were usually rebel defeats and did not redound to his credit, Holt might have preferred to leave them unrecorded; and perhaps because he had, at that time, entertained the idea of extricating himself from the Rebellion. But the most pressing reason for the omission would surely have been that a description of his activities would have left the reader in no doubt of Holt's long-standing membership of the United Irishmen.

There is no evidence that Holt took part in the battle of New Ross, at Corbet Hill on 5 June, but it is almost certain that he was in New Ross at the time: a page in Commissary Dieman's book of accounts refers to him having been allocated provisions by the Commissary there, and accords him the rank of colonel. Since it is virtually impossible that he would have been entitled to the rank, this may have been a courteous gesture offered him; although, given his own account of his assumption of the rank a few weeks later, and that 'General' Garret Byrne had managed to get out of Dublin only on 4 June, it could be earlier evidence of Holt's pretensions to supreme leadership: thrusting himself forward, he may have claimed the rank. After all, who else from Wicklow was in the running but for Byrne who, Holt might well have reasoned, had been dragging his feet?

For further evidence of Holt's gratuitous assumption of the rank, although his actual rank was that of captain, see note 55 and Appendix 5.1.

Other 'promiscuous' engagements which Holt fails to mention, and in which he took part, were the first battle of Hacketstown on 25 May and the battle of Newtownmountkennedy on 30 May. Nor does he mention the battle of Arklow on 9 June, the outcome of which was critical to his movements.

Holt's account of the 'conflagration' in the vicinity of Glandisoun and the engagement at Ballinvalla Hill seems intent on representing himself as by no means relieved of his responsibility to uphold law and order, as does his reference to Andrew Price who, by inference, would be ready to commend Holt's operation. This Janus-like attitude will persist throughout much of Holt's 'History'. At this early stage in the Rebellion did he maintain some contact with his 'dove' landlord?

In saying that he was 'much surprized' to find himself on Blackmoor hill, does Holt infer that he had detached himself from his company? Perhaps they detached themselves from him because he seemed equivocal about his commitment to the rebel cause and had yet to gain their trust. Once having 'wandered down' to Whelp Rock and having decided to assume command, the die is cast.

That, until this stage, Holt may have wavered about his allegiance seems implicit in his reference to the 'Moving Magazine'. If Colthurst has been so indiscriminate as to lump in every woman in Roundwood as a 'United Irishman' what chance would there be for him if he held off from commitment?

I then proceeded promiscuously through the mountains, not knowing where I was going; at length I perceived a smoak arising out of a glen. I then crossed to the further side of sd glen and discovered about 70 forlorn creatures who were gratified to see me. They were cooking some fresh beef which hunger and fatigue compelled them to procure. Nor was I in less need of it, not having taken any for 24 hours.

There was a little fellow there who was titled Colonel McMahon. The poor creatures adored him as a little king.[50] The first thing he proposed to me was that there was a house near Rathfarnham who possesed a large quantity of money. I answered that it was no affair of mine, that I was no robber. I kept myself quite cool, minding their maneuvres. As McMahon saw I wouldn't comply with his burglarious designs,[51] he would have me taken under pretence of being a spy, only I was identified by several of the partie.

I stopped there from Thursday till Saturday evening, when I proposed to sd creatures it was more safe to remove to a more elevated party of the country.[52] The creatures seemed to think my advice was sensible, but McMahon sd that I might go

[50] Holt has blatantly misrepresented the truth. Colonel McMahon was a lawyer, who practised in Aungier Street, Dublin, and was held in high esteem by the United Irish executive there. Father John Martin, of Drogheda, an emissary from the Thomas Street Committee of the Irish Directory in Dublin, had been sent by the Thomas Street Committee to 'co-operate at a fixed time and to excite the people to act'. He met Holt between 6 and 8 June to discuss plans for an attack on Dublin, on the assumption of a United Irish victory at Arklow. After his capture, Father Martin gave 'information': Holt 'knew me as soon as he saw me,' testified the priest. The meeting, he said, took place at Holt's brother's house in Ballinascorney, when Holt had claimed that he could show him three hundred rebels, which he commanded, in the vicinity (see Appendix 5.2 for relevant informer reports). It would have been at this time that Holt would have run into McMahon. [51] Whereas, in their quest for food, Wicklow rebels could draw freely on the farms held by other United Irishmen, or turn to their own homes, McMahon's party, having been recruited largely from Dublin city, were forced to rely on raids to secure provisions. This obviously offended Holt's law-abiding principles. If, adopting the manner of a barony sub-constable, he rebuked McMahon, the colonel might well have been antagonised by this 'upstart'. [52] Probably to Cloghogue, to the south-west of the Sally Gap, below Duff Hill. SPO 620/18/1 (a report to Under-Secretary Cooke) says: 'Holt has sent to Dublin to say that he will not act without orders from the executive.' Having learnt of the United Irish defeat at Arklow, Holt seems to have thought it prudent to bide his time. Ruan O'Donnell has suggested that the real reason for the 'division' between Holt and McMahon was that the latter was reluctant to postpone the attack on Dublin. I would suggest that the lawyer, McMahon, may have suspected the former sub-constable, Holt, of wearing two coats: having learnt of the rebel defeat, 'might not this upstart have decided against precipitate action, and be contemplating going over to the loyalist camp?'

alone as none of them should go with me. I answered, 'As they are at free will, they may judge for themselves and do as they think most safe.'

I then, with lively motion, stepped over a small brook, saying, 'My boys, any of you who wishes to save yr lives, come with me.' I At this time there were 118, and 116 of which came across sd brook to me, leaving McMahon with 2 men.

We marched on to the Old Iron Mills, where we killed a bullock, we being in much need of it – this being the 15th of June. In the morning of the 16th I marched to Fancy Mountain,[53] over Clohogue [Cloghogue]. I then heard from my disconsolate family. I then sent out a foraging party, who brought a bullock to camp, belonging to Andrew Price, Esqr. It happened to be a beast I reared indeed.[54] It hurt my feelings. However, necesity compelled me to have him killed.

Sd forageing party brought 8 prisoners in before me. I now refer to several of sd prisoners who yet survive, namely Joseph Thomson,[55] Richard Barry, David and William Edge, and others. First investigation was on Thomson, who was woodkeeper for Francis Sing, Esqr. I found nothing criminal against him, save only being atested with the oath of a United Irish man, so couldn't accuse him of more the negligence of duty. Barry was proved to have taken the oath [of] secrecy. I liberated him.

The two Edges were accused to be Orange Men, but, on strict examination nothing but bare accusation. However, I detained them till evening, when I let them go. That night they told Lord Powerscourt what happened with me. They instantly joined his corp.

On the 17th inst. I marched to Glandisawn [Glandisoun] – situate over 7 Churches, Co. of Wicklow, where I discovered 180 creatures abandoned as myself.

On the 19th inst. – Got information that there were some Yeomen burning the adjacent neighbourhood. I instantly called to arms, ever wishing to be instrumental to prevent destruction. I then asked an opinion of some of the most sensible of my company. The[y] all wished to put – if possible – a stop to the conflagration. So – instantly examined the quantity and state our firearms were in – found only 13 guns fit for duty. I eagerly wished to try the pikes. However, the places the yeomen were committing sd inhumanity was 5 miles distant necessitated me to go on rapid.

We met on the side of Ballinvalla Hill. When in view of each other, both parties got quite serious. I took winward of the army and commenced quick fire. I endeav-

---

53 Adjacent to Luggala.   54 In 1799, James Casey was court-martialled for stealing two bullocks, worth £17, from Andrew Price.   55 Thompson was a wood ranger on the estate of Francis Synge. In a long deposition, held in the National Archives (see p. 154f below), Thompson, who had probably been enlisted as a United Irishmen by the Roundwood innkeeper, James Kavanagh, casts doubt on Holt's right to be ranked as a colonel, his tone suggesting that Holt is an ambitious upstart. He also states that Colonel McMahon was in command at Whelp Rock, perhaps an implicit comment on the rivalry between Holt and McMahon. Another interesting feature of the deposition is that vicious sectarianism was already rife in the ranks of the rebels: Thompson says that they were about to execute him at the foot of the Round Tower in Glendalough when one of the rebels [William Lennon] rushed forward to protest that it would be sacrilegious to spill Protestant blood on holy ground.

oured to force down the pikes, but to no affect. My amunition being very scarce, I soon discovered the distance betwixt the army and me was to long to force the pikes to action – which was worse of my side, having no determined person to mind the motion of the enemy. So, not liking the possition I was in, I sent two of my best men over to the left of the partee. When stationed, they began to play, or fire balls across; which threw them to confusion. I then ordered the Pike men to retreat and go down the hill, as the Yoes [Yeos][56] could follow them – by which means I obtained a safe retreat, tho' so few, without missing one man.

The next Bulletin, tho, stated that the Rebells retired behind a ditch, but I am confident that there never [was] a ditch in same place since the birth of Christ, but to the reverce. Some of my men ran after their enemy till quite out of breath.

And same day, some of my enemy's horsemen going home, got their horses shod by a Felim Sally.[57] And, when they asked him what was his charge, on Sally answering, they shot him at his anvil. I refer the whole of this occurrence to Andrew Price, Esqr.[58]

I then marched over the mountain till my limbs grew quite weary. I lay down and slept, and when I awoke in the morning, I was much surprized to find myself on Blackymoore [Blackmoor Hill][59] on a heap of stones that made fast the fixture where a Walter Read was gibbeted.

On the 20th of June I wandered down to Whelp Rock[60] where I found a vast number of creatures , but no sort of uniformity appeared among them. I spoke to some of them who bore the name or title of Captain, asking that, in case they were attacked, what form did they mean to proceed? There answer seemed to me to not have the smallest oeconomy.[61] I immediately endeavoured to set them to rights, as I of couce could expect nothing but immediate death.

Being resolved not to lose my life dastardly,[62] I commenced exercising them. And every day the number was augmenting.

I next commenced providing gunpowder. I chose a la[r]ge, rather an ill looking weoman, whom I titled 'The Moving Magazine',[63] and sent her to procure two large earthen crocks, some saltpetre and sulphur. I directed my men to pull heath in order to make it into coal.[64] I infused the coal in the crocks – which process enabled

---

56 Yeomen.   57 The surname Sally still occurs in the Roundwood district; Sally Gap probably owes its name to the family.   58 Does Holt imply that his landlord may have been sympathetic to him?   59 Mountain ridge close to the Wicklow-Kildare border, to the east of the present-day Blessington reservoir, stretching from Carrig to Lackan, as far as Sorrel Hill.   60 Colonel McMahon often set up camp at Whelp Rock. It may be that Holt behaved high-handedly, claimed the rank of colonel, and attempted to wrest command from McMahon, and even that he succeeded in the attempt. On 24 June both men would take part in the second battle of Hacketstown.   61 Holt uses the word to mean efficient use of resources.   62 Stupidly, or wantonly.   63 She may have been Susy, the daughter of Phelim O'Toole, of Annamoe. Thomas Crofton Croker's vivid description of this Amazonian lady may be a figment of his imagination; on the other hand, it may have been relayed to him by Sir William Betham, Holt's friend and neighbour in Kingstown (Dun Laoghaire).   64 That is, the heather was burnt to a powder.

me to make some powder.[65] Though soft, it anwered my expectation by placing a better sort for priming. This usefull creature, or Moving Magazine, went through many camps to procure amunition. She obained many from such of them as were disaffected. I procured her a basket of ginger bread and some fruit to prevent suspicion. We must here observe that she was metamorphosed into a United Irish man from a respectable personage's testimony – namely Wm Coletrust [Colthurst], Esqr., who declared that every weoman from Tinahinch bridge to Roundwood was a United Irishman.

After Vinegar Hill: Holt's prospects for leadership
Since Holt fails to put what follows into context, at this stage in the 'History' we would do well to pull back and survey the national and indeed the international scene.

Napoleon had kept the English in an agony of suspense. The large fleet he had assembled in mid May was rumoured to be bound for Ireland and the prospect of a massive French expedition would have given a great boost to the morale of the United Irish forces. It would probably have been many weeks before the news was confirmed that the fleet was actually headed for Egypt.

On the other hand, by his time the new viceroy, Lord Cornwallis, had taken over from Lord Camden and, at once, offered an amnesty to any man who, provided he had not been guilty of murder, would lay down arms and return to peaceful pursuits.

And the catastrophic defeat at Vinegar Hill on 21 June 1798? Would not that have encouraged defection among the rebels? Perhaps not. Now that their blood was up, most of them were probably bent on revenge and all the more determined on victory. Capping all other considerations, the most encouraging harbinger of victory for many would have been the persistence of the glorious summer weather, surely a heavenly benediction of their cause?

Although he never mentions the words, 'Vinegar Hill', reading between the lines it seems obvious that Holt would have been looking for a scapegoat for that defeat. In his eyes all of the lately arrived leaders have been found wanting, Edward Roche being the prime culprit, while the scarcely fledged Garret Byrne, no matter that he may be a scion of the most distinguished Catholic clan in Co. Wicklow, is unschooled and inept, and with his 'misconducted influence' hinders Holt's 'designs'.

---

65 'Holt's "mixture" would have been perfect gunpowder, if he could have granulated it. From the want of granulation a considerable portion must have been blown away unfired in the explosion' (Croker).

I remained there unobserved, till Garret Byrne, Fitzgerald, Captn. Perry, Esmond Cane [Kyan], with many more, came to us;[66] and a Captain O'Neill,[67] who I found to (deservedely) bear the title of a Captain of a corp of robbers, but quite destitute of the least military oeconomy.

Several small scirmishes happened with us and Yeomen. Some of our most respectable men concluded to go to the County of Wexford.

The same morning I was invited to breakfast with Father Donolan [Donnelan] of Black Ditches.[68] I went accordingly and, at my returning, I observed the men in a circular position. Thinking my presence might be instrumental to prevent misconduct, I hastened my steps. When I arived I [was] much surprized to find, inside said circle, a young man on his knees, name of Pillsworth, who said he was clerk in the Ordinance Office. The pieteous look he gave me shall never be erased from my recolection.

I asked what was aledged to him, desiring him to arise. That diabolical minded wretch, Neill [O'Neill], said he was a traitor. I asked him his proof. He handed me a letter, which he had taken from the young man, saying, 'That's sufficient to seal his crimination.' On reading the leater, I observed that he had nothing to do with the dictation, being only a mesinger.

I next asked Neill, 'Did this young man fire on you?'

He answered, 'No' – that he hadn't arms.

I told Neill that I would have him tryed for willful murder. I then asked the trembling captive to cease his fears, and only requested hede relate to me the sequel. He said, 'Sir, I am a servant who was going with that letter from my master, who happened (unfortunately) to be observed by Neill – who robbed me of my watch and five guineas.'

Then Niell, in order to shadow his wicked deeds, said that the prisoner was an Orange Man.[69] I asked his proof but could find none. I then said that he diserved

---

66 Two days after the defeat at Vinegar Hill, having camped the previous night at White Heaps, at the foot of Croghan hill. It is typical of Holt that he should fail to make sympathetic mention of their marathon journey. Garret Byrne, of Ballymanus, adjutant-general for the Wicklow United Irishmen, had been in hiding in Booterstown, Co. Dublin, until 4 June. The fact that only Anthony Perry is accorded a rank by Holt – and a mere captaincy at that – suggests an intriguing sub-text: the entitlement to leadership is still in a state of flux.   67 Holt's judgment on O'Neill may be coloured by some resentment that, in September, O'Neill would break with him and go his own way.   68 Black Ditches is at Lockstown, about three miles south of Valleymount, the latter being situated on the edge of Poulaphouca reservoir – an arm of Blessington lake.   69 Ponsonby Pilsworth was the illegitimate son to a Captain Pilsworth, from Greney, near Baltinglass; a man of this name was listed on the rolls of the Dublin lodge of Orangemen. Holt may here be confused in his chronology. One of Luke Cullen's informants, putting the incident in the second week of July, at the outset of the march towards the Midlands, gave the following account of the confrontation: 'a man named Dowling said that "there was none so indignant at this inmanly expression as Joe Holt he immediately leaped from his horse, rushed into the ring and in a very bold and determined manner said no man shall be put to death here for being a Protestant. I am one born and reared myself and am as true to the cause going forward as any man here but if he be an orangeman let him die" ' (Luke Cullen Ms 8339)

punishment for his baneful conduct – which caused him to absent, in a lurking manner, continually robbing.

I then called a Wm Lannin [Lennon], whom I observed to [be] a man of good conduct, and committed prisoner to his care. (Same young man still survives near Dublin Castle). And you may see this reward of cruelty – as sd Captain Neill died by the Almighty causing a bit of meat to obstruct the passage to his stomach on the Curragh of Kildare. N.B. His late dwelling was in Francis St., Dublin.

Recolect we were at this time at Black Ditch [Black Ditches], from whence we marched through Hollywood Glen & Donard. We observed there the ruins of many burnt houses on our way. I went to the house of Justice Hynes – as I had a particular acquaintance with him these many years, at the assizes and sessions of Wicklow. Likewise he rode many miles with me in quest of Rogers, that noted robber [see pp 21ff, above]. I advanced to the door of sd Mr Hynes, leaving the most formidable part of my company in the adjacent road. Two female servants appeared to me. I asked if Mr Hynes was at home. The[y] answered: Not. I told them my name, saying that no depridation should be done to his place, in return of gratitude for his repeated good actions. Several of my unruly company commenced breaking windows. I instantly drew my sword, standing on the steps of the door, saying, 'The next person that attempts to commit the smallest outrage or crime here shall die by my hands.' It was at this time my company discovered the description of man I was.

I called to the servants for some drink, saying that Mr Hynes never let me from his house without refreshment. The sd two female servants instantly brought me some spirits and a bottle of wine, which I divided with Captain Perry and Garret Byrne.[70]

We marched on, but at the end of [a] little village was a man hiding in a remote part of a potatoe garden. He was taken and received imediate sentence, was brought inside a field, situate on the left side of the road leading from Donard, at the end of a small cabin. I wasn't by at his trial. It was very short.

At this time Edward Roche was General of the Rebels, which rendered me not liable to support of his inhumanity.[71]

At this time I assumed the title of Colonel, having only 960 men[72] – which were inhabitants of the County Wicklow. Gentle Readers, these occurrences happened only twenty, years ago. Should any doubts dwell an your minds I am able to refer ye

---

[70] Not very subtly, Holt would like to suggest that the shared libation was symbolic of the equal status which he presumes as his due.   [71] I suggest the paraphrase: although this unworthy man may have held the rank of general there were limits to my subordination.   [72] Previously, Holt had been able to play cock of the walk. Now, confronted with these senior officers, crushingly defeated at Vinegar Hill, the Wicklow man, Captain Holt, is expected to defer to the men from Wexford, and to General (?) Garret Byrne, who had been in hiding in Dublin since 4 February and has surfaced again only a few weeks ago. It won't do. Although he lacks the statutory qualification of 1200 men serving under him, which would have entitled him to the rank of colonel, Holt *assumes* the title of colonel.

to to many surviving eye witnesses and I shent fish for the smallest undeserved merit.

We then marched on, and that evening arived at Ballymanus,[73] and then got orders from (then) General Roche, each man stationed by his order. I was appointed to over look the night guards. I placed my advanced guards, posts and picquets. Having them stationed, I sent in quest of Wm Lannin and the former captive, Pillsworth, whom I saved from an undeserved death. He was brought to me and, after a conversation of about half an hour, he related to me the cause of his misfortunes. I told him to make himself content, that that God who always brings something to clear the innocent would still protect him. I instantly wrote a pass to protect him on his way to Dublin and gave him part of what money I possessed to support him. I sent Wm Lannin and another to conduct him with safety through the out posts. I took my leave and wished him safe to his journey and I never heard more of him till I was a State prisoner in the Castle of Dublin and sd Jn O'Neill taken. The same young man was sent for to identify what he knew concerning Neill and, in the presence of Major Sir [Sirr],[74] he stated verbatam what I am after relating concerning him.

We shall now return to Ballymanus. We stoped there till about 12 oclock. Next day our picquets informed us that a vast number of army was observed in quest of us, marching from Rathdrum. From thense we moved slowly to Redna [Roddenagh] Hill. The sd army appeared to us over Aughrim.[75] I procured a spy glass, which enabled me to asertain their number. I asked General Roche what he thought best to be done. He said they had two field pieces that probably would play too heavy on us. I answered, if 11,000 was terrified to meet 200 men, 'how should you expect ever to obtain the smallest victory?' I then offered myself and the few I commanded to take the front of the engagement and the rest to make two divisions and to flank them, right and left. A Madg[e] Dixon[76] exclaimed, 'Shame on Roche!'[77] saying, though a weoman, that she would take command of either right or left wing. Some said amunition was scarce. I answered that cowardice was the chief means of making it scarcer, but that I hoped I should soon have plenty, with two field pieces. I directed my standard to be displayed, advancing towards the army.

Began to advance, but weren't it for the misconducted influence of Garret Byrne, I am confident I would have accomplished my designs.[78]

---

73 Near Aughrim, where Garret Byrne had his estate. Not to be confused with the townland of the same name, near Gleneraly. The house, which had been sacked by the Tinahely Yeomen infantry corps while Byrne was lying low in Dublin, was burnt during the Rebellion and later rebuilt. It still stands.   74 The chief of police. Sirr's rank was a civil, not a military one, that is, he was the *town* major.   75 The engagement was reported in the newspapers.   76 A ferocious Amazon of a woman; Roche's sister. Her brother-in-law, Father Dixon, was the first Catholic priest to be given permission to say Mass (on 19 April 1803) in the colony of New South Wales.   77 A very broad hint from Holt that he is being given a cue to seize command.   78 Another broad hint that Holt feels Byrne is not worthy to be thought of as General and that he, Holt, should hold supreme command. Holt was acutely conscious of his social inferiority. It should be borne in mind that he

The army fired two shells at us, but didn't fall nearer than 150 perches. So their trumpet sounded and they marched away.

We moved from this possition, but there aroese a difference in opinion among our company. The majority accused our chief with cowardice and on the night of same day, a John Arundel [Arnold][79] was called to duty by sd Chief General Roche. He said, 'Sir, I was on duty all last night. I must know from Colonel Holt, to whom I belong, whether he will allow his men to suffer in sitch a manner.'

Genl Roche, most ungratefully and unprovokedly, discharged a pistol at Arundel. The ball pass through the crown of his hat. A man, named of Cullen, from his stature, induced me to direct him to carry our colours. He told me of the misconduct of Gl Roche, as have never felt the dread of a Court Martial.

Went to General Roche, who was sitting in company with Garret Byrne, Captain Perry and Colonel Fitzgerald. The[y] requested of me to sit down and [I] told the gentlemen that I wished to address General Roche on a very serious business. They said, 'Sir, speak yr sentiments.'

'Ask Roche what induced him to purputrate so cruel an action as to disharge a ball at one of my men?'

He seemed to deny it, but Arundle was at the door at the house of a Patrick Kavanagh of Tallio [Tallyho]. I desired him to come forward and specify the truth. General Roche, finding my accusation fairly proved, he endeavoured to appoligize with me. I answered my intention was 'Not to be be appeased with less than a exchange of a shot with you.'

The gentlemen (beforementioned present) entreated me to sit down, but I refused, retiring to an aajacent place with my own men, where I remained till morning, when we marched to Wicklow Gap,[80] from thence to Monaseed,[81] where we halted.

Holt's victory at the battle of Ballyellis

It is probably true that the battle-weary Edward Roche, sensing that his star was on the wane, found it prudent, and perhaps politic, to hand over command to the brash, overweening Holt rather than to the novice Garret Byrne, for all the latter's distinguished lineage. However, Holt's assertion that all of the other leaders 'absented' from the battle of Ballyellis is not only absurd and untrue but positively megalomaniacal. In his account of what follows we are meant to assume that, now

is probably writing this twenty years after the event, and, braggart that he was, may be retrospectively inclined to put himself on the same footing as his 'betters'. One of Luke Cullen's informants said that Holt was always respectful of Byrne. Another recollected that Holt addressed Byrne as 'Yer Honour'.   **79** From Ballycurragh. As a neighbour of Holt's, who had been close to him after the burning of his farm, Arnold is entitled to protection from his soi-disant colonel. The challenge to a duel which follows is ludicrous enough to be staged in a farce. Perhaps, like some of Luke Cullen's informants, we should doubt whether it actually took place.   **80** In Wexford. There is another Wicklow Gap, further north, and west of Glenmacnass.   **81** About five miles east of Ballyellis, where the critical battle will soon take place.

that he has proved his mettle as a leader, the Wexford men are only too ready to defer to him as a leader. This may have been true.

Byrne and his men headed north, where the engagement at Ballyrahan, three and a half miles south-west of Tinahely took place (see notes 22 and 24).

At this time all our men were in much need of refreshment. These that were most vigilant in procuring food on their march were best off. I shall never forget the sudden death poultry of every description met with on our march, plucking them as they moved along – which clothed the leeward side of the road with feathers. I cannot but remark that several of the Co. Wexford inhabitants [behaved] with great kindness and respect; in particular, one young man says, 'Sir, as you are not used to such hard living as the generality of us are, come along with me and I expect that you shall get a warm reception.' I departed, left orders with my party where they should find [me], in case my presence should be required in my absence.[82]

We went to the house of Knox Grogan, Esqr.,[83] where I was sumptuously received. I was refreshing my much exhausted spirits with mulled wine when one of my men came to me, saying that General Roche required my appearance in haste. I soon reached his tent. He told me the enemy has made their appearance and requested I would take the command on sd day. I complied, saying, 'I shall endeavour to use my utmost dexterity, hoping the Almighty would direct me.' I directed each officer to be immediately stationed at the head of their party.

The enemy was a mile distant. My men, by directions, fell in 12 deep. I ordered 500 of the best musquet men for my front guard, followed by 1000 pikesmen, and that three cars and horses should be stationed right across the road. I directed 100 musquet men to stand behind the cars which were to defend us. I had 1000 musquet as reserve. I directed each officer how to act. I marched in the rere with 1000 muskets.[84] I made the remainder of the pikes men to march before us. The three horses beforementioned were so fast tyed that they couldn't quit their possition.

The ditches[85] of sd road on each side were quicked impenetrably with crab and thorn. The dykes[86] were five feet deep, so that a middle sized man's head would scarcely appear over sd dykes. I order several of the pikes men to make as many holes in the hedges as possible, so that all might retire – to induce the enemy to come in.

Every thing I directed being put into imediate execution, I kept the enemy back while the vacancyes in sd hedges were making – I gave orders to the pikes and

---

82 County rivalry might be detected in the sub-text. Holt, the Wicklow man, is now only about three miles from the border of his native Wicklow; and yet, despite his being a 'foreigner', the peasant folk of Wexford recognise his worth and defer to him.   83 The rebels may have taken over his residence. Knox Grogan had been killed by rebels at the battle of Arklow an 9 June. His brother, Cornelius, might have been expected to inherit the property. However, having been, held under arrest – probably quite unjustly – for high treason, he was executed on 28 June, perhaps on the very day that Holt was being wined and dined in his house.   84 Holt has the insouciant habit of 'rounding off' his estimates to the nearest dozen, hundred or thousand.   85 Irish usage, that is, hedges.   86 In English usage, ditches.

musquet men to retire back. The army was approaching with great precipitancy and, seeing my men giving way on every side, they were sure they had nothing to do but hew down all before them. But, to their great surprize, the[y] immediately found themselves close confind in the centre of their enemy. The musket stationed in rere of the cars fired on them with rapid motion. Several of the pikes men, not having time to quit the dykes, necessiated them to take an active part in self preservation. I then ordered the remainder of the musquettry to close the ranks behind, so that the enemy could neither pass nor repass.

There was a black trumpeter,[87] who belonged to the enemy, who had the life of a cat, as he took more piking then five white men. I saw his ears taken off before he expired. Having in them two gold rings induced a man to put them in his pocket. This black man, during his torture, exclaimed the pass words of a United Irishman. This skirmish, from the moment of action, was not more than 20 minutes, leaving 370 of the enemy dead. I lost only 2 men – who were wounded before. And only 4 wounded in this action, who soon recovered.

During the action, I perceived a young boy who, from one of sd dykes, passing his pike into the side of a horse soldier who couldn't immediate draw it back, the soldier fell to the ground. The boy put his hand in soldier's pocket and took from it a purs containing 35 guineas, which was some of the plunder they made the day before. The boy was instantly seized by one of his comrades to wrest the money from him. He cried to me for relief. I instantly restored him his well entitled prize, taking it into possession till I delivered it to his father, name of Gough, residing within one mile of Clone, the well-known residence of Charles Coates, Esqr.

There was one instance happened during sd action which I must remark: One of the Britons[88] whose horse received a stab of a pike in the haunch, which animated

---

87 Anthony King was his name. According to Luke Cullen's informants, King also pleaded that he was a Catholic. Being one of the hated 'Ancient Britons' his pleas for mercy were ignored because 'the remembrance of his flogging was too fresh'. 88 Meaning the 'Ancient Britons', a notoriously cruel Welsh regiment which had run amok at Newtownmountkennedy on 8 April. Of that day Thomas Parsons wrote to his brother, Sir Laurence Parsons, that they took 'six of the inhabitants selected indifferently from those they met in the street and without any trial whatsoever or previous suspicion of guilt, hung them ... others were half strangled, others beat and wounded' (Luke Cullen). In the New South Wales section of his 'History' Holt compares those atrocities to the savage inter-tribal ritual warfare he had witnessed near Sydney: 'I could not compare the native battle to anything, only the Ancient Britons cutting the haunches and eyes off of the young women in the fair of Newtownmountkennedy in the year of ninety eight.' The victory at Ballyellis may have been all the sweeter for Holt because of his chagrin at the belated arrival of his forces to participate in the battle of Newtownmountkennedy on 30 May. On 2 June, 41 of 61 prisoners held in Carnew guardhouse, one mile to the west of Ballyellis, had been summarily executed on the orders of Lieutenant Patten of the Antrim Regiment. The recollection of that atrocity must also have made revenge taste the sweeter for the United Irishmen. Mr Lee, headmaster at Carnew secondary school, 1997, says that the site of the battle was closer to the town of Carnew than where a monument commemorating it has been erected. He took me to a field where he believes it actually took place and pointed to some humps on the ground, which, locals say, mark the graves of the slaughtered Ancient Britons. For many years after the battle it was the custom of Carnew Protes-

the animal with such vigour as caused him to fly over the seeming impenetrable fence, which purchased an escape for his rider to Carnew's malt house. There was a company of soldiers and infantry in sd malt house, which held a constant fire on us. I steped forward to descry the situation and found it impossible to cease their fire. I am able to announce that ¾ of my company never saw one of the aforementioned men fall. The only officer was to appear after the action was Garret Byrne, who chided me for standing in the road.[89] I concluded with Byrne to draw the me[n] to Sleebuey [Slieveboy],[90] hoping it should induce the enemy to quit the malthouse; which we accordingly did. It had the desired effect – the[y] immediately quit their nest, made a feint to follow us but, as soon as they heard one valley explded, back the[y] flew. It was 'De'el take the hindmost.'

In about three weeks after the aforementioned action the Briton (described to have effected his escape by his horse flying over the sd impenetrable fence) deserted to me – by name James Kelly, who gave a particular acct of what happened during sd action.

From thence I, and such as accompanyed me in sd action, moved foward to where the rest of my dastardly company were, at Slebuey Hill. I was received by the Co Wexford gentlemen with acclamations of applause. The party who adhered to me in sd action most severely rebuked ther dastardly company, say they were deserving of severe punishment and not even an individual officer or leader, save Colonel Holt, but absented.[91] Mr Byrne steped up to me, asking if Ide join the Wexford Company. I answered I don't think it oeconomy to do so, as at this time that country is quite destitue of provison, it is so long in a convulsed state and ravaged by the army.

I then gave orders to hoist my colours,[92] and such as wished to cleave to me, to step forward. The[y] obeyed my command, and instantly I found myself at the head of 1000 an sixty men. We gently marched to Wicklow Gap – going nearly the way we came. Halted at a small village that night.

Next morning we marched on through Ballymanus, from thence to Ballycurragh

---

tants to lay wreaths on those graves on 29 June. The Catholics' retaliation was to let cattle loose in the field to chew them up. 89 Luke Cullen's memoirs include a description of this episode, in which Holt addresses Byrne as 'Yer Honour' (see p. 151 below). 90 In Wexford, directly south of Carnew. There is another Slieveboy mountain in Wicklow. 91 At least forty-seven loyalist troops were killed in the battle of Ballyellis. Some of Luke Cullen's informants were lothe to grant Holt credit for being in supreme command, one suggesting that the tactics employed were quite simply dictated by the nature of the terrain, but there can be little doubt that he was. However his claim to have been the only 'individual officer or leader' present is absurd. In his memoirs, the reliable Miles Byrne writes that General Roche (who, according to Holt, had resigned his command) was very much on the scene, 'brandishing his sword with alarming ferocity'. Michael Dwyer also took part in the action as did the other leaders, Garret Byrne and Edward Fitzgerald. 92 Instructions from the United Irish military committee specified the requirement for 'A standard to be got for each company 10 feet long, with a pike in the end the flag to be green about two feet square.' Holt personally carried a green serge flag, the size of a handkerchief, adorned with a yellow harp and inscribed with his own initials, J.H.

and forward to Aughavannagh, where we halted to refresh our much exhaused spirits. From thence we proceed by the head of Glenmuller [Glenmalure],[93] and thence by the 3 Lough mountain; from thence to Nockault [Knockalt]; and arived at my former station (Whelp Rock) about four in the evening. I was most agreeably received by the inhabitants, though I am certain with many of them their kindness was more for fear than real love. I then ordered a foraging party to make out some provision for us. We at this time had a vast number of good horsers whom belonged to the fallen army, with carabines, swords and pistols and many ball cartridge, which rendered us secure from the effects of all the yeomen and infantry in the country.

I rested only one day when I took a particular acct of the strangth and number of my men, quantity of arms, amunition &c. – the better to asertain what strength of enemy I might (with safety) oppose. I next ordered 24 of the best men and horses to be ready at a certain hour. We mounted and rode through the country, leaving the remainder in sd place, with instructions how to act, in case their enemy should appear during our absence.

We the[n] advanced through the country. Crossed the commons of Broad Lays [Broadleas]. We called at Ballymore, where we got refreshment. From thence [to] the house of a Mr Bradley, who was not at home and, if he was, he should remain unhurt. Some of my men entered the house. Mrs Bradley gave them plenty of drink. They carried away a suit of his military clothes, and sword, with 13 fat cows; drove them across a hill leading to our camp, who shewed towards Kilcullen. There was a military camp there who, on seeing us, bet to arms, but didn't quit their station. I ordered they should proceed to our camp.

We on our way received information where there were two flitches of bacon and four sacks of oat male [meal]. A party immediately brought them to us. On our way we took nine oxen belonging to a Cuddy Hornidge's. I said I hoped Mr Hornidge wouldn't be angry. The wall enclosing them was instantly broke and we joined our flocks, not forgeting the old joker's bacon.

We soon arived at our camp, delivering our dead and live stock to the commisary. I order our picquets to be stationed half a mile more distant than usual so that if allarmed, the[y] were to fire signal shots an each station, which would give me immediate notice, as any person taken by surprize cannot act with oeconomy. I continualy gave repeated caution to have a strict eye an the picquets, lest the[y] should be absent from duty, this being my third night's absence from the numerous party we left on Slibuey Hill, who went on to Corrigroo [Carrigroe], where they were fiercely attacked by the army and put to flight an all directions – which necessiated them to send me information that there were 11,000 of their men coming to join me.

I instantly sent to Ballymahown [Ballymahon], where Mr Radcliffe's factory was situate, where I obtained two mettal boilers. Each would contain 6 hundred

---

[93] Baravore.

[weight?] of beef. I then ordered out a foraging party on all directions. Mr Finnamore, having 79 head, my men soon left them in the possession of the commisary, with seven vale [veal] calves, six large swine, a quantity of oat male [meal] and potatoes. I next directed that all houses within the circle of four miles to be searched for salt; next got turf kishes[94] to hold the meat and set the butchers to work – the summer being remarkably fine and dry, which gave us plenty of fuel, so that we hadn't the smallest delay in cooking. When the beef was all boiled I ordered it should be put in sd kishes in small pieces. So that I was provided with so much provision that, when the formidable company of sd 11,000 men joined me, I was able to satiate their much anhungred stomachs and languid spirits.[95]

My new company being much fatigued, I order[ed] my former men to perform duty till they were recovered. I next directed my men to improve their knowledge of military maneuvres by making sham battles – pikes against guns, &c., which explained to me the superiority of advantage the pikes had of the guns on a charge. There were a great number affecting the title of officers, but General Roche was missing.[96]

The United Ireland defeat in the battle of the Midlands
Holt's escape to the glens of Wicklow

Holt does not like to dwell on defeats, and the disastrous battle of Clonard, and the later skirmishes further north, are only sketchily described by him.

Scattered remnants of the United Irish forces were met with at Dunboyne, Kilcock, Summerhill and Tara; others had moved as far north as Ardee. One newspaper report – probably unfounded – said that Holt was wounded at Nobber, which is not far to the west of Ardee. What might be called 'mopping up' operations took place at Beauparc, Dollardstown, Stackallan and Garristown.

A psychological lure magnetising United Irish forces towards the Boyne–Drogheda areas could have been that, as the scene of Cromwell's mass slaughter of the Drogheda population, and the shattering victory of the Williamite forces in 1690, there they might they have the opportunity of avenging those monumental defeats. The magnetic attraction of the sacred hill at Tara is obvious enough. They could also have been drawn north by false reports that comrades-in-arms from Ulster were heading south to link with them.

---

94 Baskets; from the Irish *ciseaín*.   95 The *Hibernian Telegraph* of 9 July described a group of rebels 'hastening to join their General Holt at the Seven Churches, on their way to Blackmore Hill ... more than one third wounded ... who rode supported by two men on the same horse, and were every moment dropping down upon the road.' The men were in a state of 'absolute famine', which forced them to eat the carcasses of animals lying by the side of the road.   96 A sub-textual reading suggests that Holt means there's one less Wexford man barring his way to supreme command. In 1799 General Roche was captured and put in prison, where he committed suicide by taking poison.

Next – 24 sd officers consulted with me what was best to be done. I proposed the following: to go to Newtownmountkenedy, where was a quantity of amunition and two field pieces, which I told them we could easily obtain, and then march to Wicklow and free the prisoners; from thence to proceed to Dublin. But Father Carnes [Kearns] opposed it,[97] saying if we went to Clonard our augmentation would be numerous, aided with a large quantity of amunition. It went to a poll. The majority favour of Father Kearns was only 2.[98]

Next day we commenced making ball cartridges and had our own amunition distributed. We got everything ready for our intended journey. We commenced our march about 11 oclock that night, accompanied by 13,700 and eighty men and, by the time we got to Prosperous,[99] we lost by desertion 2000 five hundred.[100] We there sat down and took some refreshment, where we wer[e] alarmed by our pickets that a party of army was approaching us. We instantly spied them and discovered it was but a few corps of cavalry. I ordered 200 hundred men to go meet them. Away they flew.

At this time we had taken a vast number of cattle from a man, name of Wolf. There was a large bog which we should pass through where there was a gulph cut across the road, which rendered it seeming impossible to pass. However, I ordered the cattle to be drove with precipitancy into it, so that such as first got in should

---

[97] Although the barony of Talbotstown had the highest percentage United Irish enrolment of any in the county, one pressing contributory reason for moving out of the Blackmore Hill district would have been the need for food: the barrenness of the soil not only precluded the sowing of crops, but allowed of limited grazing. Father Moses 'Mogue' Kearns had once been parish priest at Clonard. Having suffered at the hands of some of the bloodthirsty anti-clerical Jacobins in Paris it is surprising that he was ready to play such a leading part in the Rebellion: a massive man, Father Kearns had been strung up on a lamp-post which buckled under his enormous weight, thus saving his life. When executed at Edenderry, an observer noted that the scars on the priest's neck bore evidence of that near-hanging.   [98] As a soi-disant reluctant rebel, Holt has been at pains to 'cover the tracks' of his traffic with the United Irish Executive in Dublin who, in any event, must have been lying very low as the trial of the National Executive and the rest of the eighty-two state prisoners loomed; indeed perhaps all communications with Dublin had broken down at this time. Whether Holt had grounds for believing that a direct assault on Dublin from the south was viable seems doubtful. Teeling (*Sequel*, p. 287) noted that Felix Rourke, the Rathcoole commander, spoke of his plan to march 'through the various counties in order to raise them – to avoid fighting as much as possible, but to harrass small parties'. After this, they might be able to link with the forces of William Aylmer, of Painstown, in Kildare.   [99] South of Timahoe, which was the site of the Kildare United Irish camp.   [100] More precisely, the truth seems to have been that many of the Kildare rebels were not prepared to throw in their lot with the Wicklow-Wexford men. Through his influential father, the leader of the Kildare men, William Aylmer, had already made soundings in Dublin about terms for a surrender and hoped that Sir Fenton Aylmer would enlist the support of the marquis of Buckingham for his petition. Those of his army who suspected this might have been all the more wary of joining forces with the Wicklow-Wexford contingent when they sensed division among them about who held supreme command. On the other hand, some would have been buoyed up by hopes of concerting forces with rebels moving south from Ulster, and by reports from Dublin that a French expedition was expected to land in Ireland on 24 or 25 July. In all, probably about three thousand men would have marched north towards Clonard.

form a bridge or way for the rest to get over. We proceeded to a village, name of Robbertstown [Robertstown],[101] where we halted and got refreshment. From thence we advanced to Clonard,[102] where we divided.

I headed a company to the rear – of about 3000. I had to cross a millrace and, at the foot of the bridge, there was a guard house and a small house opposite. I entered betwixt them without any opposition but, immediately after, received a warm reception from the garrison, which I meaned to surprize. Garret Byrne and Fitzgerald was sent after me as assistants in the attempt. Byrne, observing the danger I stood in, cried out, 'Holt is there any use for to get you[r]self and men killed?'[103]

A few of my men fell on discharge of the first volley. I retired and set the two small houses on fire. The smoke kept us for some time in obscurity. I rallied again, but to no affect. Then I crossed the bridge, bringing only 50 men with me, losing 8 men – before I got at the other side. I found no hope of victory. I changed to the front of the barrack, the gates of which was very strong, but we forced it open and got in several loads of straw for the purpose of communicating fire to sd barrack, which by repeated tryal we entirely consumed, but hadn't the desired affect. Then we prissed [prised] of[f] some of the cieling with the points of pikes, which compleated our design and consumed it prior to our commencement of attack.

The Flying Artilery received orders to come there. We had 15 men placed inside a wall in a shrubery. The Artilery discharged a shot at them which killed eight. The Artilery continued fire so warmly we were obliged to retreat. Captain Perry[104] and I stopped 500 men which we had lodging in ambush which, from ther warm fire on the Artillery, the[y] thought prudent to retire though I must acknowledge myself to this day much thankful to them for so doing. Had we sufficient ball cartridge we could have completed a victory, with the loss of some men.[105]

We marched on to Castlecarbury.[106] That night was partly spent in drissing our wounded. Next morning we marched to Corebuey [Carbury] Hill.[107] We got some

---

101 In Co. Kildare; the Grand Canal passes through Robertstown, on its course from Dublin to Monasterevan.   102 Although there is little left to bear witness to it now, in 1798 Clonard was one of the most impressive monastic sites in Ireland. In a field adjoining the east side of the Boyne, and only a few hundred yards from the site of the guardhouse, a Croppy monument marks the graves of some of the rebels.   103 A sub-textual interpretation points to the logistical problems resulting from divided leadership; the persistence of Holt's pretensions to supreme command; and perhaps to a reflection on Byrne's fainteartedness.   104 Anthony Perry and Father Kearns would be executed on 25 July. A monument marking the site of the execution stands on a hill overlooking Edenderry. It was said that Perry almost expired from fear before the moment of execution and that Father Kearns chided him for giving too much information. If so, it would not have been the first time that Perry had 'confessed' while under threat of death: on 23 May at Gorey, having been subjected to the excruciating 'pitch-cap' torture, he had given a great deal of 'useful information'.   105 This is probably true. However, Holt glosses over the ignominious truth that hundreds of United Irishmen had been held at bay by the stripling Lieutenant Tyrell and twenty-seven yeomen, who succeeded in killing more then sixty of the rebels.   106 There the rebels plundered the mansion of Lord Harburton. In his *United Irishmen*, Madden says that, at Carbury, 'some sharp words' were exchanged over the defeat at Clonard.   107 Corebuey being mistaken for Carbury:

sheep killed and was getting dinner ready. We had in our possession two puncheons of spirits. It was observed to me the intoxicated state the men wer getting into. I instantly repaired the [to] where the spirits was and with the breitch [breech] end of a mu[s]quet I struck in the head of both of them. I turned them both upside down and discharged their contents before I was observed. When what I done was observed, a vast number of them arose, quite exasperated, saying I deserved death. I endeavoured to appease their undeserved anger, and some of my sensible friends declared I shouldn't be insulted for saving their lives. They all sat down. I went [to] them whom I conceived had the best sense, telling them my observation on the effects of drinking freely in our situation. In a few minutes after, we heard a signal shot from our Picquets. I called all men to arms, but to my misfortune, I didn't find in my company as many as were in a state to fight 200 men. There were lying on the ground 500 in a state of intoxication, which raised such confusion in the rest they began to fly on every direction. I endeavoured to harange them, which caused as many to detain as kept us from falling victims as we affected a retreat.

By opposition from the conduct of the men, I got so iritated that I forgot all tenderness and began to burn every house as I went on, that the army might [n]ot trace me by the smoke. Captain Dalton, with a few horse men, came up to join the body. The Army brought on the artillery and we gave them a smart opposition. I rode inside of the adjacent field to keep the rebels men in order. It was boggy ground and I got a fall from my horse by crossing a ditch, the top of which gave way. Both horse and I came to the ground.

At this time the Army got in betwixt us. I got up as speedy as I could, and before I could reach any of the party to retard their motion to save the languid and fatigued, which disaster I met with gave the army an opportunity of shooting the tired men as fast as they could load and fire. I received a sleight wound in my head, which I have to this day.

I saw a vast number of men fall around me, which struck me with an idea of droping down. It happened to be where was a runing stream. My head was bleeding. The Army, coming on rapidly, never observed those that fell but continued firing on the living. But, as the[y] crossed the drain, I heard some of them exclaim, 'There lyes a brave parcel of the Devil's Dead.'[108]

---

another example of one of the phonetic errors of Holt's 'scribes', suggesting that this section of the 'History' may have been written to Holt's dictation and that he slurred the word when he spoke it: To make the facts even more obfuscated, it seems likely that Holt's memory may have misled him into compounding two engagements. Ruan O'Donnell argues persuasively that this débâcle may have occurred at Ryndville Hill. Colonel Gough wrote to Colonel Vereker that he found what he estimated as about 4000 men on Ryndville Hill who were 'prepared to give me battle' and 'yelled most horribly' (SPO 620/4/36/1). It seems possible that Holt has telescoped two separate engagements. He speaks of boggy ground in the vicinity: the terrain immediately to the north of Carbury hill is boggy.   108 This incident probably took place at Longwood, four miles north-east of Clonard, where there is a Croppy grave – a massive pile rising high above the surrounding ground.

As soon as the Army got a distance of[f] I ventured to look about me and espyed a vast crowd of weomin crying, as the Army spared no one the[y] met in their way. I was of opinion I couldn't be worse then I was, so ventured over sd stream. I perceived a weoman who happened to be a yeoman's wife, a very genteel looking person who said, 'Sir, I am sorry to see such a man as you in such a condition,' saying, 'go up to that house and make the girls take off yr sircoat. They will wash it.'

I went to the house and she followed me. She instantly ran and brought me some spirits, bread, butter and cheese. Seeing her kindness, I gave her my silver mounted sword, a silver mounted bridle, saying to her, 'Go to where my horse lyes fast in the ditch and under his side you will find a case of silver mounted pistols.' She wash[ed] my head and gave me a handkerchife and, in exchange of my broken helmet, she gave me a hat, saying, 'My husband is a yeoman, but I hope you may escape.' I answered, 'The Almighty is able to do more than that.' The maid that was watching came in & told the mrs that there was a great number of the police coming. This good weoman wished me safe and so I disappeared.

I passed through the back of her garden, but hadn't traveled far when I saw 8 of the police coming towards me. I advanced boldly up to them, asking them which way did the Army go? One of them answered very fiercely, 'What do you want to know about them?'

I said, 'The rebells robbed me and took my horse and hat, and I know if any gentleman getts my horse he will return him to the right owner.'

'You are right,' says another.

I shewed him my head that was scalped by a ball, which saying put a cloak on suspicion.

I moved forward, looking on every side, but couldn't see any of my party. I then sat down and concluded that it was all for the better and, when I saw the bog clear of my enemy, I reflected on which way I had better steer my course, for I was quite out of my latitude and wanted to take a Leener, or Pilot.[109]

At this time I began to make my observations on the sun, steered my cource by it, and came to a small house on the edge of sd bog and began to talk to the man of sd house & to my great surprize, discovered an old weoman from Newtownountkenedy [Newtownmountkennedy], wife to Andrew Carnes [Kearns], who was shipwrecked as myself. The man pointed which way we were to go. We couldn't pass ourselves for anything but what we realy wer, whis was a pair of most unfortunate Rebells, but still my [prayers] were wrested in my Redeemer to protect me. I knew I had done some deeds which I hoped would be pleasing to the Deity, and that of young Pillsworth was one.

109 One of Luke Cullen's informants reported that Holt deserted his men. It seems more likely that such confusion reigned that there was no longer any possibility of coordinated United Irish action at Longwood. Probably no more than 200 men continued to be 'in action'. Luke Cullen's *Personal Recollections* reported that Garret Byrne and his forces attempted to press on after fording the Boyne but were roundly defeated by Captain Archbold's dragoons, after having put up 'a feeble resistance'.

Night approaching, we arrived at a Gentleman's ground.[110] We got on a very high quickset ditch. We lay down, but our rest was as much disturbed by bulls and oxen as by our wretched situation. In the morning the first man we met was what I may call a friend, who put me on a path and told me how to act. I followed his directions and soon came to a small hous on the edge of a road and had just time to get in when up came a corp of cavalry. The owner of the house trembled at the sound of the horses' feet, saying to me I was lucky in geting into the house; for if any of them should have came in, 'both you and I would lose our lives.' The poor weoman of the house got for us some warm butter milk, saying she had no better cheer. The man of the house said, 'Sir, I shall get you a good breakfast.' He then conveyed us to a wheat field, desiring us to remain there. We lay down, and about 9 oclock the man returned with a large jug of tea, bread, butter and some cold meat. Gentle Reader, I shall refer to your feelings how much it was wanting, not having taken any support for 30 hours. He told me that his landlord, Mr Jn O'Neill, would come to see me in the cource of the day. He also confessed to [me] that sd O'Neill was a United Irishman, though in a corp of cavalry.

After breakfast, we lay down and slept till about 12 oclock. Mr O'Neill came to us and, after an hour's conversation, he commenced reflecting on what could induce me to [be] in this wretched situation. I answered, 'It's hard to acct for the viscisitudes of this life, and, sir, have you not read in History the many distressed people of the best information had to wade through?'

He said, 'But that creature of a weoman! What the Devil brot her here?'

She answered 'Sir, I came with my husband, for fear of the soldiers.'

When departing, he said he would send some present to me by his man, wished me safe, and parted.

About 2 oclock he sent his man with a nice fowl, a plate of potatoes & a bottle of whiskey, with some bacon – which formed a sumptuous feast for Katty and I. When Katty had taken a glass of the spirits it created in her such clamour as caused me to be alarmed lest it should lead to discovery, being near the road. About half an hour after night-fall the poor man returned, giving me a pistol and ten rounds of ball cartridge, which reanimated me again. That night he came nine miles with us, untill he left us on a path leading to a farmer's house, whom he said was a United Irishman, parted me and wished me safe.

I went straight to sd house, accompanied with old Katty, whom I frequently wished was with Old Nick from me. When I reached sd house it was just sun rise. I raped at the door. I was asked, 'Who comes there?' I answered, 'A friend.' The man arose and let me in. I pass him a signal, which he observed, on which he brot me into a room. He desired poor Katty to sit in the kitchen, which much iritated her, tho her conduct was as refined as a baboon. He ordered me refreshment to eat, which was instantly brought, and after, spirits and milk.

110 A large estate?

Night approaching, I wished to go forward and he was good enough to bring [me] to a part of the neighbourhood where he thought he might leave me with safety, but told me the man was cautious and stuborn, leaving me at a certain place near the house aforementioned. About eleven oclock I rapped at the door. He asked, 'Who comes there?' I answered, 'A friend.'

He replyed, 'You shan't come in.'

I said, 'You purjured villain, if you don't get up I will burn you in your bed' – with a tone of voice as if a great company was with me [to] set fire to the house.

With that, he changed his mind, saying, 'Sir, I will get up.'

He came out. I took [him] by the neck with one hand, my pistol in the other, asking him, 'Are you not a sworn United Man?'

He says, 'Yes, Sir.'

I said, 'I will let you know that, you perjured wretch. Come, march on before me.'

The creature thought I was going to take his life and began to beg for mercy.

'Yes, you ungrateful creature, on proviso [you] pilot me across the Boyne to a James Kenedy's [Kennedy's] house, of Navan, but should I be attacked on the way, you shall die by my hands – as the contents of my pistol shall pass through yr body.'

The only way to make a rogue act honest is by subordination.

I then commanded him to go on before me. So we traveled to the house and, on our way, we never heard the least noise. When I came to Kenedy's it was near sun rise. Kenedy arose and conducted me to his barn. Katty attempted to follow me, but Kenedy didn't permit her, but desired her to go into the dwelling house. He placed me under a large mow[111] of peas. On his going out he was met by two soldiers who bid him Good Morning. Those two had came from Navan. Kenedy asked them, 'What news?'

The[y] answered, 'The Rebels are all killed. We will now be at ease and get rid of these damed militia so much torments us.[112] Come in, landlord,' says they, 'give us a drink of new milk.'

Kenedy answered he would. They went in. On getting the milk, lit their pipes and went away. Then Kenedy sent for some spirits he and I drank with new milk, over which we related various things. He said he thought I was the most fortunate he ever saw. Say he hoped I should get the rest of my road with safety.

In the mean time Katty, wishing more fess chat than to get home, annoyed Kenedy so much that Kenedy said that hede tye her in a sack and throw her in the river Boyne. This terrified Katty. Kenedy continued, saying, 'If you travel round the world, no man would molest you. Stay here and I will send you on Monday on some of my corn cars to Dublin.'

So I got rid of Katty. Reader, this woman was wife to Andrew Carnes [Kearns], resident of Nockria [Knockrea], near Seven Churches.

111 A stack.   112 No doubt the soldiers were of the Yeomanry.

So Kenedy conducted me over the Boyne water, giving me directions to a house whose inhabitants would take care of me.[113] From thence I traveled on a path, at the end of which I found a large farm house, where I was kindly received by a young and an old weoman, who instantly brot me some oat bread and butter. Next she got me some hot water to bathe my feet [and] shewed me a bed. She observed that my stockings and shirt was dirty, bringing me clean things while she was washing my dirty ones. She then began to ask me about my misfortunes and, among the conversation, seemed quite sorry for the death of General Holt, saying several of the men was very sorry for him, saying, he was shot crossing Longford [Longwood?] bog, saying, 'Avourneen, he was a sore loss.'

After these word I told her Holt wasn't dead. She claped her hands with joy. I said, 'My good weoman, I am Holt.'

I shewed her the wound on my head, and another on my left arm. She was so overjoyed that she kneeled down to prey for my succcess. I looked upon her to be a real, innocent old right Irish weoman.[114]

She no sooner quit the room than 24 of the poor forlorn creatures came in. They wer all desired to sit down at the table. I observed when I came in about twenty large kakes of oaten bread on sd table, and the young weoman making more. She told me that that was their employment for several days.

In these creatures' discourse they related some of what occured during the late action, principally their great misfortune in losing their leader. Say[s] the old weoman, 'Agrah, who was he?'

The[y] answered, 'General Holt.'[115]

She answered, 'Avourneen, he is not dead, he is a sleeping.'

They wouldn't believe her till she brought them in the room. When they saw me they [were] much astonished. Having but a short time to stay, the[y] eagerly wished that I might arise and come with them. They even proposed to carry me was I not able to travel. I thanked them, saying I would go by myself. The[y] wished me a Good Night.

They brought the first news to County Wicklow that I was alive. These very men were the first I saw when I arived at Glenmuller (Glenmalure].

Though I was abed and much fatigued, I slept but little. I began to consider how I should get through Dublin as I been so well known, but I reflected as I had such success through the perils I passed strengthened my further hope of safety.

113 Holt has stated previously that, in order to reach Kennedy's house, he needed someone to 'pilot me across the Boyne'. It may be that he meant the Blackwater. Having crossed that river, he would have reached Navan. Then, in order to gain the road to Dublin, he would have had to cross the Boyne to the east of the town – perhaps at Kilcarn.   114 Holt here adopts the condescending tone of one of the gentry.   115 It is very unlikely, but just possible, that, at this stage, Holt was known popularly as General Holt. However, Bartholomew Connolly stated that the rebels in the Midlands were 'commanded by Garret Byrne and Joseph Holt' (SPO 620/39/73). Stephen Murray, of Gorey, and Daniel Doyne thought Esmond Kyan held supreme command, with Garret Byrne, Kearns, Fitzgerald and Holt serving under Kyan (SPO 620/51/48).

I arose early next morning and asked the old man was I near the road leading to Dublin? He said, 'Yes, Sir, it is at the head of this field.' I turned in, taking leave of the good old weoman and daughter.

I hadn't gone more than a quarter of a mile when I met with a public house. At this time it was about six in the morning. On going to the door, I met the landlord, asking had he any spirits? He replyed, 'No, Sir, I have a very good ale.' He said, 'Sir, I shall mull a quart of it for you.'

I threw him a signal, but [he] seemed not to mind it, though I knew he did. He said he wasn't a United Man, 'nor do I belong to any party, but I wish every description well.' He said, 'Go into the barn where is some new hay and I shall follow you with the drink.' So I obeyed his direction. He accordingly brot me the drink.

I said, 'Should you see any loaded cars going by, please to let me know.' He said he would. He brought me a second pot of ale and, before it was drank, he told me there was cars going by. I ran to the door and hailed one of the men. He came to me. I passed him a signal, which he answered. We finished the ale. I put my hand to my pocket, handed the landlord a shilling, which he refused, saying, 'I wish you safe.'

We traveled on towards Dublin. This young man was from Castlepollard,[116] with three cars loaded with eggs. Their name was Kenedy. There were four in company with me, three of which were 'United.' Gentle Reader, I think it my duty to let you know as great a number of military forces as could be spared from duty were in pursuit of me and my fellow sufferers.

I made it up with the owners of sd cars that I should personate the owner, and every party of army I met I seemed quite busy doing some security to my loading, and when I purceived any army drinking at a door, I stoped and called for drink, wishing them every success in their pursuit, and in all the men I met that day, not one seemed to know me – but one, who smiled a knowledge of me.

I arived save [safe] to Park End Street, where Kenedys and I went into an alehouse, drank half a pint of punch. So we parted. They wished me safe through Dublin.

I directed my way over Old [B?]ow bridge and passed by Old Kilmainham, through James's St, Thos [Thomas] Street and Francis St, turned at the Cross Poddle through New St, through Harold's Cross, but was known by a weoman, name of Susy Needam [Needham], who was reared at Delginny [Delgany] in the County of Wicklow, who sent word to Mr Berresford [Beresford],[117] who sent his corps after me. I heard the sound of their horses' feet coming up. I instantly scaled the wall. I lay down close by its side.

A little above me, they met a man whom the[y] asked did he meet a person giving my description? He answered, 'No.'

Says they, 'He is gone towards Crumlin.'

116 Perhaps travelling via Athboy and Trim. Holt may have boarded the 'loaded car' at Dunshaughlin.   117 Probably Brigadier-General W.C. Beresford, but possibly the very powerful John Beresford, Commissioner for Revenue, who had a finger in many pies.

As soon as the[y] advanced at a convenient distance, I rescaled the wall and crossed the wall opposite.

I then took the field up to Holly Park, crossing over by Lady de [C?]ily's[118] and up to Mount Pelia [Montpelier] – that enchanted house.[119] Gentle Reader, I passed by the house that day where my dr wife an children were. Had I called to see them, I should never see them more, but I hope the Almighty shie[l?]d[ed?] me to die a happy death. When I arived at sd enchanted house I was much fatigued. I considered that I was arived once more in a country which I knew. I composed my[s]elf that the name of Inchantment was not able to deter me. I contemplated, 'There is nothing worse than I am,' and, in God's name, I said my prayers and slept soundly.

Next morning I aroes, came from my arched room. I viewed it, an then advanced to Pipers town, a small village, where I found a piper who played 'Erin go bragh'[120] at end of the former late Rebellion. I saw a small girl, whom I asked did she know Holts of Bonabreena [Bohernabreena], or the Chaper [Chapel] House. I instantly wrote to my brother, requesting of him to send me a loaf of bread, some cheese and a pint of whiskey. On receiving the note he said to his wife, 'Joseph is not dead, as here is his hand writing.' He sent the contents of my note and a note with it to meet him near Carys Field.

On coming to sd field I found him in company with a Richard Johnson, a farmer who lived in Kipper [Kippure]. We sat together and talked of part of my adventures. Johnson proposed to go to Mr Beresford to obtain my pardon. I was afraid of him, which I had reason to be, as hereafter will appear, as in my later absence he took a cow from my distressed wife and never paid her. His ungratefullness was dowbly criminal, for he had 5 horses taken by my men to Whelp Rock, which I caused to be restored to him, which convinced me that his proffered kindness was but to deceive, together with the large sum was offered to whom should have me taken.

I now once more had the gratification of seeing my much afflicted wife. At this time my hopes despaired much of obtaining an escape. I said to my wife should I hear of His Majestie's Pardon, I should then resign. So I bid her farewell and commenced recruiting on[c]e more.[121]

---

118 This is my shot in the dark. I am unable to decipher the manuscript. 119 Known as the Hellfire Club, and built by Speaker Conolly in the early eighteenth century, it was a hunting lodge constructed from the stones of an ancient cairn, and was reputed to be the scene of wild orgies held by 'the sporting gentlemen'. "Local tradition states that in this house, a man named Bevan, murdered his wife; and the peasantry will seriously tell you, that to the interrogatory 'Who killed his wife?' an echo from this ruin will answer 'Bevan' " (*The Angling Excursions of Gregory Greendrake, Esq. in Ireland*, 1824). 120 Ireland for ever. 121 Holt glosses over this discussion lightly. In fact it was crucial. Had he surrendered at this time the Rebellion would probably have been at an end, for there was no other candidate for leadership with mettle sufficient to muster an army. Holt must have dreaded that, having been responsible for executions (murders?) he might not be eligible for the amnesty offered by the newly appointed viceroy, Lord Cornwallis; and yet other rebel leaders, such as Garret Byrne and William Aylmer, had received conditional pardons. The overwhelming reason for the likelihood of his not being treated with such liberality would surely have been that he was the only leader who was not a gentlemen. Acutely conscious of his social 'inferi-

On leaving Glenasmole I crossed Butter Mountain, going Ballyfolen [Ballyfolan] Pass to Scorleck's Lep [Scurlock's Leap], halted in Adown [Athdown]. I went to a widow Kirwan's house,[122] asked hur for some refreshment. She declared she was destitute of any thing save some cabage leaves which were in the pot. I drew my sword and with it examined sd pot,[123] found that part of her confession was right, but knew she told me a lye for, in a few days after, I directed some of the men, with liberty to strictly examine her house, where they discovered two pieces of bacon, four sacks of oat male.

Notwithstanding her ungratefulness to me, some time prior to it I had hur cleared of ten pound fine for depredations she committed on a plantation of Peter Latouche [La Touche], Esqr. at Lugalaw.[124] Her explanation I insert to let the reader know her ingratitude and how I treated her at my return. I proceeded to Ballydonnell, to a Simeon Kerney's [Simon Kearney's], where I was received with the warmest kindess, the[n] was instantly furnished with plenty of good refreshment. They entreated me to stop all night, but I refused. I bed them farewell, going to Ballylow, from thence to Whelp Rock.

They received me with acclamations of joy. They wished Ide stop there but did not think it prudent,[125] as I was informed many wounded creatures was in Glenmaller [Glenmalure] and knew they were much in want of one to dress their sores.[126] I then passed over the Three Lough Mountain. Crossing it, I came up to a young woman whom I knew. She collected for me some froughins [froughans], a small black fruit whech grows on elevated places. We bot[h] sat down, and pass[ed] part of sd evening pleasant, as we were in such a retired place.[127] I saved this young weoman's life in Longwood by rescuing her from the army. I recieved two small wounds. One of her brothers was killed at Clonard, and another wounded at Castlecarbury.[128]

Sd young woman advanced with me to Glenmuller. We stopped at the house of Pierce Harny [Harney].[129] Sd Glen is about 21 miles in length, its breadth is uniqual

ority', Holt was probably right in assessing his chances. One perhaps 'mischievous' suggestion I would make is that he may have been just a little influenced by his commitment to an assignation with a young woman whom he would meet shortly. 122 Later in his 'History' Holt seems to confuse this lady with Widow McGrath. 123 One might imagine the 'aristocratic' posturing that went along with this gesture. It might also have been threatening enough. 124 'In summer, scarcely a day passes without Luggelaw being visited by parties of pleasure, which, on presenting a ticket from any member of the La Touche family, are accommodated with beds, and receive every other attention which the lodge can afford' (*Angling Excursions of Gregory Greendrake*, op. cit.). 125 Colonel McMahon, previously dismissed contemptuously by Holt as 'this little king', had abstained from the Midlands campaign, and been left in charge of two hundred men at Whelp Rock; when Holt arrived he was probably still there, which could have been why Holt decided to pass on to Glenmalure, where his entitlement to supreme authority was less likely to be in question. 126 Holt takes some pride in his skill as an amateur surgeon. 127 Where they coupled? Holt is not given to poetical flights, yet the 'small black fruit' seems symbolic and brings to my mind an ancient Irish poem. 128 The only mention in Holt's text that he was in action at Longwood. 129 The fact that the girl stays with him at the cottage suggests that the meeting on Three Lough mountain may not have been accidental, and that she may have been accorded rather more status then a camp whore. Was this the 'libidinous prostitute', Croppy Biddy Dolan?, 'the handsome

– the widest not more than ¾ of a mile. The mountains forming sd Glen is remarkably high and many parts inaccessable, treatning to crush the beholders by their fall.

Refugees converge in Glenmalure

Because work had not yet started on the construction of the Military Road the rebel camp at Baravore in Glenmalure would have been extraordinarily difficult of access for the loyalist forces; furthermore, Glenmalure's reputation as a stronghold where English forces had been routed in Elizabethan times would have made it a favoured choice for a rebel camp.

Writing of 'the whole country from Ballymore-Eustace and Blessington, to Glendalough and Rathdrum', Saunders News Letter of 13 July said:

> *Strange to tell, the tract of country now occupied by the rebels, though little more than from ten to twenty miles distant from the city, has long been and still continues to be as little known to us as any of the wildest parts of America; a rude and barren extent of heath, moor, bog and mountain, it has been hitherto considered as scarcely penetrable by the most adventurous sportsmen.*
>
> *Confined to such a spot and daily wasting with epidemic diseases this band of wretches would soon cease to be of consequence, were it not for the perpetual recruiting of their ranks from every part of Ireland ... the direct roads to Dublin are not attended to ... the consequence is that the first stage of every rebel recruit is this city; he makes the necessary observations on the state in which he finds the metropolis and marches off in undisturbed security to carry off his aid and his information to the armies of treason. In this way we can account for the perpetual influx of strangers to Dublin, and the continual intercourse between this city and the rebel troops.*

Next morning, about 300 men came to sd Harney's house, 150 of which were part of the surviving creatures who returned from below the Boyne. I ordered them to bring forward the wounded till we should see what was best to be done. On examining their wound I found none fatal. On investigating sd 300 men I found the majority of them to be creatures who fled thither for refuge, as thier houses were consumed. The[y] all vowed to me that, should I become thier director and commander, that they would to the last moment of life obey my commands. I answered them that I should prefer being a full private, on proviso I shouldn't be reduced lower; which excited laughter in many of them, but mutually agreed that I might please to take general command.[130] I told them to look out for gunpowder as we might be supplied

---

young woman' , Ann Byrne? Neither? The ruins or Harney's cottage can be seen at the western end of Glenmalure, at Baravore. Situated on the left bank, they lie a few hundred yards beyond the causeway, and just short or the youth hostel.   130 William James reported to Under- Secretary Cooke that many hundreds of 'straggling parties dispersed at the Boyne passed through Dublin

with enough of lead from sd Glen Smelt House, and to recruit as fast as possible, saying whoever rises 100 men shall be appointed Captain. From this plan I discovered the best oeconomists.

I now once more saw my absent friend, the Moving Magazine. I now once more furnished her basket as usual with gingerbread and fruit, directing her to form two satchels to hang before and aft, to carrey ball cartridge. When ready, she proceeded through different military camps in order to accomplish her instructed designs.

My next step was to examine for the most suitable ground to oppose or retreat, as by this time I had purchased experience dear. I soon saw the advantageous situation which saved my life in some time after. I next examined the road of sd Glen. At each end I found a pavement in the upper end of it. I direct[ed] the men to roll great stones down side of sd Glen which formed sd causeway (or pavement). From the stones been away, the ground underneath being soft, the water answered my desired effect, cutting a gulph across the road 30 feet deep in 24 hours, so that neither man nor horse could pass nor repass. Then I went to the other end of sd Glen, whis is near Ballyboy, where I had the bridge thrown down, which assured me would give my enemys an obstruction. My company well approved of sd plan.

Holt's guerilla warfare. The French landing on Killala Bay

Holt's close familiarity with the terrain and his ability to shift ground swiftly between camps at Glenmalure, Whelp Rock, Black Ditches, Knockalt, Knockadroose and Glenbride often baffled Loyalist forces trained for conventional methods of open warfare, and represents an early example of the technique of guerilla warfare. His many 'hair breadth 'scapes' gave rise to the legend that he was in league with the devil. At Clone Hill Holt's army literally vanishes into smoke.

and thence into the mountains or Wicklow ... groups of three and four – all unarmed, and appear like savages with long beard, little clothes, and ... appeared half starved'; at Glenmalure were 'seasoned veterans, many bloodthirsty and intent on revenge' (16 July, SPO 620/39/90). The *Courier* of 4 September, reported that 'Holt is endeavouring to collect the scattered remains or his forces in the county of Wicklow, and, I am informed, has again appeared in considerable force ... disaffected soldiers, deserters, and desperate rebels, have found a resting place at his standard.' Holt's show of reluctance at the offer of leadership seems no more genuine than that of Shakespeare's Richard III: 'Will you enforce me to a world of cares?' Luke Cullen was told that, although there were others eligible for the leadership, and with superior military skills, it was Holt's close knowledge of the terrain of Co. Wicklow which swung the decision in his favour. But then Cullen's informants, not to say Cullen himself, often grudge giving Holt his due. Miles Byrne who, with Michael Dwyer, had 'held the fort' at Baravore, says that Dwyer was not a candidate, preferring to confine his movements to the familiar environs of the Glen of Imail (see Appendix 1.3). Holt has now become 'General' Holt, although the title was not an official one conferred by the United Irish Directory. Indeed, in Dublin Castle after his surrender, he would state that he held no commission; but then, at that time, he might have thought it to his advantage to disclaim responsibility.

In August, Saunders News Letter *featured a letter from Tinahely dated 7 August which referred to 'General Hall, the famous rebel': no doubt they meant Holt. The letter is interesting on another count: 'On presumption of his being a Protestant, he [Holt] was taken prisoner and threatened with instant death. He had, however, sagacity enough to persuade his myrmidons that he was a Catholic; and to prove his sincerity offered to lead them into positions among the mountains of Wicklow, which they might maintain under entrenchment against the infantry below.' While the writer of the letter may have been susceptible to propaganda emanating from Dublin Castle intended to precipitate a Catholic-Protestant schism in the United Irish ranks, it could have been based on fact. Soon after becoming viceroy in June, Lord Cornwallis noted that common parlance equated rebel with Catholic and loyalist with Protestant.*

Holt's chronology is unreliable in what follows. The engagement at Clone Hill took place in September, probably towards the end of the month.

Chronological factors which might help to put this section of his 'History' into context include the fact that, by 6 August, General Sir John Moore was offering pardons. Against this we might set Holt's statement that 'during this time my numbers were augmenting,' lumping, as it were, stragglers from the Boyne with those coming over to him with revived hopes after Humbert's landing at Killala Bay on 22 August with 1,099 troops. Among the many deserters to Holt are 28 members of the Antrim Militia, many of whom he may have secretly enlisted in May, when he had arranged the billeting of members of that company, and lodged one of their sergeants and his wife under his own roof (Appendix 6.1).

During this time my numbers were much augmenting, several returning from the Boyne, some nights 30 or 40. In a short time 28 of the Antrim Militia,[131] with several others came from Arklow, some from Longford, but, in fine, I had different men from 13 ridgements who all endeavoured to come well prepared. Some brought 60 rounds. When I found myself grown somewhat formidable, I says, 'Come, my boys, we shall go get something to do.'

We advanced to EEmale [Imail] where we pitched our camp, where we stopped about ten days. 3 corps of cavalry came from Hacketstown. We soon dispersed them, taking a few prisoners. When sd prisoners were examined I found the[y] were United men, wearing two faces each – one for their country and another for thir King. However, my men were ever partial to United men.

From thence we went to Whelp Rock, where Blessingtown [Blessington] cavalry, some regulars Donard cavalry, with some of the 89th Reegment of foot came after us. I gave orders to march, leading them through EEmale [Imail] and on a side

---

131 This tallies exactly with the figure given by Holt in an interrogation at Dublin Castle on 16 November (see p. 162 below).

of Lugnacullagh [Lugnaquillia.][132] We stationed ourselves in the centre of sd hill. The army advancing, we were all behind a rock. I wouldn't let them fire one shot till the army was within pistol shot of us, when quite suddenly we let fly a volley which killed 35 dead on the spot, but had Captain Hughes taken my directions not one would have escaped, for I sent him round sd hill to cut off their retreat but he wasn't as expeditious as was necessary, so they retreated with the loss of 35 killed and 3 prisoners – whom I liberated, as they dedn't fire when ordered to submit.

I gave them choice, to go [to] their reigments or stay with me. The[y] chose to join their reigments. I then told them they should go without arms or amunition. Then one of them, by name Connel [Connell], said, 'Sir, if I go without my arms I will be shot.' I told him I would write to his commanding officer to let him know it was the rules of my camp, on which the sd three stopt, and immediately furnished them with pikes. Two of sd three, passing through Glenbride, were killed; and the other deserted, so I know no more of him.

In staying there I found I could do nothing, being out of amunition, so I went to Aughavanna [Aughavannagh], from thence to the Gold Mines and halted at Croghane [Croghan], near Arklow, to see to procure gun powder. One day [I] took a notion to go reconoiter, ordering 24 of my horse to come with me. We went down by Kilmanor [Kilmanoge], where we saw a few corps of cavalry at exercise. We beared down on them quickly, in hopes to get between them and barrack. They too soon perceived us and immediately got into it, being situate at Coolgrany [Coolgreany]. We pursued to sd barrack, when they quickly fired on us.

In any engagement I always quit my horse, and in scouting partys carried a light furce [fusée]. A McDermot [Luke McDermott], from the County Antrim Militia, with me took one square of sd barrack and received a ball in his nable [navel], of which he expired that night. However, I can assure ye that the man who killed sd McDermot was same instant killed by me, for I saw him discharge his piece at sd McDermott. I, same instant, fired at him and saw him drop.

They continued firing through the windows of sd barrack. We at length broke in and set the house on fire. A John Moore, from the Antrim Militia, shot one and dashed out the brains of another. I came back to Croghane, and much concerned at the loss of McDermot. Next day I moved, as I knew there would be a sharp look out for me and party. The place sd skirmish happened was within 2 miles of Arklow, a large Barrack town.

I next pitched my camp on the side of a hill over Cloan [Clone]. General Scerad's [Skerrett's][133] camp was fixed in Killaduff (Kiladuff), within 11 miles of me, & General Craig [134] came sd evening, pitching his camp on the side of Aughrim Hill. The third camp was pitched Aughrim side of Tinakilly [Tinahely] Hill – I cannot not identify, tell, the chief officer's name. All situate within 2 miles of me! I perceived

---

132 The highest mountain in Co. Wicklow.   133 At this time Skerrett held the rank of colonel.   134 Lieutenant-General Craig, commander of the Eastern District of Wicklow.

the substance of their intentions. Such of my men as I made free with came to me, saying, 'How shall we make our escape?'

I said, 'My good men, how many leggs has each soldier?'

They answered, 'Only two.'

I answered, 'Well, hasn't God given two leggs to you and equal use of them?'

Says they, 'Yes, Sir, but we are surrounded.'

I endeavoured to retrieve them, saying, 'We shall fight our way and, with God's help, we shall get clear.'

This was about 5 oclock in the evening.

I walked about. The men observed my convulsed attitude, but on a sudden I made up my mind, directing them to make 150 piles of thorn bushes and furz which were convenient; which was accomplished in half an hour. I directed 4 serious men to go to 4 four adjacent farm houses and desired each house to have 3 hundredweight of potatoes boiled precisely at seven oclock. The[y] sent their respects to me that the should willingly obey. I walked about making myself hearty, saying we should have sport would the enemy's officers next day. In this position we remained until the approch of night.

They had one small fire to lighgt the piles and, all on a quick motion, ordered sd 150 piles to be put in a state of conflageration. Next I ordered every one of them to come in front of sd fires and to pass throgh and fro in rapid motion. When done, and maneuvring them, I ordered every one to the rere of sd fires. Then I gave order for every individual to march on in so silent a manner as not to make the smallest noise, and to strictly oberve that any person who raised his voice higer then his breath, that the man next him should instanly put him to death. My advanced guards and picquets were stationed with directions not to fire unless they should come too near their enemy. In this possition we marched forward to where I directed the potatoes to be prepared, and took refreshment. When done, I gave orders to march. We were but a short distance when my picquetts were obstructed by General Skerratt's. They fired at each other. My picquets said that they observed one of the enemy fall.

I continued to march, and got safe between the enemy's camps, marching on to a village called Sheals town [Sheilstown], which was six miles distant. I instanly ordered my men to [be] enclosed in six houses of sd village, securing the doors so that they couldn't get out. Next - leaving them vessels to hold their necessary occasions as, [135] wasn't it for this plan, I never could keep them in secret from their unruly and wild disposition, reserving with me 36 of the most active and sensible for picquets.

The army, on repairing next morning to where the[y] saw the fires, but to their great mistake had nothing but the ashes of sd fires. The[y] made a strict enqury

---

[135] In which to deposit their urine and excreta.

where we were gone, but it was impossible to get sd information as I passed so silent, not leting any one know my intentions.¹³⁶

Reader, there was so inducing a sum at this time offered for me as rendered me to be as cautious as possible to keep my self from the power of desception, being always accompanyed with a number of such. The enemy? After a long and fruitless search, the much fatigued and harrassed army were obliged to retire to their rendervous, exclaiming that Holt dealt with the Devil. The poor captives – or men enclosed in sd house – remaned so for three days. My picquet informed me that the enemy's camps were all retired away. I then said to my party, 'What we cannot destroy by battle we will harrass by fatigue.' So when sd generals saw my enginuity they augmented they reward offered for me.

General Craig proposed £3000 for my head.¹³⁷ I received the specification of sd reward on parade. Says I, 'What an unthinking creature this must be – to only offer so diminutive a sum for a head that is worth a million, for should His Majesty have known the value of it, he should have me at least in his room, but with God's assistance, before they get me in possession I shall more conspicuouly let them know the value of it;' adding, Gentlemen, shall any of you bring that brainless head (Craig) to me, I shall give you ten thousand pounds – though it isn't worth one farthing, as I am assured his impotent conduct was of no injury to me.'

I then directed spies to bring me a strict acct of the situation of the country. On ariving, the[y] tould me that General Dundass [Dundas] proclaimed that protection and pardon should be given to all offenders, on coming to him and giving up their arms and recant there former disobeydience by taking an oath of faithfullness to His Majesty. I instantly issued a proclamation that all or any of my enemy who should come to me, that they, on giving me up their arms, taking a vow of fidelity, should have from me a protection.

The French surrender. Ireland's 'golden summer' coming to an end. United Irish enlistment continues. The Protestant Holt's dilemma. Sex in the ranks of the United Irishmen.
On 8 September General Humbert surrendered. The presence of the Frenchman, François Joseph, together with the authority he appears to have assumed, suggests that, at the beginning of the following section, Holt's memory has lighted on a period about the middle of September.

Writing to her brother, the duke of Richmond, from Castletown, Celbridge, on 2 September, Lady Sarah Napier, aunt of Lord Edward Fitzgerald, said:

---

136 According to Luke Cullen's informants, the idea of setting fire to the furze and heath came from Michael Dwyer and other of Holt's comrades. Begrudgery? Holt has taken a leap in his chronology. The engagement took place in September.   137 Craig's offer of a reward (of £300, not £3,000) was published daily in the Dublin newspapers from 12 September until 13 November. This more or less confirms the chronological 'leap' Holt has taken in the text that has just gone before.

They watch to take the ton *from Dublin, their constant traffic with which makes intelligence come like lightning – to* them, *though not to us. They at first disbelieved the surrender of the French; they now believe it, and put a good face on it, still hankering after a new force which is collecting in Wicklow, under a clever man called Holt, who* rejects mob *and* chooses *his associates. This keeps up the flame, and while it burns, all those who persuade themselves that they acted on principle only, and those who have gone too far to retreat, besides those whom ill-usage has worked up into revenge, all reluctantly give up hopes of success. Yet their own judgments now have fair play; they see the lower orders quite tired of the business; they see a* vast number *who loudly proclaim their determination to stick to the promise they made to old General Dundas, who is their hero; for not one of those he forgave has returned to the rebels. They see the tide is against them; and, in short, I can perceive by their countenances that they are low, and sorry, and fearful. But, if they once give the point up, they will return to all their work with a heavy but not a sulky heart; for they are nearly convinced they are conquered by* fate, *not by* force, *and you must know that all the common people are predestinarians, which is a great cause of their hardy courage for moments, and their seeming indifference about death. They have very little shame about running away, being convinced they are reserved for another fight by fate, and not by their running.*

Humbert's surrender released many of the loyalist forces from their commitment to the north-east and to the Midlands, so that most of the loyalist potential could now be concentrated on the Wicklow rebels.

Against this we may set the fact that, although Holt's efforts to recruit men from the Blackwater region of Wexford met with little success, many highly trained soldiers from the Leitrim, Sligo, Antrim and King's County Militia had come over to him. In his deposition at Dublin Castle on 16 November he would enumerate them (see Appendix 6.1).

Despite the prospect of a further French expedition, many of Holt's men must have lost heart and this, together with the need to take in the last of the harvest and the impending cold weather, would have decided many to lay down arms. Holt's attitude to this was remarkably magnanimous. (See Miles Byrne's comment in the last paragraph of Appendix 1.3).

This may be as good a juncture as any to put in another word to the credit of Holt, the man, who, from the reports of Luke Cullen's informants and often out of his own mouth, transpires as blunt and overweening. Even though self-advertised, the courtly, chivalrous Robin Hood aspect of Holt's character emerges in the incident where, coming from Roddenagh bridge, he intercepts a party travelling towards Aughrim. The Courier *newspaper of 11 October reported a similar incident of gallantry at Kilcullen:*

[*Holt*] *the person who seemed to command the rest, and to whom a very marked deference was paid, addressed the passengers in terms rather polite, and said, that a want of shoes and boots, which was experienced by the party, obliged him to lay their purses under contribution – the affrighted captives accordingly laid the several sums of money which they had about them on the table, and were agreeably surprised on beholding the rebel leader take a guinea only from each sum! Mr Dudgeon's purse alone contained sixty guineas. This instance of moderation in what are termed* banditti, *and said to be connected for the purpose of rapine, I could not bring myself to credit, but that it has been had from Mr Dudgeon's own mouth.*

There was probably a fierce resistance amongst the 'diehards' in Holt's army against those who had their leader's blessing in electing to lay down arms. In taking 'the law' into his own hands, the Frenchman, François Joseph would have had their support; whereas Holt was probably canny enough to recognise that to threaten death to men who, though sworn as United Irishmen, were reluctant to take part in armed combat, might so alienate them that they would withdraw more covert forms of support, such as offering food and shelter.

The contradictions in Holt's equivocal allegiance to the United Irishmen are becoming more acute: the Protestant former sub-constable finds himself commanding a group of predominantly Catholic men, some of them bigots, some opportunistic banditti, using the United Irish emblem as a cloak for looting and wholesale burglary: Rebels transformed into terrorists, a phenomenon common to most rebellions. Although there was a rationale to justify the burning of some Protestant houses because, unlike those of their Catholic neighbours, the roofs of their houses were often roofed with slate, and so more easily convertible into barracks, there would have been times when he was expected to condone and even lead raids to burn down houses merely because they were owned by Protestants.

The most formidable threat to Holt's personal safety would have come from potential turncoats lured by the prospect of £300 which was on his head. With the exception of his friend, Matthew Doyle, Holt rarely mentions the names of other leaders, such as McMahon, O'Rourke, Murphy, Nugent. Only once do we hear of Hacket, the man who was sometimes his second in command, and then it is clear that Holt regards Hacket as a criminal.

The transmutation and consequent polarisation, whereby the United Irish cause was tending to become exclusively Catholic while Protestant and Presbyterian veered towards the Orange Order, would have been cause for satisfaction at Dublin Castle. It has been argued that 'the Castle' planned to 'divide and conquer' by propaganda that, from the outset of the insurrection, the United Irish cause was fundamentally Papist, albeit that its original principles were firmly entrenched in Presbyterian casts of mind and the transcending ecumenism of Wolfe Tone. If Holt is to be believed – and I find him convincing on this score – this actually came *about as the insurrection progressed; in which case it might be seen as the great watershed for Irish Nationalism and Republicanism, a result cruelly at odds with Wolf Tone's intentions (see Appendix 6.2).*

Holt is discreet, even prudish about speaking of sexual matters. In the New South Wales section of his 'History', he feels bound to draw a veil of silence over sexual behaviour on Norfolk Island out of respect for 'the females who will come to read my history'. Notwithstanding, he seems to have had at least one mistress, one of them Croppy Biddy Dolan(see Appendix 4).

A report in the Hibernian Telegraph *of 19 October, throws some fitful light on sexual behaviour in the rebel camps. The writer, who had been abroad many years as a lieutenant-colonel in the army, speaks of visits to Wexford and Wicklow: 'I called at Coolattin, on the poor wretched woman who nursed me and 22 others ... her husband had a call (so they term joining the rebels) ... 3 sons hanged at Wexford, her 4 daughters who 'went with the mob' were all diseased ... 2 sons killed at Vinegar Hill and three at the Battle of Arklow.'*

It was now the time [of] Earing, or Harvest, so that many of my enemy who were in town and barracks wanted to come home.[138] Their appearance often excited me to laughter when approaching me for protection, furnishing me with their nice fowling pieces, powder flasks, &c. and I had them treated with every kindness but – my men being short of tobacco money – so I appointed a clerk to form protections, charging only the moderate sum of ten shillings for each. When sd sum was paid their protection was signed – when atested to Fidelity. The form of which was that:

I, A B, do swear that I never will sell, set, deceive or betray a United Irishman, or cause to have done, & further I will to the utmost of my knowledge and power make known to you whenever I shall see any impending danger, which I think sd information may be of use, and that as speedy as in my power lyes.

So Help me God.

Gentle reader, this scheme was of infinite utility to me as it procured both amunition, arms' watchers and informers. Moreover, these new friends of course didn't let their fellow Loyalists know the substance of their vow, so that they stoped with contented safety at home finding both familyes' lives and properties safe, which rendered them quite faithfull to me, as afterwards their repeated fidelity gave me convincing proofs. Gentle Reader, lest you, the reader, should be in doubts of the aforementioned relation concerning giving my enemies protection &c. I now refer you to some of the places or towns: Ballymanus, Ballycurragh, Sheals town [Sheilstown], Nockalt (Knockalt) and whelprock [Whelp Rock] &c.

---

138 Due to the 'Golden Summer' the crops would have ripened early and reaping would have begun in August. With the news of the Humbert landing on 22 August, the morale of the Yeomen and the Militia would have been affected, and more of them likely to desert.

I marched to Nockalt, my head quarters at Oliver Hoey's [Hoyle's][139] – who was to us a good and faithfull man who shewed great compassion and kindness on coming to see me. One morning, as I was instructing my men how to exert themselves in case of engagement, I directed their officers to form some of their men in form of opposition against others in order for a sham battle. It was instantly done. I observed that a musquet and bayonet would have no more effect on a pike than a musquet ball would have against the walls of Gibraltar. I can't help making this observation: that disciplined men, if armed with pikes, and under proper jurisdiction, were, when come to a charge, are the best men in the world, but I hope – from the juniorship of my recruits – it will plead for their unruly conduct as every individual thought himself on a level with quite his superior.[140]

On this morning of sd sham battle my picquets informed me that at least 300 of the army were marching from Blessingtown towards us. I answered, 'My desire is [s]port. Ye cannot expect support unless you endeavour to earn it.' Gentle Reader, as I hadn't a drum to beat at this time, it is my duty to shew you the mode I contrived to call my men to arms – each officer under me having a knowledge of a private signal to enable them to know at any time when I wanted all men to arms, which signal was two shots quick from my pistol, which brought them all in an attitude of defence. I next had a place of safety erected on the side of sd Nockalt Hill, and in such a form that it would hide 3000 men.

A picquet came in, telling me the army was at Black Ditch [Black Ditches]. At this time I had 380 resolute, well disciplined, armed men, all deserters. I placed them in sd entrenchments, under the command of Francis [François] Joseph, a French (deserter) man from a Hession [Hessian] Reigment,[141] who lay in EEmale

---

[139] Hoyle was a Protestant.   [140] The news of the Humbert landing had been conveyed to Holt at Croghan on 26 August, by Nick Murphy of Monaseed; this would have encouraged more young men to enlist with him. The *Courier*, 5 September, reported the 'most alarming progress of Holt ... since he learned that the French had effected a landing. Although Humbert surrendered at Ballinamuck on 8 September, the news might not have filtered through to many parts of Wicklow for some days; and even when it did, the rebels and potential recruits knew that there remained the possibility of a further French expedition, led by Wolfe Tone.   [141] It is an extraordinary lapse on Holt's part to fancy that this Frenchman may have belonged to the regiment of German mercenaries, the Hessians. The lapse is gross enough to make one wonder just how *au fait* Holt may have been with the national, and international scene. I am inclined, however, to think that the passage of time between writing and the event accounts for the lapse: although, only once in his 'History', does he speak of the 'French factor', it seems likely that Holt had some contact with William Duckett who was regularly in touch with the French Directory; and various documents in the National Archives leave no doubt that, in October, he had meetings with the United Irish Executive in Dublin.   François Joseph had been sent from Mayo to Wicklow on 25 August by Colonel Dillon. His 'levity and irreligion' were frowned on by one of Luke Cullen's informants: he was said to be 'a Deist' and 'much disliked by the men', 'extremely immoral and his language blasphemous'. Joseph may also may have become involved with Croppy Biddy Dolan, which could explain Holt's personal antagonism. On the other hand, it was said that he was 'a man of distinction'. François Joseph spoke English and was reputed to to be 'an expert swordsman'. In all then, a typical child of the French Revolution. In 1799, destitute in Dublin, Joseph wrote an abject memorial to Lord Cornwallis claiming that he had been drawn into the Rebellion against his will. The wording of the memorial throws doubt on his mastery of English.

[Imail]. There was with me 400 pikes men, which I placed at the convenient end of my ambuscade, then gave orders how to act. In a short space I perceived my enemy appear. The halted and commenced asking questions at the opposite side of an adjacent river. They were answered by an old weoman:

'Perceive that place yonder. Faith, he is there, for I saw him this morning in yon two green fields, and be me shoul he seemed quite busy.'

They asked her had he much me[n]? She answered, 'By my shoul them two fields I shewed you was full.'

'Has he much deserters?'

She answered, 'By my shoul, two Read coats for one grey.'

During which time I was viewing their maneuvres. I walked in the rere of my men, which was (to them) imperceptable, drawing my sword, brandishing it as a figure of defiance. Sd Frenchman placed a distance of [illegible] with his pikes men.

I perceived the enemy in a state of meditation. I cried out, 'Have I any volunteers to cross sd river and give them seeming cowards a broad side?'

I received a unanimous answer; particularly the Leitrim Light Company, with most courageous vigour and activity, crossed sd river. I first replyed I should do my utmost oeconomy in protecting them, in case they should be compelled to retreat. On coming close to the enemy's line, [we] gave them a volley, which left many of them dead & wounded. The cowards were so terrified that they forgot to answer a return to my Leitrim Volunteers. Mean time I stood observing their motions, and [they] soon sounded their trumpet for a retreat. I gave orders for all to pursue and, if possible, make a rapid chace, which was put in execution – which continued about 80 minutes and about four miles distance, at which time I thought proper to retire.

At our return we found in our possession 18 guns, 24 cartorich boxes, 13 bayonets, 10 dead. And as for the wounded, I couldn't asertain. I wish to remark that I am sorry to this day that [I] couldn't find out their chief's name, as from his dastardly conduct on sd day should exclude him from any enterprizing appointment under His Majeste, for had he made an obstinate resistance, I should [have] retir[ed] in fifteen minutes for want of amunition.

We then returned, coming by Black Ditches. We purchased some liquor, of which we drank hearty to reanimate our victorious spirits. At my return I had the pleasure of the arrival of my 'Moving Magazine' loaded with 300 rounds of ball cartridge, giving me as brief an account of the state of many camps as she could conceive. I called her my chiefest treasure, and procured for her nourishment of the best in my power.

I gave orders for all to be ready next morning at one minute's notice, as I knew that there would soon be a formidable army to attack us. The news of my subtelity transpiring through my enemys on all directions, of course it was their duty to take every means to catch me, which they endeavoured to put into execution, employing as many setters and pointers as had Buck Whaley when he had in possession the due [duke] of yourks [York's] mis, wife.[142]

One day walking, I saw a smart looking girl coming towards me (she had a basket on her arm), who approached me, saying, 'General, I have brought you some very fine apples from Rathfarnham.'

I said, 'Have you?'

She says, 'Yes,' and continues, 'there will soon be out a large number of the boys who are gathering gunpowder th[re]e weeks, and sure they bid me come and tell you.'

I stared her earnestly in the face, saying, 'What are their names?'

She answered, 'Faith, Sir, I don't know. You know them yourself.'

I continued to ask her questions, and finding a visible criminality in all her answers, I directly desired the Drum Major to call her to trial, as I imagined her to be a spye. She was found guilty. I ordered the following punishment: Her basket to be kept; and to receive one dozen from the cat; then to be ducked. Some of my party wished to cut of her ears, which I didn't allow, as she went through her punishment. So I never heard more of her.

A boy came to Whelp Rock on the same deception. When observed walking through my camp, I asked him what was he about? He answered, looking for his father. I ask[ed] him his name. He answe[re]d, a 'James Connor from Hacketstown.'

There was a strict and immediate enquiry made for sd man, but found no such person. At length he was known to be a basket weoman's son, well known to be the name of Murphy. I then ordered Lieutenant Pluck[143] to tye him to the threelegged horse[144] and give him a dozen when, on receiving only three lashes, he confessed that he was sent thither by a Captain McDonnel [McDonald],[145] who gave him three guineas for so doing, which he gave to his mother, with a promise of a suit of clothes on giving an acct of our situation &c. at his return. He was tried, found guilty and received immediate sentence of death, which was put in execution in 12 hours after.

Next day we moved to Ballybrocka [Ballynabrocky], near Adown [Athdown] and, on my coming there, my men asked me what conduct they should observe. I answered, 'Free [Three] quarters of the inhabitants of this village were all sworn United men who usually resorted to my camp to procure plunder, steal horses &c. and then give information of our state to my enemy to cloak their theft – which formed my resolution to punish them. I appointed Edward White's house for head quarters, who had four grown up sons, all 'United'. I next recolected the inhumanity of aforemention Widow Magrath of Adown.[146] I gave strict orders that my men should take from her anything they should find useful.

I, accompanyed with a guard, advanced to Edward White's aforesd. I was seem-

---

142 Mary Anne Clarke was the duke of York's mistress. Buck Whaley, of Whaley's Abbey, was a flamboyant devil-may-care 'character'. Whaley's father was known as 'Burn Chapel' Whaley, a nickname which speaks for itself.   143 Probably William Pluck, of Ballycotton.   144 The triangle.   145 Captain Roderick McDonald, of the Glengarry Highlanders. The boy executed was named Murphy.   146 See note 122: this lady seems identical with Widow Kirwan.

ingly kindly received by Mrs White, saying, 'General, I am extremely sorry you didn't call last week, as I haven't even a bit of butter in my house.'

I said, 'Madam, we can't expect impossibilities. You can't give what you haven't.'

There were some potatoes put to boil. Meantime a young weoman, a friend of mine,[147] went to examine and found a cool[148] of butter and, from Mrs White's refusal, she of cource couldn't claim it, she knew it was no use to try to regain it. We then made divides of the butter.

She replied, 'I am sorry I have no spirits in my possession.'

I said, 'Well, Madame, you have a good substitute, that is, plenty of money.'

She said, 'Sir, I am afraid to send for it.'

I said, 'I shall rid you of that. I shall procure a mesinger,' adding, 'hand out the cash.'

She replied, 'Perhaps you may go be[fore] the spirits hath time to arive?'

'No, Madame, I don't intend going till [I] see this village in a state of conflagaration,' adding that, 'you and [your] neighbours are long enough living by plundering this country.'

Replyed she, 'Musha, the General is angry. Here is half a guinea.'

I says to one of my men – name of Dougherty – 'Here is another. Bring us the worth of them both of whiskey.'

Which he did expeditiously. We passed sd night pleasantly.

In the morning I called Captain Hollogan [Corragen or Corrigan] and company desiring the[y] would repair to the hill over Mrs White's house. When done, I shewed them a large flock of sheep, desiring that they should bring as many of them as the saw marked with the letters *E W*. Reader, observe that at this time, from not having a variety of food, it was impossible to observe days of abstenance. I sent fifty men, who brot a large flock who contained 86 mark[ed] with *E W*, which was instantly killed – which so agrieved Mrs White that she came to me, saying that she was ruined, that she believed there were 100 of her sheep killed.

I answered her, 'O, if that is all, you have no reason to complain. You had nothing yesterday, but now I let my men be their own providers,' adding that, 'when yr sons was plundering my camp, taking horses &c. to sell, you was not heard to murmur. Likewise, giving deceptionable information on my harrassed creatures who were destroyed before. But you imagined their actions of deciet would not come to light, but, if your lives are spared, think you are superfluouly complimented.' [149]

I had proof of this Mrs White's conduct, which assured me she was no less than fatal deception.[150]

In a short space a Mrs McGrath [Mrs Kirwan?: see p. 57], who refused me of refreshment on my arival from the Boyne before mentioned, came forward, stating

---

147 Ann Byrne? Croppy Biddy Dolan? **148** 'In Irish, cuíl, a shallow tub holding from twenty to thirty pounds of butter and put by as a store, or for sale' (Croker). **149** You are being treated better then you deserve. **150** That her deception has cost men their lives.

that my men were after plundering her of 4 sides of bacon, 4 sacks of male [meal], some shoes, shirts and money, saying, 'Sir, I hope you will have them restored.'

I said, 'You know, Madame, it's my duty so to do from the kind and gratefull treatment you bestowed on me when you offered me the green cabage leaves,' adding, 'Madame, observe yon tree. Instantly disappear, or it shall be yr gallows.'

She was rejoiced to get off. I am to this day gratified to have sd opportunity of inflicting punishment on so many sons of deception.

Gentle Reader, at this time I completely discovered the disposition of the sort of people this country produced. They were externally quite Puritans but internally quite the reverse, as their conduct was a proof, really attached to nothing but mere lucre.

On knowing that the news of us being here by this time had transpired to Rosborough [Russborough],[151] where a large number of Army lay, I now think it necessary to observe that, before my departure from Ballybrocka [Ballynabrocky], I received information of a large banditi who was robbing in my name. On strict enqiry, I discover[ed] their rendezvous, on which I wrote to the chief commander at Rosborough[152] as follows:

That it was a particular indignation to me for a well known banditti to be commiting violent acts of Burlgary in my name. As I am on leaving this neighbourhood, I hope you may have the goodness to send some of your men to Ballystocking [Ballynastockan], where you will find sd banditti of 24 men. By so doing you will extremely obleege your very humble servant

Grl. Jos. Holt

On receiving my letter, he sent a party to sd place, where the[y] discovered sd banditts, shot 11 and took eight prisoners. Among them was a Garret Eustace, who was much celebrated for activity and pipe playing, who had in his possession 97 guineas in gold and three guineas in bank notes – which entirely done away that false criminality alledged to me.[153]

I next received information that the army was to endeavour to surround me next day, which induced me to move my quarters to EEmale [Imail], where I remained three days. On one of sd days I sent Francis [François] Joseph, the aforementioned Frenchman, through the inhabitants of sd EEmale as knowing them to be 'United',

---

151 The country seat of Lord Leeson, of Milltown. During the insurrection it was comandeered by the army, who tore up many of the parquet floors to use as firewood. It was never burnt down during the insurrection, perhaps because Lord Leeson was thought to have some sympathy with the rebels. In more recent times it was owned by Sir Alfred Beit, who died in 1994.   152 This letter was addressed to Lieutenant Thomas Hugo, son of Holt's sworn enemy of the same name.
153 Newspapers of the time often referred to Holt as a desperado, or one of a banditti. Nothing would have stung the former barony sub-constable more then to be classified as a criminal; and he is often at pains to protest the distinction between a rebel and a criminal.

to come fulfull their vow and become our assistants. Sd Joseph, on going to the house of a James Byrne, he asked the man of sd house where were his sons? The old man's answer was, 'What's that to you?', on which Joseph took forth his pistol and shot him dead on the spot. When I heard it, I caused him to be taken prisoner in order to bring him condign punishment, and tryed.

On Tryal, it was proved that said Francis shot the old man without any more cause than the aforementioned. I then asked Prosecutor [154] if he knew of any conversation to pass betwixt deceased and prisoner? He answered, 'No.' I then asked him was he continually present, so that nothing could occur betwixt them unawares of his observation? He answered that he was.

A second Prosecutor came forward, declaring that he saw the prisoner come up to sd door and ask for 4 men who were sons to the deceased; that some more conversation took place but didn't hear the particulars; that he saw the prisoner take forth his pistol and shoot the deceased through the breast; that he saw him fall, quite dead, to the ground. On cross examination, he said he believed that prisoner's rash conduct arose from deceased's sons not joining my camp.

The evidence on behalf of the prisoner swore that he accompanyed prisoner from camp to Byrne's house; that the prisoner told him that he was going to order in all the United Men of sd place to come fulfill their attested duty; that on asking for the four young men of the house, the old man answered that he would 'sooner see them shot at the door than see them going to sd camp'.

Prisoner asked the deceased, 'Are you a United man?'
He, answered, 'Yes.'
'And was you sworn?'
'Yes.'
'Was you forced to do so?'
'No.'
'Was your sons sworn?'
'Yes.'
'Was any of them forced to do so?'
'No.'
'So, you rather commit perjury and stay at home, even have your sons shot at yr door, nor to assist us?'

Evidence continued that more conversation passed that he couldn't asertain, when prisoner drew forth a pistol and shot him, saying that it was too easy a death for all of his disposition. Three more evidence on behalf of prisoner proved the same. The jury brot verdict Not Guilty, so prisoner was acquited.

---

154 Holt, who in his days as a barony sub-constable, must have spent a lot of time in court, giving evidence, fancies himself as an amateur lawyer; by 'prosecutor', he means 'witness'. Although his pretensions are sometimes comic, it is to his credit that he allows prisoners the advantages of what he believes to be 'the due processes of law'.

Now I was apprehensive that the friends of the deceased would take every proceeding to betray me, which occasioned me to retire to Glenmuller. Stationed my quarters at a Pierce Harney's. Stationed my picquets.

I received information of a quantity of gun powder being procured for me at Cronebane.[155] I disclosed the subject to Colonel Mathew Doyle.[156] We concluded to go that night in quest of it. I directed that 300 of our best men should make ready for sd expedition, as I conceived that number would be sufficient.

Reader, before I relate what occurred to obtain sd powder, you must know that an Antrim soldier, name Peter Kavanagh,[157] best known by the name of Goodpay, had a miss or girl with us, whom he disclosed to her what we were about. Lucre being so tempting, she instantly hied to Rathdrum with the sd information.

We were 5 miles distant from sd Cronebane. So we proceeded just at dusk, but, on passing down by a wood, [I] called the flanks. I gave orders that the Antrim, Letrim [Leitrim] and Kings County Militia should march convenient to me, and strictly observe a profound silence, accept obstructed my advanced guard, being only 8 perches before me, in which possition I thought myself safe. There is a bog each side of sd road. At the end of sd direct road was a cross road. Some time before, the Yeomen had burned several houses at the end of sd cross road, where my instructed enemy lay in ambush.

We got so near them as pistol shot, when they discharged a volley at us. Though not a man of us was killed, several of us had our garments singed from the burning heat of their balls. There was a part of the sole of my foot taken away, and 7 more slightly wounded. At the event of sd explosion, I cried out with most determined voice to 'Surround the bridge at Greenane and we shall have them all!' My men gave them a speedy return, an which my affrighted enemy immediately fled and, from the confession of Lieutenant John Sutton who accompanyed them with such rapidity and confusion, that they rolled over each other. Some of my men came to sd plaice next morning and got several of their accoutrements. Reader, for the identity of the above, I refer you to sd Lieutenant Sutton who yet survives near Rathdrum.

I gave orders to my officers to desire my men to mind the bridge, as I new the form of the ground and the command of the bridge and each man that was there new me of old, so that I struck them with the greater terror.

I returned to Glenmuller and Mrs Holt. When she heard of the buisness she said, 'My dear, you were sold[158] but, thanks be to God, they were disapointed.'

---

155 The Cronebane Corps had originally contained many United Irishmen. Luke Cullen reported that 'many of the Cronebane corps were connected by consanguinity' to Holt. Later, after it was purged, Holt might consequently have had a special reason for detesting it.   156 The only man serving under him in whom Holt seems ready to confide. Their friendship may have been of long standing. Several of the Doyle family were enrolled with the United Irish movement. In his *Memoirs*, Miles Byrne says, 'Matthew Doyle, who resided on the way between Ballyarthur and Arklow, was appointed by the provincial chief to travel in the adjacent counties, to give instruction to the societies' (see Letter to Doyle, Appendix 6.7).   157 Kavanagh had deserted on 31 August.   158 Hester Holt's comment may refer to an incident reported by Miles Byrne (see Appendix 1.2),

I pulled off my stockings and dressed my wound with [a] turnisuat [tourniquet]. Mrs Holt said, 'They were near you, for your stocking is burned.'

Next morning I was up early and called the men to parade to see who was missing, and found our loss very small. A man of the name of Casker came to us to get a musket ball extracted from his cheek. I felt it with my finger and found I could not force it up. I then took out my lances and cut the cheek just under the ball and, with the assistance of my new invented pivoted a goose quill, and [with] my finger I extracted the ball and then dressed the wound, and remarked to him when he would get a few more hits of this sort he would make a good soldier.

The next that I assertained to be wounded was a woman by the name of Ann Byrne.[159] She received it in the thick part of her arm near the elbow. I soon perceived that the ball passed through her arm. I exammined it carefully with my prope [probe] and passed a sutair [suture] through the wound and made a perfect cure of them in fifteen days. The remainder were but slight flesh wounds, and as for me, the ball took only about half an inch off the left side of my left foot, which did not prevent me from doing my duty. The account of this engagement and all other occurrences was of course transmited to the different depotts of the Army - and expresses going backwards and forwards every day.

I received an account that Mr Allen, the clother, was going to make a barrack of his house – to intercept reinforcements coming to me. I called a Council of War to see what was best to be done, and it was agreed that the house should be burnt. I kept the matter secret, as I was in dread of being betrayed,[160] and immediately fired

---

although, in some particulars that report does not match with Holt's. Byrne says that Holt had proposed a raid at Glendalough. His men, fearing that their leader had betrayed them and would be leading them into a booby trap, proposed a raid at Cronebane. Holt's reference to 'my instructed enemy' implies that Miss Goodpay had given 'information' which led to the ambush at Greenane bridge: hence Hester might be thought to have meant, 'You were sold – *by Miss Goodpay*.' In any event, as Byrne points out, Holt could not be held responsible for the ambush since it was not he who had proposed the site of the raid. It is significant that Holt chooses to quote his wife's comment, since, in Miles Byrne's account, she was under suspicion. Holt says that he 'cried out with most determined voice,' while Byrne says that Holt struck terror into the hearts of the enemy with 'the voice of a stentor'. The two descriptions are so close in their focus that I wonder whether Byrne, writing many years later, may not have been influenced by reading the Croker version of Holt's memoirs, published many years earlier, in 1838. The ambush at Greenane probably took place in the first few days of September. There may have been yet another confrontation, in mid October, in which Holt and his wife were threatened. This could have been triggered off by a letter, mistakenly addressed to 'Captain Corragen', and written on 11 October, by William Hoey, of Edgeworth Street, Dublin. The letter gave the following warning: 'Mrs Holt has been in Powerscourt this week past and has General Holt's pardon if you and Captain Dwier does not mind her and him you are all lost' (SPO 620/51/238). **159** That a woman was among the party which set out to get gunpowder at Cronebane is remarkable. Sir William Betham passed on to Thomas Crofton Croker the following description he had been given by the boy, Ryan, spared by Holt, and who, Holt tells us, visited him in Dublin Castle: 'At one time he was constantly attended by a very handsome young women, dressed in a green habit, a kind of uniform with epaulets, her name was Byrne, she was the daughter of a farmer, and was called "the general's lady".' **160** Betrayed by someone who wants to collect the reward on Holt's head; or, with the growing pre-

Maintaining discipline 75

my signal to arms, and marched down to Greenane.¹⁶¹ One of my pickets observed a man of the name of Whelan runing in front of us. He was well nown to be an ennemy. John McEvoy, of the County Antrim, and a man that went by the name of Antrim John ¹⁶² – I gave them the command of field officers. On this occasion MacKevoy seen the man running, and fired at him and lodged the ball in his shoulder. That did not kill him, but in half a minute he loaded and fired again and shot him through the heart.

We marched on to Mr Allen's house. I sat on horse back near the house while the men were seting fire to it, and heard the voice of a female, seemingly in distress. I soon suspected what was the matter and, turning about my horse, I leaped over a large quickset ditch and, advancing to where I supposed the voice came from, I found a lady, the daughter of Mr Allen, in the greatest danger of losing her honour.¹⁶³ I drew my sword and cut the villain from the top of his shoulder down to his ribs. I left him for dead and, turning about, I found his sister, mother and aunt in the same sittuation. The ladies, altho nearly frighted out of their lives, most generously thanked their deliverer. I then conducted them out of the garden and called a gaurd and ordered them to convey them safely to a small village within two miles of us, near Rathdrum, where I knew the army would protect them.¹⁶⁴

The house was supposed to have a great quantity of money in it. The men, after plundering all that was loose, the[y] found the form of a cubboard in the wall, in cut stone, with an iron door and three locks on it. This they then concluded the money was depossited in this place. The fleams were raising very high about this time. I enquired for a few men I found missing, as I wanted to keep them together, least the army should take us in surprise, as I expected would be the case every moment. Those men were not to be found. I dismounted, went in to the house, and drew my sword, commanding them to turn out, which they refused to, as they said if they were to loose their lives they would open the cubboard, and when it was effected their was found contained in it several promissory notes for small sums of money, some bonds and laices [leases] on parchment.

My Good Reader, the reason that I can give so particular an account of this busnes is all those papers were packed up in a small box, and when the men got it out of the cubboard the[y] would have murdered each other for it but, to prevent this, I told them I would tie it up in my pocket handkerchief and cause the man that carried it never to qu[i]t my sight untill we arived at the house of a man of the name of Kelly, in the glenn. When we arrived there I called three of the best clerks to

dominance in numbers of the Catholic faction, by someone who thinks Holt likely to be a traitor because he is a Protestant. A third possibility is that, although he has not yet confided it to his reader, Holt knows that, through the agency of Mrs La Touche, Hester has made overtures to sound out terms for her husband's surrender, and fears that his men may have got wind of this. **161** Site of the ambush which Holt has only recently described. **162** John Mooney, appointed by Holt as an officer (Luke Cullen: Ms 8339). **163** Luke Cullen's informants refuted this account. According to them the threatened lady's name was Collins. **164** Although not the county town, Rathdrum, four miles to the west of Greenane, was the seat of the military establishment in Wicklow.

examine the box and found it to contain the papers I have mentioned and, of course, was not worth one farthing to the men.

This Mr Allen was reported to be a United Irishman very early in that buisness, and then changing to the other side caused him to have no friend. He has called on me since my return from New South Wales and asked me if I would make an affidavit that he never was a United Irishman. I stared at him and, said, 'Mr Allen, do you want me to swear to a transaction I saw nothing about? No, sir. If I was to swear at all, I should declare I was told you were a member of that body by twenty different people, and alow me to remark to you that you should return me thanks for protecting your wife and daughters at the time your house was burned in the year 1798 in place of making a requisition of me to swore to a transaction I know nothing about.'

On the day after the burning of Mr Allen's house, my old Moving Magazine arived, with two hundred and fifty rounds of ball cartridge and, early on the following day, my pickets came in a great hurry, leting me know their was a most powerfull army marching towards Balliboy, and the pickets from Faninnuran [Fananierin] quarter brought me the same news. I walked out to my observatory, or look out place, and found they could not come in on me in either ends of the glin, on account of the bridge being thrown down at one end, and a gulph that I had cut across the road in the other. I took out my glass and viewed them, but their number was so great that I could not possibly take it with any correctness. I called all my men to arms and ordered them to fall in to line. I walked in front of them and spoke to them as follows:

My dear fellows, our fate this day depends on God and your conduct, as our enemies appear to me to be twenty to one. Divide your amunition equally amongst you, and when I see the moment for your safety, you shall get notice.

I walked about for some time and then called on the Shilmileers [Shelmaliers][165] to examine their guns and get them in order – there were long pieces for shooting fowl on the great lakes; they carried a ball one fourth farther than a musket. I bid them fall in. My number was seven hundred and eighty-six. I placed the long pieces in front, the muskets to follow and the pikes in the rere. I ordered them to march slowly and the band to play 'God speed the Irish.'

I watched the motion of the enemy. We advanced about one mile. I then guaged the ground, and ordered the Shilmileers to fall on their knees and suppose them selves at Blackwater, shooting geese. Sixteen of them fired, an I seen a gap in the ennemie's line. Immedately I cried out, 'Charge again, my brave boys! The line at Ballyboy is breaking!'

[165] Quoting Sir Richard Musgrave, Thomas Crofton Croker tells us that 'in the attack on Arklow, their [the rebels'] front rank was composed of those who had fire arms, and who were mostly from the barony of Shelmalier, on the Wexford coast, where they subsist during the winter by shooting barnacles and other sea fowl, which makes them excellent marksmen.'

The remainder of the men that was in the rere – I never tould them my design, least the might take-french leave of me. I advanced slowly and gave the ennemy another volley. The trumpet sounded, and I seen the hurry in their lines and made my desent towards Elmale [Imail], watching their motion. I ordered my men to advance in quick time, directing that no man should go before me, as I hoped to God I would this day disapoint my enemies.

We had a great advantage of our enemies on this occasion as we were not encumbered with poutches, cross belts an a heavy load of aminution, together with the advantage of a good road. The ennemy had the most intricket boggy mountains to cross, the practicable passes on which was unknown to them, so that we could retreat ten perches for their one. Notwithstanding all those advantages, I found the ennemy surrounding us in all directions, so that I ordered my men to retreat and still keep up a regular fire so as to check their advance.

I originally planed the place to make my desent. It was over the Smelter House in Glenmuller, on an old path that the minors formerly made in coming down of the mountains to their work. The army had advanced at this time so far towards Emale that they could not be in time to intercept our retreat. We got near the top of the mountain. We found a few of the Light Briggade of the ennemy but they were much fatigued, I suppose from forced marches perhaps for three or four days. I gave orders to the Shilmileers – with their long pieces to give them a volley to let them see who they had to contend with. They poor fellows immediately gave way, which I asure you, my good reader, was more then I expected, and much more my enemies, but I asure you I was determined to fight while we could stand, as I was well aware if we were taken we would put government to the trouble of becoming a customer to some ropewalk in Dublin.

When the army advancing from Balliboy seen this transaction they began to run, both men and officers, but could not stop the advance of my Shilmileers. I must do His Majesty's troops justice – the[y] run hard, striped in their shirts, to get within shot of us, and often fired, but to no effect.

The army from Faninnuran were also advanccing in quick time. They had several guns and, when they seen the soldiers from Balliboy running stript in their shirts, they thought they were rebbels[166] and began to fire on them with small grape shot, which had they desired effect in my favour. The first shot killed sixteen men. The trumpet sounded immediately, and the firing ceased about this time.

We were on a hill at about a mile and half distance from the ennemy, perfectly secure, so we gave God thanks for our safe deliverance, and sat down to rest, being much fatigued. The army from Balliboy still pursued us and, when ever they came within shot of a Shilmileer, I ordered them to advance and give them a volley to reward them for their trouble, but the enemy from Faninnuran quarter were to far

166 The confusion may have been compounded by the fact that some of Holt's men wore uniforms of the regiments from which they had deserted; or uniforms from the corpses of the men they had slain.

behind to [shew?] for the chace. The army drove me off the first hill or, in pleon speaking, I went off to save them the trouble, but at every time the[y] came within shot of our long pieces, we gave them a round in the retreat.

In the evening of this day I was reinforsd by one hundred and forty men, who brought with them two prisnors of war, of the name of Marks and Chapman, from near Ashford bridge. I had not then time to try them, but told them they were the first two men that ever attimted to take me after my house was burnt. As soon as my men heard that, the[y] piked them immediately. This transaction took place on the mountain over the Seven Churches.[167]

This put the army in a great rage when they came up to the dead boddies, but the shadow of night put an end to the scene and left us perfectly secure from our ennemies. I then found it necessary to take the advice of my officers and men to know where would be the most elligible place to fix on for our head quarters. It was agreed that Oakwood, Nockenadruce [Knockadroose] and Nockalt [Knockalt] should be the place.[168] And, notwithstanding the darkness of the night and the intricket rout we had to take, we had no occasion to fire a signal for a pilot as we had the best in the country marching with us.

On this night we met with a flock of sheep belonging to the following persons: Saml Snell, George Manning of Ballyteague [Ballyteigue] and my 'old friend', Tom Hugo.[169] Notwithstanding it was far advanced in the night, we put the butchers to work and had for supper mutton chops and potatoes, a repast very acceptable to us after the fatigues of the day. After supper we retired to our respective quarters, but had no occasion to put out pickets, as no spie or informer could possibly know the rout we took.

I was up early on the following morning, and fired my signal for marching. Each man fell in. I changed the countersign and then walked in front of the line and asked the men several questions concerning the day before, and they were thoughtfull enough to return me thanks for the manner in which I conducted the business and vowed themselves to obey my orders on all occasions.

---

167 The reader will recall the incident early in Holt's 'History': on 12 May, with John Arnold, Holt had set out over Ashford bridge to get some whiskey. Having been given 'refreshments' by Mrs Kavanagh, she had rushed in to warn them of the approach of Marks and Chapman. Anxious to disclaim responsibility for this 'criminal' execution, Holt ascribes it to the loyalty of his men.
168 As a result of Humbert's surrender at Ballinamuck, it has been possible to step up the campaign against Holt's men. He finds it necessary to retreat to more remote headquarters. On 16 October, the *Courier* published an extract from a letter, dated 9 October: 'The fastnesses of those blood stained miscreants are situated in a range of wild mountains, for a chain of above twenty-five miles, and the scenes of their depredations are in the vicinity of those mountains. Twenty thousand troops would be insufficient to form a cordon to surround them, and so long as there are cattle, corn, or any other species of sustenance to be procured by plunder, within their range, they cannot be starved out. The mountains, rocks and ravines, among which they range, and with which they are familiarly acquainted, afford them numberless points of security and facilities for escape, inaccessible to cavalry or artillery ...'   169 Holt's enemy owned vast tracts of land in the county, much of it barren and boggy.

My headquarters was now at Olliver Hay's [Oliver Hoey's]. I walked about all this day, reaconnoitering; and, in the evening, I was informed that Hunter Gowan had taken up his quarters in Aughrim, with several corps of cavalry, and that he said he 'would make a sixpenny loaf be a sufficient supper for Holt and his men on the Satterday following'. I smiled at the comparisson, but took no more notice of the intelligence at that time, as I was aware that those that fetch news can generally carry the same. I began to consider on the most prudent time to pay my brave Hunter a visit and spent the whole day and night in contemplating.

Early the next morning my Moving Magaseene arived with 300 rounds of ball cartridge and brought me an account that my son was killed on the side of Macredeem [Macreddin] Hill by the cavalry. I fired my signal immediately for marching and gave orders for every man to be ready in thirty minutes and put in his haversack two days' provisions.

We began to march at about 9 oclock in the morning. I lead the van, and at about two oclock, we reached Ballahonal [Ballyconnell?], a small village within one and a half miles of Ballamanas [Ballymanus], and three of Aughram [Aughrim]. I gave directions for each man to coock his dinner, and that no man should quit the mean boddy without leave. I ordered Antrim John to place the pickets and outposts, and then despatched a messenger to inquire if my son was really killed. He returned in a short time and informed me my son was living, but their was a young boy killed supposed to be him. This child was met by a corpse of cavalry and asked whe[n]ce he was. He endeavoured to make the best reply he could, and, at the last, said he was looking for his father. They then asked him what his father's name was. He said, 'Tom Howlet.' This being so like Holt, without any more hessitation, th'e[y] struck him with a sword and clove him down through the head. I new the father of this child for many years. He lived at the Stamp Mill bridge, near Newbridge, and was a miller by trade. I regreted much that this boy lost his life on acct of his name being supposed to be Holt. He was but eleven years old and just the same age of my son whom he was supposed to be. These wicked and abomonable practices caused a great number to be killed on both sides without considderation, and I am sorry to say it came to my lot to witness too many seens of it practised by both parties.

One of my pickets now came in and informed me that four of my men were cut up in a most shocking manner in a sheebbeen house (that is, most properly speaking, a house that sold whiskey), in Ballimanas [Ballymanus]. I instantly fired my signal to arms. The men fell in immediately. I gave orders that no man should ride or run from his comrade. We advanced in quick time and soon came in sight of Aughrim, where my brave Hunter Gowan was stationed. We immediately perceived him advancing to meet us. I took up a position on the side of Redna [Roddenagh] Hill. John McEvoy, of the County Antrim Militia, was standing by my side. He perceived the flashes of fire from the pass of the ennemie's muskets and immediately called out, 'Down with you all!'

We fell on our backs, and I asure you, gentle reader, the ground was cut to pieces within a few feet of our heads, and must acknowledge I never in my life seen a volley better directed. We were soon on our feet again, and returned the compliment. I then ordered 150 men to go down by anacurira [Anacurragh] along by the river side, and get in to the wood, but to be compelled never to fire a shot untill Gowan had advanced as far as Redna [Roddenagh] bridge, and then get between them and the barrack. But the party were to heasty and fired too soon. When the ennemy found themselves attacked from the wood, the(y] immediately retreated, both foot and horse, back to the town. My brave Hunter,[170] seeing the dangerous sittuation he was in, abandoned his barrack and retreated across Aughrim bridge, and over Killaclora [Killacloran] we were still in pursuit of them.

Once, seeing the rout they took, I cried out to my men, 'Can any of you swim, boys?'. In less than two minutes I perceived about 40 men in the river, holding up their muskets and amunition in one hand and swimming with the other. As soon as they got on the other side, they commenced firing across the enemy's line and I kept up a regular fire in their rare. The Hunter, perceiving this, took his course another way – on the road to inakelly [Tinahely], in direction of Whealley's [Whaley's] Abbey. It gave me some pleasure to see my brave Hunter dismounted twice, but they third horse carried him off, and from that day to the present he never headed a corps. I was tould he received a wound, but am not certain as to the fact.

I pursued the ennemy as far as Mr Coatses of Cloan [Clone]. So that, my good reader, the sixpenny loaf that Gowan said should serve me and my men for supper on the following night should be of the same materials of the barley loaves and fishes mentioned in the Holy Writ.

After our chace we returned to Aughrim. My men were very impatient to burn all Loyal housees, and their lived in the town a sister to my wife., and lives there still. She came to me and said, 'Brother, protect me and my house.!' I promised her I would, and I asure you, gentle reader, I never had a more difficult engagement to fulfil in my life time.[171]

There also lived in this town a man of the name of Bolan [Boland]. He sometimes sent me supplies of provision, but I am not certain whether it was through love or fear. I caused his house to be protected also and, in order to prevent the army from burning it in retalliation, I broke every window on the concerns [?] and cut himself with a sword in several places. The barrack was completely consumed, with all other houses nown to be our enemies. We took some refreshment in the town and then returned to Ballahora [Ballyhara]. About sun set I gave orders to put out pickets in several places round the camp; and then retired to bed such of us as could procure one.

170 See note 21.   171 As the distinction between Protestant loyalist and Orangeman is becoming blurred in the eyes of the (now overwhelmingly Catholic) rebels, Holt's own Protestantism threatens to make him a marked man. Hester Holt's sister's situation would have been made the more uncomfortable – as would Hester's – by the fact that their mother, née Manning, had come from a family believed to have Orange sympathies.

Early on the following morning one of the outposts brought me an account that there was a small party of army marching towards Tinnehaly [Tinahely]. I ordered a party of cavalry to mount and we set out in pursuit of them. We soon came in sight of them, at about one mile and a half's distance. They were 24 in number, with a commissary and fourteen cars and horses, and a gentleman of the name of Croats [Coates]. This gentleman and the commissary were in a coach, and I was afterwards informed they were going for wheat, belonging to Mr Croates, to Tinikerley [Tinahely].

The road they were marching on was along by the Derry river, so that they soon perceived us and instantly, stripd in their shirts, abandoned their firelocks and threw away their carterage poutches, and began to run, except four men that mounted behind some of the drivers and road off with the coach. We pursued them in all directions, and I ever will remember I [c]ame within pistol shot of the coach but, when I attempted to fire, to my great astonisshment on snaping my pistol, I found no priming in the pan. Immediately shouted, and two of the soldiers that was riding double leaped down of the horses, left their arms lying on the road and got over the ditch in to a srubbery, or plantation. When I came up to these muskets I dismounted and, taking up one of them, I fired after the two soldiers. One of them I heard give a loud shout, but I am not certain whether it was fear or a wound he received caused him to do so. The remainder of the party were pursued in all directions by my men and, at our return, we had three men prisoners, with fourteen horses and cars. The horses were of a good kind, and I added them to my cavelary. The cars were burned in the road.

The men were brought to head quarters and, on the following morning, brought to tryal. Their was sufficeint proof that two of them were ennemies, as they were Airange [Orange] men. The jury returned a verdict that they they were guilty and should be put to death, which was of course carried into effect in a short time after their tryal. Their was very little feeling for these two men as it was well understood they were in the habit of informing agains United Irish men.

The third prisnar – I caused his life to be saved, as he was but twelve years of age. His name was Ryan.[172] Since my return from newsouthwales he called to see me,

---

[172] At this point in his edition of Holt's memoirs Croker provides a long note about Ryan supplied by Sir William Betham. It contains a detailed account of his capture. In the course of the episode, Ryan recalls, Holt said to one of his men in an angry tone, 'Do not make war against children, this poor boy could never have had a hostile feeling against us: God forbid we should hurt him unnecessarily; and killing unjustly is murder, and will bring down God's judgments and vengeance upon us sooner or later, and with His blessing I will protect every child's life that falls into our power, and if any man commits murder, or cruelty towards the helpless, I will have him tried and found guilty of murder, and he shall surely die. Neither shall any prisoner be put to death without trial, unless he be taken in arms and in uniform, and let me see the man who will dare to act against these orders.' 'He then turned to me,' Ryan recalled, 'and in a kind manner and voice said, "Don't be alarmed or afraid, my boy, no one shall harm you; you shall be with me, and I will protect you!" He then ordered me food, and as I was indebted to him for my life, I felt attached to him, and have ever since been grateful. [...] I continued some weeks with the rebel army, and was witness to several

and is a well-looking young man. He returned me thanks for pleading for him and saving his life, on his knees. And I asure you, my gentle reader, it was a great consolation to my mind, on cool deliberation, as the seens of cruelty practised at the period of my life that I am now treating on were beyond comprehension.

On the Sunday morning following, we marched to Nockanannaga [Knockananna], a mountainous place where there was a Roman Catholick chapel. Several of the men wished to hear Mass – it was then celebrating. We acordingly went in, as many as could get room, and brought in our arms with us. When the clergyman seen the fire arms, he said, 'Gentlemen, you never seen such weapons as those brought in to the house of God before.'

I replied to him and said, 'Sir, you never seen such times as those, and you would oblige me by going on and finnishing the sacrafice of the Mass, as probably those men would never see a priest or a chapel again, so that I think it is your duty to comply with their request.'

One of my men, called by the name of Antrim John, then spoke and said, 'Sir, if you don't say Mass this day I will take care you never shall at any other time.'

The priest took the hint and then proceeded, and indeed it was well for him he did, for I afterwards heard this Antrim John declared, if he did not, he would have shot him at the altar, which I certainly believed as he was a violent tempered man.

When prayers were over, the priest sent for me, requesting that I would take some refreshment with him. We had some conversation, in company with two or three other gentlemen, and the[y] were all aware that I was not a Mass man. [173]

I returned in the evening to quarters, when an express came in that twentyfour of the King's County Militia were coming across from Aughram. I ordered my horse to be saddled imediately, and set out to meet them, in company with five of my chosen men. Previous to my laving the camp, I ordered a partey to be prepared to give them a salute of arms while I escorted them in. When the[y] arived I gave them up to Captain Hacket and ordered a good beif cow to be killed for their sepperate use, at the same time tould them they should have double allowance for one week, and that I would make them earn it at another time. After dinner I went to see them. Two of them played different instruments of musick, the violin and flute. I requested they would play us a tune, and we had a dance. So that you see our sittuation, gentle reader: We were merry one day and sad another.

The army were about this period breaking the coocking utentils in every house they came to, in order to starve me and men, and I gave orders to my men to do the same. In the mean time [I] contrived a plan to send a letter to send to General

---

extraordinary instances of General Holt's bravery and humanity, as well as of his determined character.' See also note 159.   [173] Ruan O'Donnell tells me that Luke Cullen gives another version of this incident. Antrim John (John Mooney), devout Catholic though he may have been, may have been ready to carry out his threat to kill the priest. Luke Cullen's memoirs report him thus: 'It was a rebellion & no war & there was no way of keeping pris[one]r[s]' SPO 620/17/30/73.

Jones[174] to stop this proceeding and the burning of houses, together with requesting that he would give orders to the different corpses under his comand to protect the honnour of all females, and suffer no man to be shot under the age of sixteen; and if he agreed to these regulations I would do the same. And further stated, although my number was small,[175] it was large enough to do good or evil. I received the answer to this letter in the course of a few days, stating to me that he was sorry this was not thought of sooner so that we had no more of those wanton and barboures acts commited.

I remained in camp untill the Sundy following, as I expected to see my second eldest brother, William Holt, an architect by trade,[176] on that day. I ordered twentyfour of my best cavelry to be readdy on that morning to go meet him. We set out tollerable early and crossed over Balimanis [Ballymanus] towards Redna [Roddenagh] bridge, where we perceived eight soldiers and a sergant, with some baggage, traveling towards Aughrim. I said, 'My boys, their is some game.'

We bore down on them and, coming up close to them, they soon perceived what we were. I rode in front and, perceiving they were but nine in number, I turned down my fire arms, signifying to the sergant that I did not intend to fire on him, and as I drew near them, the[y] stoped trembling with fear. I ordered my men to halt, and advanced up to the sergant. He presented me with his sword, which I refused to take. On turning my head towards the cars, I perceived a very well-looking woman and five children. She was seemingly swooning away, much terrified. I asked the sergant if she was his wife. He answered, his, 'Sir.'

I went over to her and took her by the hand, saying, 'Maddam, stop your lamenting. I am not going to hurt your husband or injure you.'

She still kept crying, and also her little children, saying, 'Sir, don't kill my Dada.'

The poor little ones induced me to think of my own. I orderd the soldiers to drive on the cars to Aughrim, and turning about to Mrs Jones, said, 'Maddam, did you ever hear of such a man as General Holt?'

She answered, 'Yes, air, but shoorly you are not that man, for I am told he is a terrible man.'

'Well, Maddam, the Devil is not as black as he is painted. I certainly am the person whom you so much dread.'

When we arived on the town I halted at a man of the name of Mr W. Bolon [Boland] and ordered one gallon of ale to be given to the eight soldiers, and desired the sergant, his wife and children to come in to the house. I had bread, butter and cheese provided for them, with some ale and punch. The poor woman was still in trouble and had her eyes fixed on me.

I then told the sergant I should search his baggage and if I got any fire arms, flints, powder or ball catterage in them I would be very angry with him. He then

---

174 At this time his rank was colonel.   175 See Appendix 5.2 for an informant's report (19 September) about the size and morale of Holt's force.   176 He was a builder.

replied, 'Sir, in order to give you no trouble, I will give you my oath their is no such thing in my possession and, if you find their is, shoot me immediately.

I then asked the sergant if his regiment 'was to meet eight of my men in the same situattion that we found you, don't you think they would put them to death?'

Both him and the wife answered, 'Yes, we believe they would.'

'Well then, I will treat you in a more humane manner. And give my compliments to General Jones and tell him I hope he will follows this example.'

I then called for pen, ink and paper and gave him a pass, as follows:

I command all and every United Irishman to let the bearer Wm. Jones and company pass from Aughrim to Rathdrum unmollested and any person acting contrary to this requisition shall be punnished in the severest manner. Given under my hand at Mr Boalon's, Aughrim, Sunday evening.

(General Joseph Holt)

I ordered twelve of my own guard to conduct this party as far as Whealley's [Whaley's] Abbey, as I much feard if the[y] were attacked the[y] might be killed before they could produce my pass. However, the[y] proceeded unmolested, and my men returned with my brother. He had but two miles to come see me from his own house.

I had the pickets placed in their respective placces and then sat down with my brother and some friends to drink punch. We talked over several matters untill about two oclock in the morning, when we parted and my brother went towards home, but he was unfortunately met by a supplementary corpse called the Bond Men of Cronebane, a poor set of raskals that had neither honour, vallour or honesty in them that could intitle them to ware His Majesty's cloath. They made a prisnor of him and draged him to Rathdrum, telling him he would be hanged next day for going to see that villain, his brother. I can asure the reader that this man would drive ten of those miserable creatures before him on the road, but they were to many in number for him to contend with. They brought him to the abovementioned place and lodged him in the guardhouse, and several of them remained in the town to prossecute him, as he was to be tried by Court Martial, the country at that period being proclaimed under that law, and I can assert for fact it was eassy for any hard-mouthed villain to swore away the life of an innosent man.[177]

There was in this corps a man of the name of Thos Lewins that agreed with the description of the persons I alude to. He was by religion a Roman Catholick, but reformed from those principals to get in favour with Thos. King Esq., who was captain of this cruel corps. And to prove to the reader that crimes are punnished either on this earth or here after, this man was since murdered by his own son, and

---

[177] Far from being an innocent man, William Holt had been active as a United Irishman as early as mid 1797.

the son was tried for the deed at the asizis of Wicklow, found guilty, and hanged in the year 1818.[178] The reason that I dwell so much on this subject is to let the reader see a tipe or figure of the description of yeomen employed by His Majesty and the cruel actions they were capable of commiting' in the year 1798, and I also think it my duty to show the reader that good and humane actions meet with their just reward, and will prove it as follows: Had I gluted my self or imbrued my hands in the innocent blood of Sergant Jones and his eight companions, in retalliation my brother would of fell a victim to the existing law at that time, but when Sergant Jones heard there was a prisnor of the name of Holt in the guard house, he repaired to it instantly and enquired of him if he was my brother. He answered in the affirmative. The Sargent then replied, 'Don't fear. Your brother saved my life, and my companions' also on yesterday and I will do what I can for you this day.'

He then quit the guardhouse and repaired to General Jones and related to him the hole transaction of his being taken by me and how I treated him. The General could scarcely credit what he said untill he produced my pass, and that was not even sufficient untill he enquired from the party that was with the Sergant and, when he found them to agree in every particular, he then said it was a pitty to give me a character I did not deserve. The Sergent then intimated to the General that their was a brother of mine in the guard house charged with being in company with his brother, the Rebbel General, on the day before. He then tould the Sergant to go to the Officer of the Guard and desire him to bring the prisnor before him.

When the[y] arived, he interregated my brother and asked him if he was on a vissit with his brother, the reobber chief. He answered he was and told the whole transaction as it occured. The General then said, 'Your brother gave a pass to some of His Majesty's soldiers yesterday and I will give you one this day,' and said, 'I think it is a great pitty your brother should die in the state he is in.'

My brother then related some of my misfortunes, which he readdilly believed and, in some time afterwards, I received a letter from General Moore, which causes me to think he did – which letter will appear in its proper place in this narrative. I was informed of this transaction and eagerly wished to come in contact with the Craanebone [Cronebane] Corps to make them repent their conduct on the occasion.

Next morning the pickets brought me an acct that there was a party of Army marching towards Aughevanna and that they were marching across Ubonks [Bluebank] Hill, bearing down on Mucklar [Mucklagh] Hill. I went out immediately to my lookout place and, on viewing them with my glass, they proved to be the very corps I wished to meet with. I ordered all men to arms and drew them up at the rare of a large ditch so that their number could not be taken by the ennemy. We were at this time within musket shot of each other but I endeavoured to seduce them to come down one hill, having another to assend, on which I was posted. I walked at

---

178 A reminder that Holt is writing at least twenty years after the events he describes.

the rere of my men with my sword drawn, and spoke to Captain King, by means of my trumpet, as follows:

> I wish you may have courage enough to fight me in single combat and have our men to look on. You little thought when my house was burned and my property destroyed [179] that I could or would give you such trouble, and I swear I could die eassy if I was after setting the matter with you.

One of my men, by name Francis [François] Joseph, asked me if I would alow him to fire a shot. I told him I thought they were to far off, but he said he would engage his rifle piece would tell at the distance. He fired, and his assertion proved to be true, as I was afterwards informed by Captain King in the Castle of Dublin – as he paid me a vissit to try if he could get any information from me, but he was disapointed, as was all men that ever made the same application to me.

Immediately after Joseph fired the shot, the enemy's trumpet sounded, and I said to my men, 'That wretch thinks to trippan [trepan] me this day, but I will show him that God has given me a better head than ever he had.'

Prievous to this occurance, I sent out Patt Dougherty, from the County Carlow, as picket on the mountain at my rere, but the cowardly scoundrel run away from his post without even firing a signal.

The trumpet was still sounding. I instantly suspected I was surrounded in the rere, and gave my men orders to follow me in open and single files, that the enemy should not take off my number.

I marched across the side of the mountain over Ballahona [Ballyconnell?] towards Aughevanna. I had the good fortune to be about twenty perches of the ground to the right of the ennemy, when I was attacked by seven different divisions. I said to my men, 'Let no man run. And keep together.' And, to show them a good example, I alighted from my horse and, having a nice fusee in my hand, I applied it.

Their was a very hot fire commenced but, to my misfortune, I new the strength of my amunition and accordingly ordered my men to march, and fight as they retreated. We loaded as we walked along and turned about and fired in regular sections, so that we checked the ennemie's advance. It continued for a considderable time. I had seven wounded, but none killed. I received a slight wound my self but it did not prevent me from doing my duty.

At one particular period during this engagement I was nearly left alone and, when I perceived it, I cried out, 'You cowards! Are you going to do what I never done to you?'

I had my piece charged, droped on my knee, and loveld [levelled] it so carefully that it told well. When the men seen this, they returned as fast as they went forward and, when the ennemy seen them runing down the hill to me, it put them to a stand.

---

179 Thomas King had been present at the burning of Holt's house.

They then sounded the trumpet and returned, once more disapointed at not haveing my head, as I am certain several of them calculated on what a fine, season's work it would be to obtain it, but thanks be to God I have it my self yet and thinks it worth more than General Craig bid for it.

The corps that we were engaged by on this day were as follows: Rathdrum, Northshire, Southshire, Tinnehaly [Tinahely], Hacketstown, Dunard [Donard], and some others that I don't at present recollect.

Holt's keen appraisal of the causes of the Rebellion

Holt's apologia for those who perforce had joined the United Irishmen includes a keen appraisal of the causes for the Rebellion, even if he remains disingenuous and tendentious about the precise date of his own enlistment. He is extraordinarily frank about one of his more ruthless tactics in boosting recruitment to his own forces.

I now think it my duty to inform the reader of the causes of so much blood being spiled in those very grievous times, as I am aware that many will read this narrative that might not be well acquainted with them:

That their was a conspiracy to overturn the constitution I believe cannot be denied, and that its origin was amongst the lower order of people I have reason to believe,[180] but it would never of been followed up by so much cruelty but for the conduct of the yeomen, as the[y] generally put an unfortunate man to death without inquiring whether he was guilty or not, and I have nown instances of my own knowledge when they got on their neighbour's horse and, His Majestie's cloth on their backs, they proceeded to revenge any old spleen existing in their breasts against any of their unfortunate Catholick brethren, making use of the expression, 'Now is my time. I will have sattisfaction;' and the result was the miserable man would be shot. And the murderer's defence would be, 'He was a United Irishman,' and, of course, he had a right to shoot him. No further inquiry would then be made. When ever any of those instances would occur, the whole country would be allarmed and of course quit their dwellings, at the same time remarking to each other, 'We may as well go out and fight as to be shot at home.' A muster would then take place and, in retalliation, they would sally out and put any man in the country supposed to be an Orrange Man or Yeoman to the sword. So that I asure the reader I often thought the people considered murder no crime.

I now inform my gentle reader how I generally mannaged in recruiting. I or-

---

180 In the New South Wales section of the 'History', Holt inveighs bitterly against Defenderism, a movement which did indeed have 'its origin amongst the lower order of people' and which was later subsumed into the United Irishmen. Perhaps Holt was unaware of the distinction between the two movements, and even quite ignorant of the principles of the United Irishmen; if he had been informed of them by his friend, Matthew Doyle, Holt may have found them quite unappealing.

dered a party of men to go and bring me some gentleman or yeoman's horse, or play some trick on them. Then the result would be, in twenty-four hours after, some unfortunate man would be shot and, on the following day, I would have plenty of recruits repairing to my standard and, as matter of course, relating to me what happened in the neighbourhood – namely that such a man was shot. My reply was generally, 'I think they served him right. Why did he not come to me and probably he would yet be living?'

> **The French 'factor' remains crucial. Holt continues to hold out.**
> *The raid at Blessington described by Holt is probably that described in the* Courier *of 10 September. The raid took place on 4 September. The 'Information' given on 19 September suggests that, although his authority may be waning, Holt's thoughts are still far from surrender: see Appendix 5.2.*
> *Holt's habit of wearing the full regalia of a French officer is probably a clue to the trend of his thinking. Although he has yet made no mention of the 'French connection', other than the garbled reference to François Joseph, the prospect of a further French expedition would have been to the fore of Holt's thoughts until the end of October, and the most critical factor in his assessment of the prospects for victory.*

The reader will observe that, after the engagement with the seven corps of yeomanry, I found the army were receiving informations every day of how I was sittuated and then resolved to make short stands in every place, as the reward that was offered for my head I feared would gain it.

I marched to Oakwood and Nockalt [Knockalt], as we had nearly run the country we were in out of provissions. I received information that their was several corps of cavalry in Blessingtown, and a great quantity of cattle in the park under their protection. I fired my signal for marching. Our route was trough Blackditches, over the Kings river, in to Ballyboys [Baltiboys]; and soon got in sight of Blessingtown.

There was a man of the name of Johnathan Eves lived near Baltyboys. He was half Quaker and half Prottestant. I new him to be no party man. I also new him to harbour several wounded men in his house and, with the assistance of his daughters, made perfect cures of them, and I considdered him to be of more service than ten men in the field, and I was also aware he had them concealed in [town?] at the risk of his life. One of my men, Hennery Downes by name,[181] met him and made him a prisnor. I had to much to attend to and could not stop to have him tried and was aware that, on his tryal, I would aquit him. I ordered two men to bring him in

---

181 'Henry Downes, who appears to have been a deserter from the Kings County Militia, was ultimately taken and hanged' (Croker). Downes was hanged at Malahide, in north Co. Dublin. His memory as a national hero, was celebrated in a lament, 'Erin's martyr'.

safety to headquarters untill my return, and indeed I must confess their was but a chance for my so doing, as no man going in to the field of battle can be certain of returning. I rode on and, in a few minutes, heard a shot in the rare and instantly turned about when, to my utter astonnishment, I perceived Eves lying dead on the road. Downes cried out to me, 'General, I saved you the trouble of trying him. I tried him my self.'

'More villain you are,' was my reply.

He shot him walking between two men.

The firing was commencing very hot from the steeple of the church about this time.[182] I desired that no man should fire a shot in my party untill I would give notice. A man run out a house on the roadside. Barney Holligan [Corragen],[183] of the Kings County Militia, was riding with me. The man fired and wounded Holligan in the arm and side. He instantly turned about and nocked the wretch's brains out with the but end of his firelock. The reader will be sattisfied as to the justice of such an act, as the shot was fired at him with an intent to kill and the act commited by the latter was but in his own defence.

We had not advanced much farther when a ball struck one of my men in the breast, from the steeple. It passed through his coat and waistcoat and lodged outside of his shirt. He fell, but I believe more frighted than hurt. When I observed him still lying on the ground, I dismounted to see where he was wounded and found the ball lying outside his shirt. I laughed at his sittuation. He then cried out he was shot, and I said I believed him and immediately gave orders to have him buried. As soon as he heard that, he boun[d]ed up.

We were still advancing near to the steeple. I ordered the one third of my men to take a surctuous rout and get to the opposite side of the town to us. As soon as this plan was effected, we were prepared to attack the enemy in the steeple where ever the[y] made their appearance, both in front and rere, and kept them in this sittuation while a party of my men were driving the cattle out of the park. They drove off 150 sheep, 32 cows and bullocks and ten horses, and amongst the latter number a beautifull bay mare, three-quarterbread, the property of Parson Benson. I expected this transaction would cause the enemy to quit the steeple and give us battle but they took no notice of what was doing.

We then returned with the cattle and, as we were traveling along the road, several old women came out and asked me if I would give them a sheep. I desired them to go and catch [one] and I perceived one old woman endeavour to hold two strong weathers and, in the struggle, she was often draged in to the ditch and, after all her exertions, she was obliged to return without either of them.

182 This action was reported in *Saunders News Letter* of 4 September. 183 Another instance of the 'scribe's' ear playing him false?: Ruan O'Donnell informs me that, after consulting lists of the United Irishmen, he is persuaded that this man's real name was Corragen. This accords with a letter from Major Sirr (quoted by Dickson in *The Life of Michael Dwyer*) in which he writes: 'Captain Corragen is a deserter from the Kings County Militia and commands the deserters from the regiment.'

When we returned to camp I consulted with my officers on the propriety of trying Henry Downs [Downes] for the willfull murder of Eves and disobedience of order, but their advice was not to attempt it.

About two days after our return from Blessingtown, I received intelligence that the Marquis of Waterford's lodge in Hollywood Glen was going to be converted in to a barrack. I then took the advice of my officers on the subject and-it was agreed that it should be burned.[184] I ordered forty-nine of my best cavalry to get readdy for the excursion. I marched with them and, when we came to the head of the glenn, the men seemed very uneassy to get in to the house, and I have no doubt but it was for the sake of plundering it.

As I sat on my horse at the door, I heard the cries of a female. I dismounted imediately and went in to the house, where I found a young woman supplicating some of the men not to murder her. I ordered them to let her out, and they said they were not going to ebuse her person, but she had money about her and they should have it. I endeavoured to get her out of their hands, but to no purpose. They tore off her stays and found consealed in it fifty guineas in gould, and two watches, with some other articles of value. The lodge was set on fire. I put some tables agains the sillar door to prevent them from seeing it. They threw some loocking glasses out on the window, with feather beds and other valuable furniture. I then ordered them to quit the place and went to Miles Miley, who kept a publick house, and desired him to give them to [no] liquor, but to bring up to the top of the hill three or four gallons of spirits. Which he complyed with.

A great debate arose amongst the men. I inquired the cause, and was informed that one man had got a lace purse of guineas and every man claimed an equal share of it. I made them fall in to line and ordered the man that had the purse to give it to me. I then divided it amongst them, giving each man a guinea, after paying for the spirits, and the two men that came short I gave them the watches. They were then sattisfied. We then returned home, except a few that deserted and commenced robing, a trade that men generally loose their lives by – I never new any man that made any thing of the trade but Patt Dogherty, of the County Carlow, and James Devit [Devitt] from Ballinacor.[185]

Both of these men went to Amirrica [America] having, by that system, realised a large sum of money. As for my part in all the proceedings of the year '98 I was contented when I could get plenty to eat, and guard against spies and informers.

The morning after the burning of this house, I attended on parade and cautioned all the men against the robing sistem, telling them at the same time that such acts would 'be punnished one time of another. I then began to think of going to see my wife, and give orders to the men to get readdy for marching. We proceeded towards Glenmuller and, in one hour after our arival, my wife came to see me, as she

184 On 26 September the *Courier* reported, 'The Marquis of Waterford's seat at Hollymount [*sic*] [Hollywood] has also been plundered and destroyed.'   185 Probably Ballinacorbeg, one mile south of Roundwood.

got an acct. that I was wounded and lost one of my eyes. On the same evening I received a letter from General Moore. Its contents were as follows:

> Mr Holt – From the good account I have got /recieved/ of you I should be glad to have some conversation with you. Point out any place you think proper. Bring as many of your men as you please and I will bring with me only my servant. I will also bring with me a cold dinner and, if you let me now what will sattisfy you for your losses, I will use my endeavours to get it for you.[186]

The bearer of this letter was Keogh, the miller, from Whitetown [Whitestown] bridge. I certainly must confess I would embrace the opportunity if I possibly could. When I finnished the reading of the letter I handed it to Colonel Doyle, and he read it for the people. The moment he was done reading, my wife and I was put on our nees to be shot. I was astonished what came over the people, and inquired the cause. One of them made answer that my wife had brought me that letter and that the[y] were of opinion I was going to make my escape and sell them all. My wife answered, 'You wretches! Why don't you stop the man that brought the letter? He is now rideing down the road on that gray horse.'

They followed him, brought him back and asked him where did he get that letter? He said that General Moore sent him with it to Mr Holt and that he did not think it was a crime to carry it. We were then relaced from our perilous sittuation. *My wife could not keep her temper*, but was reprobatung thir conduct to me and said she allway expected they would treat me in the end as they were about to do on this occasion. I suspected it was the abuse I gave Henry Downs for shooting Johnathin Eves that made them combine against my life and I was resolved to be very sircumspect in how I would act in future.[187]

They fixd a watch on me, and if I attempted to go to the rere, I would certainly be shot. Before the matter was completely settled, an argument arose amongst the

---

186 General (later Sir John) Moore, who would later serve in the Peninsula Wars, was a compassionate, humane man, and reluctant to take command during the insurrection. He once said that, had he been Irish, he would have enlisted as a United Irishmen. Moore condemned the 'violence and atrocity of the yeomen', and said that Wicklow would be restored to peace 'if the gentlemen and yeomen could behave themselves with tolerable decency'. Cornwallis's decision to employ him as a negotiator for peace was wise and sensitive. 187 One story in Luke Cullen's papers (ms. 8339) has it that Michael Dwyer, convinced that Holt was a traitor, spared the lives of Joseph and Hester Holt only because he thought their execution would encourage the opinion that the Rebels were discriminating against Protestants. I think the story unlikely to be true: it should be borne in mind that, at this time, there would have been nothing intrinsically 'treacherous' in entertaining the idea of accepting an amnesty. Dwyer himself had received an offer of amnesty from General Moore but seems to have been deterred from accepting it by his perception that, had he returned home, he would probably have been vulnerable as a target for Loyalist reprisals. In this case, Holt may have been accused of being a prospective turncoat, ready to 'inform' on his comrades; especially if any of them had got wind of Holt's hopes of escaping to England. It is possible that Miles Byrne, in his *Memoirs* confused this incident with the one prior to the ambush at Greenane (see note 158).

men – which had like to end in their murdering each other for the insult offered to me and my wife, but I interfered between them and reconsiled the parties.

Next morning, on parrade, I was determined to give up the command and become a full private in the ranks but they would not suffer me to do so, and made a promise to me they would never offer any insult to me or Mrs Holt again. I was much hurt at the treatment I received and kept my self from conversing with any person as much as possible for several days. Some of my best friends would walk some times with me and endeavour to cheer up my spirits, requesting I would endeavour to forget the transaction that occurd and, if ever it was attempted again, the offender would suffer death. I endeavoured to reconsile myself and began to get in something better spirits.

My Moving Magazine arived and brought me intelligence that, if I went to the camp of the Kings County Malitia, forty of them would join me, and further said the moment I would challenge thier sentry or pickets that moment those that were to join me would bayonet forty of the Loyal men, and that would make a difference of eighty out of one hundred and sixty – the present strength of the camp. I began to consider how to act, as I was aware of the perilous sittuation I stood in with my own people and, should the information given to me by the Moving Magazeene prove to be a falsehood, it was more than probable I would be suspected to be a party in it and perhaps be brought to tryal and, if found guilty, put to death. I concluded the best mode of proseeding would be to call a Council of Warr and have the sence of the people on the subject. I then called on Colonel Doyle, as he was the only sensible man in my party, Hacket haveing quit me some time previous to this and brought 80 of my men with him – for no other reason than my protesting against the robing sistem. I must confess I did not regret much their quiting me, except on one principle: that eightty men reduced my number considerably, together with the desertions takeing place at every favourable opertunity as the men began to dread the approaching long nights and could weather.

Colonel Doyle communicated the matter to as many of the people as he thought requisite, and it was agreed to hear my observations on the subject. I then gave them my opinion and they consented to comply with any mode of proceeding I thought proper to adopt. I thanked them for the good opinion they seemed to entertain of me, and then desired them to repair to their respective quarters untill further orders. I retained Col. Doyle with me, that I might have some conversation with him on the subject. I mentioned to him that I was often betrayed and that it was necessary for me to be very cautious on this occasion, as every one of the people knows I am acquainted with the ground the camp is on, it being within gun shot of the ruins of my house and one quarter of a mile of Roundwood. Doyle made answer and said, 'Sir, I am not competent to give you any advise on the subject and therefore hopes that God will direct you to the best mode of proseeding.'

The day was wet, but the evening clerd up fine, and I fired my signal for marching and gave orders that every man should be readdy in one hour, being resolved to give no opportunity to any informer to get before me at the camp, being still in dread that the money offerd for my head would purchace it unless I was very cautious.

We proseeded without interuption untill we came to Glanmuller [Glenmalure] [Avonbeg] river. It was unfortunately very much flooded, in consequence of the great rain that day. I halted untill the rare came up and had their opinion whether it was fordable or not. They were of different opinions. I road a huntress belonging to Buck Wheally (Whaley) on this day. I leaped her in to the river and kept her head up against the stream as much as possible. I got safe across to the other side, but not without being wet up to my weast. I then dismounted and cried out, 'Come on, my fine boys! Cowards never gained any thing!'

Several came over, but the horses was obliged to go back and forwards sevril times in order to bring the footmen over. But the most unplesant thing that occurd with me was Mrs Holt was with us, and how to get her over was the most difficult part. We had to act, however. I desired her to venture in to the stream, being aware she would not be alarmed, or quit the horse's back if possible. One of the men asked her if she would carry him over the river. She desired him to jump up behind her, and then plunged the horse in to the stream. The beast she roade was not able to bear up the weight of them both and, the current runing so rapidly, they were cast of[f] in to the river and the horse came wadeing over them. They were drifted down with the current into deeper water. I jumped in to their assistance, but they were driven up on a sand bank, near the opposite side of the river before I reached them. I was nearly suffocated and found my self quite weak, not being a good swimmer. A man of the name of Niley [Miley], who was standing on the bank loocking on, said, 'I will loose my life, or save the General and his wife.'

He accordingly jumped in to the river, and soon reached us. He then took me by the hand. The other two got a holt of me by the other arm. Miley kept next the stream and landed us safe on the other side. My wife lost her baver hat, but it was afterwards taken up twenty perches lower down than where she was cast off. She also lost her shoe, but I considered it was eassyer to get a shoe than a wife, although I must confess woeman were very plenty, particularry widdows. We gave God thanks for our safe deliverance and proceeded towards a farm house at some distance.

I road up to the door and related to some young women that were within what had happened, and requested that they would try if any of their shoes would fitt Mrs Holt, and also that they would exchange cloathes with her. They complied with my request, and I paid them for the shoes.

We then marched across Cullentrough [Cullentragh], Derrybawn, Nockfinn [Knockfinn] bridge,[188] Drummeen [Drummin] and Old bridge. We halted near Balltimany [Baltinanima] wood at the edge of the river and was then within two miles of our place of destination I weated untill the rere came up and then said, 'Gentlemen, we are within two mils of the place we are to stop and, as soon as we get

188 At Laragh.

over this river, I will make three divisions of you to carry the buisns we came here on in to effect.'

Several of them was not aware of what I was about to do, and I believe it is certain if soldiers were to know what they have to encounter before they were inlisted, few of them would take the bounty, but it is the opinion of some of them they are to do nothing but walk about and receive their pay. Colonel Doyle spoke to the men and said, 'If you take directions in a proper manner, the buisness will soon be acomplished.'

I knew the river we were about to cross very well and raind about my horse in to it instantly, keeping his head up as well as possible against the stream, and soon reached the other side. I called out to the men to follow me. As soon as they heard that, one of them cried out, 'He is going to sell us all, or else he would never venture over.'

I heard the word he expresed distinctly and, turning about my horse, I proseeded to reacross the river. I soon reached the opposite side and, when landed on the bank, proseeded towards where I heard the nave. I called for Doyle and asked him where the man was that made use of that expression. He replied, 'I am loocking for him.' I then asked him did he know his name? He answered he did not but, if he could assertain it, he should suffer death.

I then spoke to them and said, 'No, you wretches, it is not in my composition to do any such thing, but I believe you will one day or another sell me to my ennimies.'

I had my sword drawn to cut a way if any of them replied. Their was a great argument amongst them. I then dismounted and walked about. It was about 12 oclock at night. Col. Doyle and some of the sensiblest of the party came to me and inquired what was to be done. I told them to go and inquire from that villiain that said I was going to sell them all, or other wise bring him to me untill 'I would run this sword through his heart.' I turned about to my wife and said, 'My dear, I wish you were at the other side of this river,' and my reason for saying so was that she would then be within two miles of a friend's house where her children were at the time.[189]

She replied and said, 'I will not quit you this night, as I dread if you can find out the person that insulted you, from the hate [heat] of mind you are in at present, you would kill him and then the rest of the men would put you to death.'

I then returnd to Nockfinn bridge and proceeded along the road leading to the Seven Churches. I then turned to my right, on Glinmiskenass [Glenmacnass] and soon enterd a little village. The people was seemingly very glad to see me, but I was inclined to think they would as soon have my roon as my company. I orderd a bed to be got readdy for Mrs Holt, and then ordered the man of the house to stand picket all night, and tould him if the army were to disturb me without geting proper notice, I would put every soul of his familly to death. 'And you must also send up to

---

[189] Oldbridge is about three miles south-west of Mullinaveigue – on the Avonmore, about half a mile before it opens out into Lough Dan to the north.

Bryan Bradey's and let him now I ordered him to send out pickets at the other end of the glenn.' I, then went to bed and tould my wife that their was too many insults offered to me, and that I would form some plan to extricate my self from my present sittuation.'[190]

Next morning I marched, but fired no signal. I suffered one of them to communicate it to the other to show them I did not intend to overloock the insult I received.

We marched to Oackwood [Oakwood]. I stoped at Oliver Hoyle's as usual. This man was no party man, but an honnest, worthy neghbour, but I must confess was badly recompenced for his attention to United Irishmen, as he was robd and murdered by a banditty of robbers that went through the mountains after I surrendered my self in the Castle of Dublin.[191]

Holt plans to 'quit the kingdom'

Holt's intention to 'quit the kingdom' is borne out by an informer's report submitted in October to John Lees: 'In my last report but one I repeated Holt's plan to his confidential friend – "If he found he did not succeed he would make to Dublin – from thence to England – perhaps would be in Dublin on Thursday next," (This day) his wound – and disappointment has brought him 2 days sooner – England will now be his object. I should lament if he accomplished it. Should not confidential men be placed on board every packet that sails (furnished with the enclosed description) at the Pidgeon House & Dunleary. I can no more ... in my last letter but one I described him accurately I here repeat it – about 5' 9 inches high – smooth faced, well looking man about 40 years of age – well made. Short black curly hair. Generally wears an officers scarlet coat ... has a very poor address'.

Holt was so alert to the safety of his son, Joshua, that he had arranged for the boy to be relocated every fortnight; he cannot have been less vigilant for the safety of his wife and his 'favourite child'. If the whereabouts of Hester and Marianne, a mere few hundred yards from the site of their burnt out farmhouse, were known publicly, some form of guard, perhaps provided by their landlord, Andrew Price, would probably have been mounted; otherwise they would have been obvious targets for reprisal (see note 41). On the day after the sale of Holt's goods and chattels the guard may have been temporarily relaxed.

This raises the question as to why Andrew Price, should have had any special care for Hester? The rumour that her mother's family, the Mannings, had Orange connections is intriguing: it was to Hester's mother, Mrs Long, that the property had originally been leased. Perhaps there was a familial, or consanguineous bond between Holt's wife and the landlord.

A report of the killing of Mr Hume, one of the MPs for Co. Wicklow, was published in the Courier *of 10 October.*

---

190 We might assume that, by this time, Holt and Hester had discussed the idea of his surrender, or escape.   **191** The significance of the murder being, of course, that Hoyle's 'crime' was that, like Holt, he was a Protestant.

Now, gentle reader, at this period I was very unpleasantly sittuated, being obliged to watch the movements of His Majesty's forses and also all informers, both publick and private, my own wretched men to pleace, not knowing the moment they might call me to trial and probably take my life. I coolly deliberated on my unplesant sittuation and made a conclusion that to quit the kingdom was the most practicable line of conduct I could pursue, and accordingly gave directions to Mrs Holt to call an auction and sell the remnant of my property that escaped the fury of my inimies. It consisted of some potatoes, oats and live stock, every thing else being burned. She accordingly went to Mr Price, who lived in the neghbourhood, to arrange the sale, which was done in some kind of form or in such a manner as was found practoble. I also remarked to my wife that, if she could make up as much money as would pay our passage to Amerrica, that we would go their, providing we could procure a vessel to carry us. At this time she lived in an old house called the Mill House.[192]

On the night after she sold the goods by auction, she was attacked and robed, not only of the money she had, but the cloathes of her back and the earrings that was in my daughter's ears. They also inquired for my watch. She told them she left it with me when she was with me last. They then replied she did not, as they seen me later than she did. I was informed of this transaction and much grieved at hearing it. Previous to Mrs Holt parting me at our last interview, I appointed a place to meet her if some unforseen accidence did not happen.

My old friend Hacket came back to me about this time and began to seduce more of my men over to his robing sistem, but he did not long succeed as he was shot at or near Arklow and his head exhibbited on a spike in the town, as a just reward for his abominable conduct.[193]

My gentle reader, at this time I was very unpleasantly sittuated, having my son to remove every second week from place to place, to avoid the vigilance of the Yeomanry. He was at this time in Aughivanna and I made a resolution that I would go see him at all risk. I accordingly fired my signal for marching and took our rout through Nockmadruce [Knocknadroose], Jumale [Imail], and soon arrived in Aughivanna. I took up my quarters at Mr Byrne's and had, in my own guard, John O'Neil of the Co. Antrim and some three deserters from the Kings County Militia, well knowing these men could not deceive me, as their sittuation, if taken, would be as bad as my own. My entire force at this period was only two hundred men, including about fifty cavalry, amongst which was my brother, Johnathin.

I was very unwell to add to my much distressed state of mind and my brother, seeing me so dull in spirits, he requested I would not be fretting, saying the first man that ever would insult me of the party the[y] would make an example of him. He then asked my opinion of his taking a party of the cavelry with him to reaconitre the country, least we should be surrounded. I consented, and he accordingly took a

---

[192] The Mill House was in the north-eastern corner of Andrew Price's estate at Mullinaveigue. [193] Hacket was executed on 20 November 1798.

small party of the cavalry with him, at the same time appointing to meet me at Jackey Byrne's.

They had not proceeded very farr when they were met by the Army and my poor brother fell a victim to his enimies and I never seen him more. I heard the firing in this skirmish, but it was only random shots. I soon perceived one of the party, John O'Niel, runing up towards me. I asked him what was the matter? He said they were met by the Army and that he seen my brother in the midst of the enemy and was shure I never would see him alive, and that he also seen Mr Hume, captin of a cavelry corps, shot.[194] I then asked him where he was situatted. He said he run up the hill and left his horse behind him. I told him I believed him to be telling truth, as it was like his conduct, and that he was allways a damed coward.

I then proceeded towards where I heard the fireing, with the remainder of my men. The day was wett and foggy, so much so that we could scarcely see any thing at the distance of ten perches, so that we found it difficult to march. The fireing soon ceased and I proceeded along the foot of Lugnaculla [Lugnaquillia], a large mountain that is sittuated between Glenmuller [Glenmalure] and Jumale [Imail]. We soon fell in with the remnant of my brother's party, who confirmed the matter as to his death, and also Mr Hume's. I then proceeded to get a full account of the transaction from one of the party, whose name was John Moore. He told me that Mr Hume was a little in advance before his corps and that he, Moore, met him and presented his piece at him, knowing whom he was. He cried out, 'Cavelry man, I am Captain Hume. What party do you belong to?'

He, Moore, replied, 'Genl Holt. And if you put your hand to your pistols, I will blow your brains out,' ordering him at the same time to dismount, which he complied with. The moment he alit on the ground he, Moore, shot him and one of the men, named Conway, came up and fired another ball through his head. The Army appeared in a few minutes and began to fire indiscriminately. They then retreated, but my brother was unfortunately shot.

I must confess the loss of him lay heavy on me, but when I began to think of the uncertainty of this world and my own sittuation, I found it necssary for me to strike out some mode of proseeding. I then called Col Doyle and asked his opinion of the late transaction, at the same time remarking to him that there must be an informer in the neighbourhood, or else there could not be so close a look out for us. He said he was of the same opinion, and then asked me should we remain where we were that night? I tould him we would, as I seen no safier quarters that we could procure at present. He then placed our pickets and out posts, giving them orders to have a close look out.

My good reader, this Jackey Byrne that I have mentioned to have taken up my quarters at his house, was a private informer and I had some suspision of him but,

---

194 Hume had been one of the members of Parliament for Co. Wicklow. The killing was reported in *Saunders News Letter* and the *Hibernian Telegraph*, on 15 October; and in the *Courier* on 18 October.

in some time afterwards, was convinced as to the fact. This man and his two sons stole several of our horses, brought them to Dublin and sold them and was constantly carrying information to the Army of where I was posted.

Holt's army 'splinters'.

The Information given on 19 September (see note 175) speaks of what the writer regards as the virtual disintegration of Holt's army. That is not likely to have been how Holt saw matters. The only other leader for whom Holt had any warm feeling was Matthew Doyle who was one of those who 'broke' with him at this time. That 'break' implies no animosity between the two men, but rather a prudent strategic decision. No longer could Holt trust his men, or be assured of having drilled and disciplined numbers capable of open confrontation with the enemy. 'The smaller our number was the safer we were,' says Holt. This was probably close to the mark and in accord with Lady Sarah Napier's shrewd assessment of him as 'a clever man who rejects mob and chooses his associates'. Of Matthew Doyle, Holt would write from Dublin Castle: 'He was the only man of his perfession that always strove to save the lives of Protestants' (see p. 165 below).

On 15 October, the Courier *reported: 'The daring and desperate ravager, Holt, has, we hear, had the audacity to send proposals of capitulation to government.' As Holt puts it, one might think his illness was the main factor prompting the desire to see his wife and daughter, but it is not unlikely that the compelling reason was to consult Hester about preliminary negotiations for his surrender.*

On the following morning we marched across the mountain between Jumale [Imail] and Nockenadruce [Knockadroose], and then halted. Some of the men regretted to see me so ill, and more of them wished to get in to the sporting company – I mean the robing and drinking party. I heard them all deliver their sentiments on the subject and then told them I was no longer able to be of any use to them, from the bad state of health I was in, but trusted in God I would soon recover. I then remarked to them that they experienced enough of my manuvering to teach them how to conduct them selves. Some of them shook their heads, intimateing they dreaded they could not manage without me there. I then stated to them that I should go to wander in some retired place, to save my life. They said I should not lave them, as it was their duty to watch me and protect me in my present sittuation, as a token of gratitude for the attention I paid to their preservation on all occasions.

About fifty of them remaind with me and, amongst the number, was a man of the name of Joseph Begly, an Englishman that was taken prisnor about ten weeks priour to this and, when brought to trial before me, I asked him if he was a United Irishman? He answered, 'Dam his eyes, if he was an Irish man, but he was an Englishman,' and 'I will stay with you if you let me.' I orderd the men to give him some thing to eat, and that we would make a United Irishman of him. He then said he had no objections – he never would wish to go back to his regiment. He was a butcher by trade and was very usefull to me.

A division took place amongst the men, when forty-nine turned out to remain with me as my life guard. The remainder went with Doyle and others. We shoock hands and parted and I wished them all suckcess indisscriminately. I marched with my little party through Oackwood and halted at the Widdow Reilley's in Nockalt, where we remaind that night and next day, at the same time takeing care to keep out our pickets, although I was aware the smaller our number was the safier we were, but the reward for my head was the temtation to induce the people to betray me in to the hands of my enemies.

I got a little relief from my complaint at this time and began to think of going to see my wife and daughter – as she was my favourite child. I communicated the matter to my little squadron. They wanted to accompany me but I told them it was better not, as I new the rout to take so well that I could get very near the place by day light, and return in the same manner. They agreed to any mode I wished to adopt.

I left Nockalt about one o'clock in the afternoon and crossed the mountain, in sight of the road. I crossed over Lugelaw, down Slimaine [Sleamaine] and through Mullinaviege, and soon found my wife and daughter. She then informed me of the manner in which the robbers treated her and the expressions they made use of, which lead me to suspect they were some of the men that quit me and joind Hacket in the robing sistem. I prayed to God that I might soon hear of the destruction of this infernal gang.

She told me she new one of them. His name was Byrne, and formerly was in the habit of working for me. He was afterwards hanged at Wicklow, and another boy she also recognised to be John Delany from Roundwood. He was sent to that country from the Foundling Hospital, and raised by William Pollard. He was transported to Botnybay [Botany Bay] for the robing sistem, in some time after.

I remained with my wife, talking of my misfortunes untill about two o'clock on the following morning. Before we parted, I apointed a place to meet her on a certain night. It was at Patt Mullally's, near Adown [Athdown]. I then took my lave of my daughter, and never seen her again untill my return from New South Wales.

I brought a boy and horse with me on this night. It was in the latter end of October. Their was a smart white frost on the ground, and moon light, and when we reached the top of the hill over the Iron Mills, near Capure [Kippure], I made the boy return, and then quit the road – shaping my course for Ballibnackey [Ballynabrocky] mountain. I came to a widdow's house that I was known by. She was glad to see me and said she was sorry to find my health so much impared. She then requested that I would go to bed and that she would send one of her daughters out to watch for me and, when I would get up, she would have some breackfast readdy for me. I then took off my coat, as I very seldom stripd intirely, and lay down.

About sun rise in the morning, I was not more than half an our lying down, when the old woman run in to the room and told me the country was full of Army, both horse and foot. I jumped up, put on my coat and hat and run out. I perceved the foot soldiers very near me, sufficiently so to kill, but I suppose they had no orders to fire. I began to run, and you may be sure they run also. The cavelry was on the other side, coming through Adown. They new me and road on as fast as they could, thinking to get before me. My pistols were emty and, as I went across under Simon Cearny's [Kearney's] house in Ballidonnel and leaped across a stream that cut a large gulf in the ground, in runing down the hill, two of Lord Pourscourt's [Powerscourt's] cavelry came up within pistol shot of me. I then said to my self, 'I am taken after all.' I turned about and presented my pistol towards them, saying, 'Dam you! Stand back, or I will blow your brains out!'

Those two cowards turned their horses about, which gave me fresh spirits, and [I] then concluded I never would surrender untill the last moment, and then intended to put an end to my own existence, that they should not have the settisfaction of hanging me alive.

I then pushed foward, and had not proceeded twenty perches when I perceived a small cavity in the ground, made by the runing water from the mountain. I was on the flank of it, and also on the desent of the hill, so that the foot [infantry] lost sight of me and the cavelry could not advance without being in great danger. I leaped in to this cavern and found it to be eight feet deep or there abouts, and took it[s] course under ground for some distance. I began to think what I would do, as I dreaded they seen me jumping in to this place. I remained in this sittuation for a considerable time, and at last put up my head and found a standing line of infantry within ten perches of me. Their was a large tuft of heath growing over this place, through which I put up my head, and the Army crossed the very place several times.

I heard one of them swear, 'Dam his eyes!' – but he seen me, 'about that very place.' Another said that I dealt with the devil. Another, that this was 'three times' he 'got within shot of him, and he escaped!' Another that 'it was not him' they seen, and a fifth that he would swear he seen me, and would swear to me.

The reader may judge my situation must be miserable, striveing to push forward in to the hole and at last stopd [by] the water. I searched about with my hand untill I found a stone, and placed it under my hip to let the water pass under me. In about half an hour after this, I put up my head a second time – and perceived the Army going through Adown, and more disapointed.

I had a struggle to get out of this dreary but fortunate asylum, my blood being congeald from the length of time I remained in the cold water and being very warm at my entering it. I would not be astonnished if it cost me my life. When I got up on the bank I could not walk, haveing lost the use of my limbs. I then lay down on the ground and began to roal on the ground as well as I could, for the purpose of bringing the blood in sirculation. When I recoverd the use of my limbs, I loocked about and found Simon Kearney's to be the most convenient place I could make for, and immediately proceeded towards the house. When I reached it, Mrs Kearney made me strip off, gave me a dry shirt and made me go to bed. When I got a sleep, she brought me some dinner.

Amnesty?

From the good care this lady took of me I soon recovered, and then began to think of my poor men, and accordingly took my lave of Mrs Kearney and proceeded in search of them, and found them in Glin bride [Glenbride], a small village at a small distance from the place I was chaced in. When the poor creatures were informed of the matter they were astonished.

The reader will observe that, when I was going to see Mrs Holt and my daughter, I was seen by a woman of the name of Byrne, whom had her husband and two sons in goal [gaol] at this period, and if she could set me for the army so as that I would be taken, the[y] was to get their Free Pardon. She accordingly gave information to Lord Pourscourt and he ordered his cavelry in pursuit of me, together with a party of infantry. But I disapointed them in a miraculous manner, as I believe the reader will admit from the manner it is described.

Hester Holt begins to negotiate for her husband's surrender. Holt stays in the field.

On 10 October Major Sirr wrote to Captain Corragen that 'Mrs Holt has been in Powerscourt and has Genl. Holt's pardon'.

The arrangement for Hester Holt to approach Mrs La Touche may have been made earlier than Holt allows (see notes 190 and 195). Despite what he says about the lady 'having no knowledge' of him Holt must have already been very well acquainted with Mrs La Touche at a distance (see note 32). Before entering into any preliminary negotiations he probably wanted firm assurances guaranteeing his eligibility for an amnesty. It would become a vexed question a few weeks later, as is evident in a letter, written on 9 November, from Under-Secretary Cooke to Lord Castlereagh (see Appendix 6.2).

At this stage in his 'History' once can sense that Holt is playing a delaying game, keeping his options open; for even if he proves to be eligible for an amnesty, there remains the likelihood of an expedition from France, with the prospect of laurels and high office for him. He says that, because of his ill-health, he intends 'to go to a friend's house' to recover his health. There was more to it than that. Reports of his movements, given to Dublin Castle, leave no doubt that he was headed for a meeting with the United Irish Executive in Dublin (see Appendix 5.2). If the French were on the seas, Holt might have elected to stay 'in the field'. In fact they had set sail from Brest on 6 September and, after having been forced to retreat into port, were on the high seas by 16 September.

At my parting with Mrs Holt I apointed a place to meet her and communicated the matter to my men, but did not tell them the place least I should be sold again. The apointment was at the house of a man of the name of Mullalley and, agreeable to promise, I went to the place but, preevious to my going, I told the men I would return in a short time and desired them to remain in Glenbride, and to be carefull in keeping out the watch.

On my arival at Mullalley's I found my poor miserable wife their before me, after walking ten or twelve miles. After some conversation relative to my esscape on the late occasion, she tould me she had a notion of speaking to Mrs Latoutch [La Touche][195] to interced with Lord Pourscourt for me to try if he would protect my life, in case I surrendered my self to him. I told her in reply it would be well done, but Mrs Latouch had no knowledge of me, or was she aware that I saved Legelaw [Luggala] House from being burned. However, I then said Mrs Latouch was a good woman and her benevollonce was allways bestowd on those in distress. My wife had a relation in whose husband was in the employment of this amiable lady and we concluded it would be well done to try the event of this enterprise. We then, after some short time spent in bewailing our wretched condishon, parted, with my promising to call to see her if possible in a few days, to be informed of Mrs Latouch's answer.

I then returned to my men at Glenbride and found my self attacked with my old complaint, so much so that I was scarcely able to walk. I took up my quarters in the house of a man of the name of Quinn. This man said he would go to Rosborough [Russborough] to see how the army was sittuated and inquire if there was any information given their respecting me. I told him I was obliged to him and requested he would bring me a gallon of spirits from Blackditches. At his return he said he would, and welcome. I gave him half a guinea in gould that I got from my wife that morning and desired him to get it of the best quality, as the poor men would want a glass of spirits that stands sentry those cold nights. This man returned about twelve oclock on this night and tould me there was no spirits in Black Ditches, and returned me the money. I told him I was sorry for it but it could not be helped. He then said he would go and bring home one of his cows that she might be milked for me, adding that boiled milk with an egg broke on it would be a good remedy for my complaint. He then went out, but did not return.

I went to bed and soon fell fast a sleep and, while in that sittuation, I dreamt or had a vision and thought the bed took fire all round me and, in the immaginary dangerous situation I was in, I thought I mad[e] a leap to escape from the fire and fell out of the bead. I came out of the room instantly and found nine of my men lying round the fire. I roused them up and tould them I had a dream that forbode to me something would happen very searious this morning. The men prepared them selves instantly for the worst. One of them went out and, as he was geting over a stile at the end of the house, a party of soldiers that had the house surrounded cried out to him, 'If you don't come here, we'll shoot you.'

The man run, and seven of them fired at him but all missed. When I heard the shots I cried out to the remainder of the men, 'We are all sold. Let us now fight like men in prefferrence to being hanged like dogs.'

---

[195] The philanthropic Mrs La Touche was popularly known as 'the widow's and orphan's friend'. I am indebted to the O'Conor Don, Denis O'Conor, for the following ditty of the time: 'Mrs La Touche / Open your pouch / And give unto my darlin' / One hundred pounds sterling'.

Each of them examined his arms, and such of them as wanted primeing it was given to them. I had my pistol in one hand and my sword in the other. The first two men that made their way out was Joseph Begly, an Englishman, and James Donneho [Donohoe] from the County Waterford. They were both shot dead. I then proceeded to the door and, perceiving the white belt on the sergant, I shot him dead and then run out, sword in hand. I leaped over the dead boddy of the sergant, when a volly was fired at me which took the leaf off my hat and shot the ploom I wore on it in to three pieces. It hung down on my shoulder, but did not fall off. This hat belonged to a French officer but the Scotch men prevented me from ever wearing it again. One of my men, named Maurse [Maurice] Macoon run out with me. He was wounded under the hip, but not dangerously. Two more followed us, unhurt.

The last two that remained in the house were Mathew Mackdonnel [Matthew McDonnell] and his brother. The former was delayed in looking for his blunderbuss that one of the former men carried out. The second sergant at this time approached the door and one of the Mackdonnals fired at him and shot him dead. They then rushed out and made their escape without injury. The reader will observe the night was dark, so that white belts and well cleaned muskets served us for moonlight.

Macoon, that was wounded, kept in company with me and, when we got, as we immagined, out of the enimy's power, I then proceeded to examine his wound and found the ball passed through. I put a small piece of tobacco in my mouth and chewed it a little and then put it in to the wound. I must confess I bestowed a laugh on the poor fellow, notwithstanding the perrilous situtation I was in a few minutes before, to see him leap up of the ground from the smarting of the tobacco duce.

We then began to lament the loss of the poor men we left behind us, supposing them mostly all dead, and in deed I am certain if we were not alarmed so soon not a man of us would [have] esscape[d]. The man of the house we were in was the informer. He knew the place where our pickets were posted and brought the army another rout silently, so as to put it out of their power to hear or see them coming. The only thing that saved our lives was the darkness of the night, as the soldiers could not see us when we once got out on the door, and consequently could only fire at random. When we were all gone out of Quinn's house, the Army came to the door and fired in, not knowing but some of us might still be within. They shot his sister and his child, his first cousin and his servant boy. During this time Quinn himself was in Glenimackinass [Glenmacnass], as he set off their the moment he placed the Army round the house, thinking I could not escape, to claim the reward for apprehending me. But at his return he found himself disapointed, togather with a decrace of four persons in his family. The Army had two sergants and four privates killed, and seven wounded. Our loss was two killed, three wounded and one taken prisoner. [196]

[196] This was reported in *Saunders News Letter* of 15 October: 'The banditti were well armed and immediately on the defensive: a terrible contest ensued ... Holt effected his escape while the re-

I proceeded across the mountain to a small little village called Ballinoultha [Ballynatona] and stopd at Wm Bradey's. In about two hours after my arival at this place, the remainder of my party joined me. We then returned to bury our dead and, in our march, seen the Army returning as the[y] come out, but less in number. After finnishing the office of burrying the dead, we marched to Scurlix [Scurlock's] Leap and remaind their one night and, on the following morning, proceeded in the direction of Shankle [Shankill] and took up our quarters at the house of a man of the name Thos. Donohoe.

I called my men togather and told them that it was impossible for me to esscape the vigilance of informers while I remaind publick in the manner I was, as the reward was temting people to betray me in to the hands of my enemies in all directions and that, to evade this, I intended to go to a friend's house for a few days, at some distance off, to recover my health and disappoint those wretches if possible. They wished to know the place I was going to, but this I gave an evasive answer to, but promised them I would return and that I would search for them untill I made them out. I then took my lave of them, desiring them to go down towards Jumale [Imail], conceiving it to be the safest quarter they could remain in.

Hints of Holt's political aspirations. His last stand.
The French naval defeat off Donegal

In his Memoirs, *Miles Byrne says that 'often did he [Holt] boast that we were the only troops under arms in all Ireland fighting for its independence at the time the French landed at Killala' (see Appendix 1.2).*

On 24 October, a proclamation issued in Kilkenny, and apparently signed by General Joseph Holt, invoked the authority of 'General Bonapart to make and enact laws'. People were warned 'not to pay any rents or tythes or excessive taxes'; and 'persons that don't abide by my laws', meaning anyone venturing to bid for goods sequestered from victimised or evicted tenants, were threatened with punishment.

Did Holt have any direct connection with the French Directory? The Kerryman, William Duckett, thought to have fomented the Nore and Spithead mutinies in 1797, was an agent of the Directory in Hamburg. Sir James Crawford certainly thought Holt knew Duckett, having written on 23 October that Duckett was believed to 'have been in correspondence with Holt, the rebel chief, who, through him, has been pressing for French assistance' (Sir James Crawford to Grenville, Castlereagh Memoirs, *ii).*

The Kilkenny proclamation sounds like a desperate last fling and hints, for the first time, at high-rearing political ambitions in Holt: was he nurturing the idea of

maining sixteen are said to have been, every man, put to the sword. The brave serjeant and several of his men are also said to have fallen in this hard fought and desperate contest.' It was also reported in the *Hibernian Telegraph* of the same date; and on 18 October by the *Courier*.

assuming political authority in the event of a successful French invasion? perhaps even the supreme political authority – in an Irish Republic? Looked at from General Holt's point of view, who could match his feats in the field; and where else might you find a United Irishman entitled to be called 'General'? Garret Byrne, Edward Fitzgerald, Esmond Kyan, Edward Roche, William Aylmer, Anthony Perry, Moses Kearns? All out of the running, either because they had accepted terms for an amnesty, had been exiled, executed, or, in the case of Roche, made himself scarce. Of the fourteen United Irish Executive leaders arrested on 12 March, by early August, five ringleaders, Emmet, McNevin, Bond, Neilson and O'Connor, having made a clean breast of their plans for a revolution, had forfeited all pretensions to credibility as future leaders. Nor did Holt want for a model of a warrior who had demonstrated a bent for spreading his wings beyond the reaches of the martial into the political arena. Absurd though the idea may sound, especially in light of the fact that Holt was a political ignoramus, it may seem less far-fetched when one remembers that, at this time, Bonaparte's eminence was based on his military achievement and that he was as yet only on the threshold of absolute political power.

The Kilkenny declaration is but one wisp of evidence that Holt might have dreamt up such a scenario. However, did it not exist, everything we know about Holt, by virtue of the available documentary evidence, and out of his own mouth, indicates that he was playing a double game, and would suggest that he might have been playing for very high stakes indeed.

On 30 October, the Hibernian Telegraph reported: 'Holt said to have solicited pardon from government upon terms of transportation ... we have not heard whether his request has been granted.'

Holt has made no mention of his contacts with the United Irish Executive in Dublin. The several emergency meetings he attended in late October and early November would have been occasioned by the following:

1. On 5 October the news reached Dublin of Nelson's triumphant victory at the Nile. A large proportion of those serving under Nelson would have been Irishmen. Dublin was lit up: the Post Office displayed a giant illuminated transparency of Brave Admiral Nelson defending with his sword the Harp and the Crown.

2. On 12 October the French fleet was intercepted off the coast of Donegal by the British Fleet commanded by Sir John Borlase Warren. Without the loss of a single British ship, Warren succeeded in capturing all but three of the French fleet of ten, carrying 2,500 troops. Among those captured on board the Hoche was Theobald Wolfe Tone.

3. Tone was transferred from the Hoche to the Robuste, with the intention of sailing the Robuste to Portsmouth. The ship was, however, blown off course and, after battling tempestuous seas for two weeks, put into Lough Swilly on 31 October. Tone was landed at Buncrana, on the Inishowen Peninsula. On 5 November, the Hibernian Telegraph reported: 'Nov. 3. On board, the Robust, among the

Irish prisoners taken out of L'Hoche, was the well-known Theo. Wolfe Tone, who has been identified by a gentleman in Derry, as [sic] *is expected to be brought up a prisoner to Dublin.'*

Holt's final visit to one of the United Executive meetings may have been on 4 November: a report (see Appendix 5.2) cites that date for a meeting of 'Holt's party ... in some street off Thomas Street' and refers to plans to be picked up off the coast at Rush and transported to 'determined enemys [of Britain]' on the continent.

Did Holt ponder that last option as open to him? I think it unlikely (see note 255).

On 12 November, the Courier *reported: 'Holt, the self-created general of the insurgents in Wexford, and Wicklow, has written a letter to government in which he offers to come in on certain conditions being granted to him, and he concludes his letter with these impudent expressions ...'*

Now the reader will observe I am once more alone by my self and, having an invitation from a relation of mine in Dundrum,[197] I thought within my self it would be a safe place for me to repair to, nothwithstanding it was on the high road leading to Dublin. I set out accordingly across Butter Mountain, Glenismall [Glenasmole], and the Three Lough [Rock] Mountain, and, finding my self very weak, I sat down to rest. This was on the top of a rock coverd with haith. I then lay down on my breast and soon fell fast a sleep, but was not long in that situation when I imagined the rock took fire under me. I bounced up and went about twenty perches lower down the hill and began to consider whether I would proceed on or return back. While I was deliberrateing in this manner, I heard the sound of horses' feet and soon perceived My Lord Pourscourt's cavelry crossing the rock I had been lying on. I lay down between two thorn clumps that grew naturally on the mountain and let them pass. I then got up and gave God thanks for my deliverance, as I was well aware they were looking for me, as I was after wards told the fact by Lord Pourscourt himself.

I then concluded I could not be in a worse situation by proceeding to Dundrum than I then was in, and accordingly proceeded. I soon arived at the house of my friend, and went round to the rere of the house and threw up some sand against one of the windows. My friend raised one of them and imediately knew me. He then came down stairs, opened the door, and let me in. He told me he was glad to see me and asked if I would take some refreshment. I told him it would be time enough when I would get some sleep. He then shewed me my room. I locked the door on the inside, left my pistols and sword on a table in the room, resolving if I was to be attacked to have some sport before I would be taken.

I slept the night tolerable well and, on the following morning, arose early and got

---

197 Holt was bound for Dublin to one of several meetings with the United Irish executive which would take place during the next few weeks. It may be that, after Hester had been robbed, Holt no longer had the funds to make good an escape to England or America.

some breackfast, after which my friend, Mr Wright brought me some books that I might amuse my self reading. I then told him I would go by the name of Long.[198] I sat near the window of my room, from which I had a commanding view of the Dublin road and, at night, came down stairs to drink punch with Mr Wright and a gentlemen that lodged with him. The latter person frequently looked very sharply at me.

I very often sent out the maid for some spirits, telling her to inform the person whom she got it from that it was for a Mr Long that lodged at her master's. I lived in this situation for some days, untill at length the gentleman that lodged in the house went to Dublin, and did not return.[199] On the same evening I asked Wright if their 'was anything suspicious in this occurrence. He said he was certain there was no danger. I went to bed at the usial hour and soon fell fast a sleep, but was not long in that sittuation when I imagined that the house was a fire, and the bed under me. I awoke with the fright and found my self geting out of the bed. As this was the third time I was forewornd in this manner of aproaching danger I dreaded the result. Mr Wright was alarmed at the noise and came in to my room to enquire the cause. I desired him to get a candle lighted and bring it to me as quick as possible and then I would inform him of the cause of the noise. He immediately done as I required, and I then related the matter to him and told him he would have plenty of Army round his house before sun rise in the morning. I then took my lave of my friend and set out. It was about four o'clock in the morning.

I soon passed the Iron Mills, an by Ballally [Ballawley] Hill to the Three Lough [Rock] Mountain. I was not two hours out of the house when it was surrounded by a corps of cavalry. They found the nest but the bird were flown. I was then aware that some information must [have] be[en] given, and whether to accuse Wright, his maid, or the gentleman, his guest, I was at a loss to know from that period to this. The reader will see by this transaction that there is a temptation in money that it is difficult to withstand.

I proceeded from the Three Lough [Rock] Mountain in search of my men. I carried in my pocket some bread and cheese and breackfasted on it near the first spring well I came to, and had no other means of takeing up a drink from the brook than stooping down over it and drinking like the beasts of the field. I proceeded across the head of Glanismall, keeping the side of the mountain with a view of the glenn.

I stoped at the house of a man named Monanee [Murnane?] and told him the escape I had from being taken. He then asked me did I recollect being in a house on the mountain that day? I answered I did. He said, 'Their was three men in it at the time, one of which gave information to Lord Pourscourt. 'In an hour after I left the place, 'he immediately ordered his cavelry out in pursuit of you and the[y] searched every house in the country for you.'

198 Long was his wife's maiden name. 199 'Various reports of Holt's presence in Dublin at about this time are to be found in the National Archives: cf. Appendix 5.2.

He then said he wondered I did not write to Lord Pourscourt to try if he would do any think for me, and said His Lordship said a few days ago, on parrade, it would be a pity I should die any shamefull death. He further said he considered Lord Pourscourt would conceive I done him great honour by surrendering my self to him. I deliberated coolly that night on what this man had said to me, and began to think how I could arange the matter. I slept but little and, early on the following morning, proceeded in search of my wife to hear what answer she got from Mrs Latouch [La Touche]. I fortunately met with her on that day.

She told me Mrs Latouch said if I would write her a letter, stateing that I would surrender my self to Lord Pourscourt, she would go to him her self in person and try what arrangement she could make. My wife carried pen, ink and paper in her pocket that I might write the letter privately. I then considered this was a good opputunity for me to get out of the power of spies and informers and, being confident their was an end to the unfortunate sistem I was implicated in, I took my pen and wrote to this lady as follows:

Dr. Maddam
god and you are my dependence and as you are so good as to take my case in to your hands I hope it will prosper as does every thing you under take to perform. let the result with me be what it will at your request I will surrender my self to Lord Pourscourt at his house on (such a day) and am maddam your Very obedient Humble Servant

Joseph Holt

to Mrs P. Latouch
Belview near Delgeny [Delgany]

When this good and humane lady received this letter, she said she would go first to Lord Meath[200] and procure his interest in my behalf, which she soon was granted. She then proceeded to Lord Pourscourt and showed him my letter. He was highly pleased, thanked Mrs Latouch and promised her my life should be protected. She drove back with speed and sent a letter to my wife in the most cordial manner, stateing the promise she was made by Lord P.

Gentle reader, my toung could not express and my pen would not be sufficent to write the many good acts done for me by this amiable lady, and Mr Latouch. However, I will explain some of the outlines of them in their proper place in this my narrative.

I am informed, naturally, of this transaction, and the reader will admit I had a painfull office to under take, namely communicating the matter to my men, which I considered my self bound to do, well knowing it would be the last subject I ever would have to explain to them.

---

200 The earl of Meath, of Killruddery, was one of the largest landowners in Co. Wicklow.

Holt surrenders. A revealing self-portrait

The Rebellion had lasted five and a half months. From Holt's point of view it might seem to have begun earlier. When Lord Powerscourt says, 'It was a pitty you were not in some corps of cavelry,' Holt recalls 'many a fine man I seen fall during the last eight months' – a clear reference to the reign of terror following on Lord Camden's proclamation of martial law and General Lake's brutal, licentious response to it; and perhaps a clue inadvertently let slip to his commitment to active military service in March, two months before his house was burned.

No longer preoccupied with detailed accounts of his feats in the field, in the following section, Holt, his braggadocio in full spate, gives the reader a pretty comprehensive self-portrait: the yeomanry, often being doubly enlisted, are, in his eyes, hypocrites or contemptible opportunists. Never does it cross his mind that he might be open to the same charge, his argument turned against him with a force redoubled by his special pleading: for if these two-faced, cowardly wretches fought badly – perhaps because they had enlisted for a cause in which they did not believe – how bizarre that Holt, who in this was at one with them, should bring to bear his considerable military skill against an enemy with whom, in his heart, he sympathised.

That may be a sophisticated, logically impeccable argument, such as a prosecutor would deploy in a court of law, but it will not stand up as realistic or even fair; for once the dogs of war have been let slip what price the rights and wrongs of the original cause? Only once does Holt put forward an argument to condone the Rebellion and it seems likely enough that he didn't give a fig for United Irish aims and principles. Many soldiers will go on fighting because there's nothing else for it and they mean to save their lives. A few, once they have drawn blood, will acquire a taste for battle and exult in it as sport as did Holt.

Holt prided himself on being a professional soldier. By military criteria, his record has qualified him for heroic status. He shows no intellectual distinction and, like so many formidable warriors, is overweening, blunt, even crass, vain, ruthless, scornful of the ordinary run of men for whom the better part of valour is discretion. It is only when he is humiliated, victimised and seen to be fiercely protective of his brood that one may be expected to warm to Joseph Holt, the man – for his experiences in New South Wales humanised him.

He had hoped to be treated as an exile rather than a political prisoner, and allowed to emigrate freely to America. His letter to Lord Powerscourt ('or Lord Monck', reads the address), conserved in the National Library of Ireland, offering to surrender, is transcribed in Appendix 6.2.

As to the terms for surrender, see Appendix 6.1 for an extract from a letter from Under-Secretary E. Cooke to Lord Castlereagh, dated 9 November.

I proceeded acording to promise and found them at Bradey's, of Ballinalough. I called them to gather and said:

Men, I am about to surrender my self to Lord P. to evade an awfull death. That hundreds has endeavour[ed] to betray me you all know, and as to any hopes of our succeeding, it is entirely out of the question, as the report of the French coming to our assistance is quite unfounded. You are all sencible that your present situation in cold and hunger is beyond human conception and I here give you my last advice, namely, to return to your respective homes and betake yourselves to your usial employment. You may be certain when I am from amongst you, the cavelry will desist from patroling those hills and vales, so much so that the traveler can pass without being anoyed by those Vulcons. I now entreat the Omnipotent Being to protect you and guide you all savely to his own fold, which shall be the constant prayer of your unfortunate commander when probably surnadering (wandering?) the wilds of some forreign land. So, Adieu for ever my dear fellows.

I shook hands with each of them, while the tears fell from their eys, and I asure the reader mine was not without a tear of sorrow for being oblig[ed] to part them. Before I took my final lave of them I told them to be aware of Hacket's party – as their trade was robing they certainly would be punnished sooner or later. The poor fellows neled down and offered up their prayers to God for my future wellfare. I then bid them the last farewell and, while I remaind in their sight, they were pitching their hats on the top of their firelocks, wavering them in such a manner as to let me see they still had me in view.

I proceeded across the side of Ballibrockey [Ballynabrocky] mountain, through Capure [Kippure], and assended Jouce [Djouce] mountain. When I arived at the corner of Lord Pourscourt's demesne wall, I sat down to rest and try if any one seen me or was in my view. After some short time, I proceeded in the direction of Behan [Bahana], to the house of an old friend, William Keegan. He was at home and received me cordially. I met Mrs Holt at this place. Our worthy host brought me some refreshment and, after partackeing of it and converseing on various subjects, Mr Keegan and I set out togother for Lord Pourscourt's, where we arrived about seven oclock in the evening on the 10 of November, 1798.

Mr Keegan sent in his name, adding that I was with him. Lord P. soon made his apearance and took me by the hand, welcomed me to Pourscourt in a pleasing and gracefull manner. He then conducted me up stairs to a spacious apartment, where he had a sumptious repast prepared for me.[201]

When I was done dinner and the cloth removed, the table was furnished with wines of every description, and some excellent spirits. The convesiation naturally

---

201 Far from taking refuge from the family seat, out of harm's way, as had most major landlords, Lord Powerscourt remained on his estate and permitted the local yeomanry, many of them his tenants, to have their headquarters there. Writing twenty years after the occasion, Holt still fails to grasp Powerscourt's strategy: honour 'the General' as the 'gentleman' he has always longed to be, and ply him with liquor to loosen his tongue.

turned to the transactions that happened in the country for the former eight months. I answered such questions as he demanded of me in a manner suittable to their requisition and, after some time spent in this way, I asked His Lordship's liberty to give a tost. He said he had no objections. I then anounced:

'Bad luck to Thos Hugo!'

Lord P. said with all his hart. Their was a friend of His Lordship present and he said he had no objections.[202]

The reader will observe my reason for giving this toast was to turn the conversation on the cause of my joining the Rebbel army, namely the burning of my house caused by this wretch. Lord P. then turned to the subject and I related the matter to him in a short manner. When he heard it he shook his head.

He then asked me what was my opinon of my fate, in case I was taken. I told him that never could happen while I was a live, as I intended to fight while I had a round and, if I was worsted, to put an end to my existence. He then said to the gentlemen that sat with us, 'Did not I tell you that Holt would do so, sooner than be hanged?'

Lord P. then asked me, if I meet him a few days ago when he was in pursuit of me, would I fire at him? I told him I would but, if I could take him prisnor, he should not be hurt and, before I would give him up, I should get ten men in exchange that was then in custody, and also remarked to him, if he fired at me with an intent to kill, I certainly would return the compliment. He then said he believed me to be telling truth.

The discourse then turned on my opinion of his own cavelry. I told His Lordship if they could not fight they could run, and then explained to him the manner in which I caused two of them to do so, with an emty pistol, while they were well mounted and armed and I alone and nearly surrounded. I then proceeded to explain the transaction to him, as I have stated in the narrative. His reply was it would be a pitty to take a man's life for going to see his wife and children.[203] He then said he was glad I was then out of the power of my enemies. I told His Lordship I might thank his humanity for the sittuation I then stood so secure in, adding that he gained a greater victory over me this day than ten thousand of His Majestie's forses could gain over me, while my force did not exceed seven hundred and eighty. His Lordship laughed immoderately, and then asked me how I got out of the glinn from such a number. I explained to him as I have mentiond in a former place in this work. He then said, 'Holt, it was a pitty you were not in some corps of cavelry.'

My reply was, 'Perhaps, My Lord, it is better as it is.'

He then asked my reason for saying so. I answered, 'I would be to wicked and

---

[202] Powerscourt probably meant it, being informed enough to realise just how many men had been driven into the ranks of the United Irishmen by the brutality of Hugo and others of his stamp. [203] Referring to Holt's narrow escape when he took refuge in the small cavern near Athdown. Did Holt sense the possibility that Powerscourt, perhaps having been privy to the meeting that had been arranged between Holt, his wife and children at Pat Mullaly's, in Athdown, took advantage of this information to arrange for his cavalry to waylay Holt?

perservereing and probably would be shot before then, as many a fine man I seen fall during the last eight months. It is true, My Lord, you have a very fine corps, for, if the[y] can't fight, they can run. And, if any of them were shot, I would recommend the surgeon, if any simptoms of life be vissoble, to proceed to examine their backs for the wound,' and further remarked, 'If I had a charge in my pistol the day the[y] pursued me on the mountain, His Lordship would be one short of his number on parrade the day following.'

His Lordship then asked me if I knew them. I replied I did not, but added they were good-natured men and I believed did not wish to take my life. The gentleman that sat in company with us, Mr Cannon [Canning], said, 'Mr Holt, you make very little of My Lord Pourscourt's corps.'

I answered, 'Yes, Sir, and I will explain the reason to you. I prevented them from a great many comfortable nights' sleep and, when they had me in view, I think they should [have] run me closur than they did, as I asure you, Sir, if I was in their place, a single man with a pistol in his hand – supposeing it to be even charged – would not frighten me.'

This gentlemen said he was certain of that.

It was then about twelve o'clock at night and, finding my self very tired and not able to drink more, I intimated to Lord P. I wished to retire to bed. I was imediately conducted to my appartment but, previous to my retiring, Lord P. and Mr Cannon wished me a comfortable night's repose. My room and bed were most commodious and I slept very sound untill morning, as I was aware My Lord P. had placed the pickets so that their was no danger of my being taken in surprize.

I arose very early on the next morning, cleand my self, and prepared for the breackfast parlour. Just as I left my bed room, I met Lord Pourscourt and Mr Canning on the stair head. They bid me a good morning. They then conducted me in to the parlour. Lord P. said, 'Mr Holt, I hope you got a good night's rest.'

I answerd, 'Yes, My Lord, I thank you, I did, and I hope my life is safe.'

He answerd, 'Yes, Holt, it is, as I have pledged my word of honour that I would forfeit my life sooner than you should lose yours, as you paid me the compliment of surrendering your self in the manner you have done.'

I thanked him and said if I had not that opinion of him, I never would come to Pourscourt.

While we were talking, one of Lord P.'s cavelry came in. His name was Buckly [Buckley]. He spoke to me in a degradeing manner, saying, 'You are welcome General Holt.'

I loocked at him and smil[e]d, saying, 'I am sorry, sir, I have not my papers about me or the list of officers that would enable me to call you by your title or rank in the army. You know, Buckley, you were a United Irishman long before I was drove to misfortune by such scoundrels as you. Stand here before My Lord P. untill I speak to you, and I will show His Lordship by your own confession – as you dare not tell a ly before him – that you are a perjured villain and was sworn both sides of the question. Now, Buckley, you come here I know to mock my missery, but, if I had a dozen like you in the lawn without, I would drive you before me.'

Lord P. and Mr Canning looked at him very earnestly. He then turned out not much pleased at the uisset [insult?] he paid me. When he went out, Lord P. came over and took me by the hand and thanked me for what I said. I then told His Lordship I was aware he considderded that this fellow was a Loyal man, but he was quite the reverce. I then asked His Lordship did he know how many Loyal men he had in his corps? He answered he did not. I told him then that I was not [*blank*] so he then asked me how many thier were in it. I refused to answer, saying they were all his own tenants, 'and will be after my departure out of this Kingdom, so I shan't say any thing more an this subject, save only that I am sure you had but few sincere men in Yr Lordship's corp.'

At this time breakfast was ready, when Mrs Holt came, who was brought up stairs where I was. When breakfast was over, His Lordship appeard to me, saying, 'Which form should you wish go to The Castle? You shall have either a horse or coach.'

I said, 'Me Lord, as I have been a visible spectacle for this country, if Your Lodship pleases, I choose the coach.'

It was soon prepared.

His Lordship asked me how many men should he bring to convey me?

I said, 'As many as Yr Lordship pleases, but you may be assured that your own valet is sufficient. From my present state I don't wish to escape, nor need you fear a rescue.'

So he ordered 24 of his corp.

I got in the coach precisely at 11 oclock the 11th day of November, 1798. We passed from Powerscourt to Enniscerry [Enniskerry], by the Golden Ball, Dundrum, Miltown [Milltown] to Stephens Green, through Grafton st & straight on to the Castle of Dublin. The coach stopped in the Uppr Castle yard, opposite the Secretary's office. From the numerous spectators, I can assure you that I conceived that, they should destroy,[204] a vast number should be smothered.

I can't help but remark that at this time the city and country for me were universally at prayer, as such as didn't wish me well wished me Evil. I was so gazed at that I could descry various dispositions stigmatized in the faces of many of the beholders as I placed me head out of the coach, saying to the multitude, 'Feast your eyes, as yr present seeming curious object will soon disappear.'

I then lift[ed] up the blinds of the coach windows and sat down.

My garments was as follows: A common round hat, scarlet jacket faced with green and gold apulets, white cassimere vest, grey pantaloons – and heart and face well stocked with resolution.

[204] Holt, or his copyist, may have had second thoughts about 'they should destroy', as it has been lightly scored through, probably with the intention of substituting the more arresting 'should be smothered.'

The instant I raised the blinds I could distinctly hear many words from the assembly, but – quite a contrast! But, reader, to be in plain, I cared not what was their interior, as my confidence was placed in the Almighty.

So, at this time My Lord Powerscourt had returned, [and] was much surprized on finding the coach blinds raised. He imediately opened its door, took me by the left arm. We walked in. He first introduced me to Mr Marsden, whom I believe was Secretary to His Excellency, the Lord Lieutenant, where I got refreshments after I was asked a few questions.

In a few minutes after, Me Lord departed, saying he would soon call to see me again. Immediately James O'Bryan [O'Brien] and Major Sir [Sirr] [205] came to me and conducted me to the apartment of Arthur O'Connor.[206] Major Sir departed, leaving James O'Bryan with me, who mad himself quite busey to obtain some interesting confession from me, but on finding himself disappointed, he looked as equally pleased as a lawyer without fees. At this time it was about four o'clock. Dinner came to me from the Castle Hotel (the keeper of which was a man of the name of Watkins), with the allowance of a State Prisoner – which is two dishes such as Prisoner pleases to order, a bottle of port, and two bottles of porter. I said to O'Bryan, 'Will you get me some spirits to make a jug of punch?' I gave him some money. He brot in a pint of spirits and some sugar. I mixed the wine and spirits togather, which afforded me nice punch.

Still O'Bryan continued to ask me questions, leting me know how he cam[e] there. I seemed to pay him slight attention. At this time it was about 12 oclock at night. I observed to him that it was time to go to bed. His wife came and dressed my bed. To be sure he introduced Mrs O'Bryan to 'Genl Holt.' So they soon departed. I went to bed.

Next morning, being the 12 inst., O'Bryan came to me. I desired that he might send in a hair dresser, who shaved, and dressed my hair.[207] About half after twelve I had many visitors, who much anoyed me with their various questions. Such as asked me propper questions in a polite manner, I answ[ere]d with equal complisance, but was firmly resolved not to vent anything prejudical to my former fidelity.

Reader, I refer you now to the Co. Wicklow, County and City of Dublin and its suburbs, who contained many inhabitants whose fears were inexpressable lest I should become a Jemmy O'Bryan, proof of which many quit their houses, but on finding no news of deception of me, there fears in a short time were dispelled.[208] I am much gratified to this day that I never deprived a wife of her husband, nor a child of his father, throgh deception, which was gratefully returned by my Redeemer shielding me from many and innumerable perilous dangers.

---

205 The *town* major, chief of police.   **206** One of the most eminent of the United Irish leaders arrested at Oliver Bond's on 12 March.   **207** Holt was meticulous about his appearance.   **208** On 20 November Sarah Tighe wrote to Ann Ponsonby: 'Tone being dead the reigning topic is General Holt and various are the inventions about what he is to disclose' (National Library of Ireland *Ms 4813*). She was allowed to visit Holt and noted that a close watch was kept an him 'lest he might be assassinated.'

For ------ poison less than falsehood fear
Rather than purchase life so dear –
Should embrace cold death,
And stain my country's love with my departing breath.[209]

On the 14th inst. Mrs Holt came to see me, accompanied with James O'Bryan. Mrs Holt beged leave to send for a quart of spirits as she knew the state of affliction my mind was in, particularly for the absence of my children, hoping it would give me at least a momentary consolation. She gave O'Bryan a guinea, which was a dear bottle, as he never returned the change, which much agravated Mrs Holt. But I endeavoured to console her, saying, 'With God's help, we shall surmount all grievances.' So she went to the country, and in a few days she returned.

At the hour of 12 oclock on the night of same day of her return, Jemmy O'Bryan came to me, saying he got orders that Mrs Holt wouldn't be permited to stop with me. I replyed, 'Why did you not let me know in a seasonable time? This is an improper hour to turn a female to the streets and, as I have ever used my efforts to protect females from Evil and prostitution, I will do so with her. Therefore she shan't quit this room this night!' – desiring him to withdraw. Which he done. I locked the door and went a bead, and then Curtain Council[210] took placce, she much lamenting that any thing should seperate us while the Almighty should please to spare us our lives.

I desired her to go to Lord Powerscourt with my respects next morning and make known to him the treatment she had received, that I hoped His Lordship would be so good as to obtain her permission to stop with me during (my aparent) short stay in Ireland.

So she performed my request, leting His Lordship know the sequel of what had passed the night before with Jemmy O'Bryan. Me Lord was good enough to make her this reply: 'You shan't be deprived of your husband's company, nor any friend you wish to introduce to him.' He instantly wrote a letter to the Secretary, the contents of which I am a stranger. But, in future, Jemmy O'Bryan became very humble and polite, saying to me that he would let Mrs Holt stop, with other conversation. I remained silent for some time to hear his deceptionable chat. At length, I desired that he might never appear there more, lest that he had a propper message, adding that 'even so, you must appear to me uncovered, tapping at the door, and in this attitude deliver me yr message. So, fellow, begone! And shut the door! So he disappered, never more assuming the smallest prerogative, but quite conformable to my request.

Next day, my dinner came to me from the Castle Tavern, composed of a neck of

---

209 Rough jottings for a poem which Holt never got round to finishing? Having given certain 'Information' about men who he thought no better than criminals, it obviously preyed on his mind that this might be interpreted as treachery to his comrades.   210 Council with his wife, in the seclusion of the bed and blankets, as opposed to the many councils held with his comrades.

mutton, some half boiled cabage, a stake from a shin of beef. I meditated for some time on sd treatment, but from being in possession of what His Magestie is gracious enough to allow in such cases, roused my resolution to act in this manner: I first placed sd diner in a cupboard, rung the bell – on which Js. O'Bryan appea[re]d, asking what was wanting? First shewing him the sd dinner. He smiled, saying Watkins wasn't 'particular', on, which I desired him to get me [a] nice fowl, giving him five shillings.

Next day I saw the former Town Major,[211] whom I informed what sort of treatment I received and how I acted, having broke one of the dishes, placing its broken partikles to garnish the secondhand cabage, which I shewed him. He then told me what I was entitled to get, i.e. to state or furnish my bill of fare, as any two dishes I fancyed should be at my service. In future I was treated to my fancy.

Mrs O'Bryan came, attempting to carry away the remnants of sd dinner. On which, I asked what was she about to do? She replyed she hath always the State Prisoners' broke mate. I said it was my usual custom to give my broken mate to the poor, in which form I meaned to continue. She layd it down and disappered. The next morning I saw a poor weoman, collecting cinders out of ashes, which I called, taking a shoulder of mutton and a loaf of bread, let it drop into her lap, for which [the] poor creature prayed most sincerely. And during my stay in the Castle I repeated sd practice, given my broken meat to the seeming distressed.

The 16th inst. I was visited by His Excellency, Cornwallis, accompany[ed] with some millitary gentlemen, who asked me several questions concerning skirmshes in the late Rebellion. My declarations seemed to afford them much amusement. I must confess that they never asked one prejudicial question. His Excellency hoped that I was agreeably treated. I replyed that I shouldn't wish to trouble His Excellency with some complaints I had against 'honest Jemmy O'Bryan', and Watkins. He further was good enough to confess that he was happy to see me look so well after my so many and perilous fatigues, adding that he well knew what it was to be in skirmsis in critical and inaccessable places, asking me had I been taught military exercise in my early days? I replyed, 'Yes, Sir, in time of the former Volunteers I was in Captain Bryan's corp, Arklow.' and that I conceived that a martial disposition was imbibed in me from my earliest period.

His Excellency said, 'I believe you, as we well experienced it from yr conduct on the mountains.'

'Yes, Your Excellency, it behoved me so to do. When I was most inhumane and opessively driven to such a labyrinth of calamity formed my determination not to lose my life in a dastardly manner, for Ide rather die by a bullet than get the death of a brute.'[212]

---

211 Another clue to the date at which he is writing. When Holt returned to Dublin on 5 April 1814, Sirr still held the post of town major.   212 We should allow of the possibility that, despite his brothers' enlistment, and despite his efforts to cover the tracks of his own enlistment, Holt may have been a reluctant rebel, driven into the ranks of the United Irishmen because, had he held off, he would have had no means of protection from the villainous Hugo.

Which caused him and company to laugh, biding me Good Morning, saying hede soon see me again.

These gentlemen were scarce gone when another company of respectability came. They thought my mind was an open letter for everyone to read, but one in particular took the liberty of asking me such an so many improper questions as spurred me to say, 'Sir, I should be glad to know where or when you formed an acquaintance with me?'

He replied, 'I never was acquainted with you.'

On which I said, 'And so you shall continue, and therefore I wish you to be absent.'

He seemed quite offended. I rang the bell. O'Bryan appeared, whom I asked, 'How come you to let a rabble of creatures to annoy a person whom you know is in trouble?', saying that I would enquire of the respectable gentlemen would they permit me to be a publick curiosity. So they all disappeared. I am convinced that O'Bryan was feed to give these spectators admission to my apartment, and from the insult he gave Mrs Holt filled me with insensed disposition for him, and knowing his influence dwelt but in a weak number of respectability.

Notwithstanding the many reproaches given to O'Bryan, he had (after) the assurance to tap at the door of my apartment, asking permission for different gentlemen to speak with me, but admission depended on whither I pleased to do so or not. I have sometimes sd, 'Let them come in,' and on entering my room Ide commence asking them questions. Be assured some of sd questions were enigmatical to them, so that Jemmy's friends had little storys of gratification to carry.

In a few days, two of Jemmy's sisters came to see him from Ballynakill, one married and the other single. The young one was much attatched to stop in my room in Jemmy's absence. The married sister['s] business was to endeavour to obtain pardon for her brother, John, who came to me to Whelp Rock, as a deserter from the Royal Artillery who lay in Edenderry, and continued with me till our separation at the Boyne. At this time he was in a state of obscurity in Dublin. Though 'faithfull Jemmy' would go take him, his sister obtained his Pardon. In a short time, he came to his brother, Jemmy, who instantly inlisted him in his diabolical employment. I must allow that, during his service with me, he conducted himself an active fellow.

Reader, this John O'Bryan, in order to become the better 'lure', got in the habit of a sailor, resorting to every public house or place likely to meet with his prey, endeavouring to extort treasonable words from inebriated creatures. He had nothing to do to accomplish his design but call for his brother Jemmy to convey them to confinement, so their punishment was inflicted agreeable to these misreants' testimony.

These two birds of prey were originated from the most sordid extraction, and disclosed to me were both 'United', and basely conceived that by becoming informers that it would be means of procuring them a more elevated station. Which fortunately and deservedly happened with Jemmy, for he was at a certain time placed in such an elevated attitude which induced many spectators to behold. And when he came down was in such a state of permanency that he valued not the influence even of His Excellency.[213]

Reader – wishing to inform you of the particulars of what I observed while in the Castle –: Early on a morning, hearing a tap at my door, I asked, 'Who comes there?' O'Bryan replyed, 'Major Sir waits your appearance.'

So I walked down stairs, at the lower part of which, on my left hand, I was conducted in a small room, where I was much surprised to behold John O'Neill, from Redwells[214] from the Conty Kildare, in conversation with Major Sir. The Major asked me if I knew 'this man?' I replied that 'This man's appearance brings me to a recolection that I have had saw him.'

The Major continued, asking me, 'Can you recolect this man to be a John O'Neill?'

I reply[ed], 'I don't know his name.' On which, the Major asked O'Neill, saying, 'Do you know this gentleman here?' He answered, 'O yes, that's General Holt.'

At the same juncture, in came young Pilsworth (whose life I was instrumental to save, when brought to me a plundered prisoner by the hands of sd O'Neill, as before is minutely specified in my History) who imediately declared O'Neil's criminal proceedings with him, confessing that I spared his life, giving him a Protection to Dublin.

The Major asked Pillsworth if he was ready to prove what he had said? He answered, 'Yes,' on which I retired to my apartment. James O'Bryan told me that it was in Neill's power to save himself, and so he was about to do. But I don't know more on that subject.

Reader, I can't help but remark that individuals who are possessed of a faithful and virtuous heart are most liable to be visited by the tempests of confusion and perplexity. John O'Niell and the O'Bryans are in co-partnership, living in splender for some time.[215]

> Ime destined now to go away
> Unto the land of Botany Bay
> And filled with Joy which should be tears
> But so many Bryans now appears
> Which makes my mind quite a contrast

[213] A reference to the hanging of Jemmy, who would eventually over-reach himself and be found guilty of murder. The grisly hanging was celebrated in a ballad, *The night that Jemmy was stretched*. Even after that 'stretching', many spectators continued to behold Jemmy: his skeleton came into the possession of the School of Anatomy at Trinity College where it, and that of a freak giant, were suspended from the ceiling. It was possible to manipulate ropes attached to the two skeletons so as to agitate them into a *pas de deux*, a frantic *Danse Macabre*. [214] It was held against Holt that, in several cases, he was guilty of ruthless killing. Here he is again tendentiously at pains to invoke the case of Pilsworth in order to prove his credentials as a just leader, who never overstepped the mark by permitting 'criminal' executions. [215] Holt's macabre sense of humour. Earlier in his 'History' he has told the reader of how O'Neill was destined to die: 'the Almighty causing a bit of meat

When I reflect on what is passed
May the deity direct our way
And from that path may never stray
Which leads too that brilliant place of rest
Where contrite souls are ever blesst

Next morning, walking in my room – and heard a great noise. I steped to the door to discover what it was. I overheard O'Bryan say, 'I can take any man whom I please', which reply I discovered he made to a poor country man that he had taken into custody who was passing by, who only asked if Holt was prisoner in The Castle?, saying, 'I have no call to him.'

Says O'Bryan, 'Go up stairs or, while this stick remains whole in my hand, I will lay it on you!' The agrieved creature passed me, before O'Bryan. I took sharp observation of the poor captive as he passed, and thought I had knowledge of him.

Next morning O'Bryan asked me if I knew any of the Farringtons from Talbotstown? I said I saw some of that name in the County of Wicklow, but had 'no recolection of the man you was beating going up stairs.' Says O'Bryan, 'If you let him come to your apartment, it may serve you.' So I gave him permission.

After some conversation I knew him, and recollected that a brother of his was in the Dunlavin Cavalry and deserted to me, at which time I was at his relations' house at Nockalt [Knockalt] – by name Reily [Reilly].

The same had with him an entire grey horse which he called Lillicks and, not wishing to be encumbered with any stranger in my room, [I] desired that O'Bryan might provide a place for him – which he done, keeping him in punishment for five days, never disclosing or discovering that he had such a person in custody.

At length, I made it my business to advise him to give O'Bryan what he demanded, which was five guineas, on which the poor captive wrote to the innkeeper where his horses were, who, after selling his [illegible] loads of barley, sent him sd sum, which purchased his liberation. I advised him to acquaint his family with the substance of his delay and to apply to some magistrate in order to obtain satisfaction of O'Bryan, but to no effect untill he barbarously murdered Mr Hoey.[216]

In a few nights after, O'Bryan, meeting with an acquaintance of mine at Watkins's Tavern, in order to exasperate him to say or do something within his jurisdiction, shot his spaniel dog. Sd acquaintance was name of Martin Byrne, who lived in Ormond Market, No. 45, in a respectable way, a Deputy Allinger [Alnager], under Sir John Blaquier [Blacquière].[217] I was in Co. 8 [?] and a Mr Bryan Byrne of Roundwood also. The sd Mr Martin Byrne was so agrieved at the loss of his favourite dog that he was provoked to vent some words, which this second Judas took hold of, procuring assistance, and forced him to the Tower, where I was. As I had permission (through the interest of Lord Powerscourt) to leave my door open or shut as I

to obstruct the passage to his stomach on the Curragh of Kildare'. So that the 'co-partners' have got their due in the 'splender' of the everlasting bonfire. 216 And was consequently hanged. 217 See note 4.

pleased in the day, I was alarmed with a noise and soon discovered it to be my sd friend – in custody with O'Bryan – with whom I have road several hundred miles, collecting His Magestie's fees, as Allingers. On hearing the conversation betwixt them, I said, 'Is that Mr Martin Byrne?'

He replied, 'Yes, Mr Holt. I am with this villain. A prisoner!' On which I repaired to where I had spirits and wine, taking a mixture of them in a bottle down stairs, filled a glass for Mr Byrne, which he took. I must acknowledge that O'Bryan didn't ask to hinder me of so doing, but I must thank My Lord Powerscourt for having such liberty, as O'Bryan was to give permission to whom I pleased to come see me. (For which Mr Byrne commenced a suit against O'Bryan. I don't know how it ended.)

A few nights after, about twelve o'clock at night, a building adjoining the Ordnance Store took fire, which much alarmed the inhabitants of this city, and the prisoners who were in the tower was permitted to go in its top. O'Bryan accompanied them, coming to where I was sitting, saying, 'Little fear of you to let Government know of this.'

I replied it was impossible to discover a thing I knew nothing of. He sayed, 'John O'Neill knew and discovered.' I replied 'The greatest tongue knows most.'

The drums beat to arms, the trumpets sounded, and Artilery stationed in several parts of the city. The engines played with such rapidity as soon extinguished the fire, which was a gratification to me. So we all retired to our respective quarters.

Next, Mrs Holt went to the County of Wicklow to see her children. On sd day I was visited by His Excellency, accompanied by Lord Rossmore, Lord Monk [Monck], Lord Powerscourt and Reverend Thomas Brownrigg, and a strange personage whom I didn't know, who said to me he had come a long journey, hoping I would inform him who burned Lady Frances's house.[218] Prior, to my answer, His Excellency was so gracious as to leave my answer at my own option, saying, 'Answer as you please.' On which I faced sd stranger, saying, 'Sir, I hope you know the road you came.'

He said, 'I do.'

I replied, 'O, there's no fear of you missing your way. My name is Twyford.[219] I know nothing of the matter.' On which he seemed much displeased, which served only to gratify me.

The respectable gentlemen then present smiled, pleased at my answer.

218 Lady Frances Beresford's house was at Ballinastoe.   219 Several villages or towns in England bear this name, including Twyford near Winchester. It may have been a United Irish password. Soon after his arrival in Sydney harbour, Holt hears a boatman say 'he should be out late that night, as they should have to "Pluck the gull". But, as for my part, I was "Twyford", I knew nothing of the matter,' Holt comments.. The incident, with its hints of an Irish conspiracy in the colony, and an allusion to Defenderism, provokes Holt to write: 'I hope gangs will be ever opprest and kept under, for I think the world never was at ease since clubs or meetings first began. It sets the people like dogs grinning at one another. I wish all subjects to be alike and then happiness would soon dispel all the gloomy aspects that appears to this unfortunate little island, who reres fine men for His Majestie.'

His Excellency was good enough to ask me how I was in health. I said, 'My state of hea[l]th is quite good, thanks to God, but my mind is most anxieted.'

He asked the reason.

'As I am reduced from an honorable title and commission, excluded from a fair tryal, as I feel myself neither guilty of cowardice or neglect of duty.'

He turned to Ld Rosmore [Rossmore],[220] saying, 'Is not that a propper answer?'

I craved pardon for my jocular reply. His Excellency said that he was well pleased, adding that he was ready to serve me with any thing in his power. I, then placing myself in a posture of thankful submission, sayed, 'That is the most consoling gratification that could be offered to a person in my situation – as from yr most superior power volunteering'such a kindness – I have no need of further interest.'

His Excly sayed to Ld Rosmore that he never before conceived that I was possessed of such abilities. I then replyed, 'Yr Excellency, I am not surprised at that, for from being compelled to fill the wretched station[221] I was in much obscured my sagacity through the County Wicklow mountains, adding that 'the only request I shall make is to grant permission to let my wife and children with me, as their absence should doubly increase my a[n]xiety now at the approach of my decline of life.'[222]

On which His Excellency was so good to reply, 'Yes, Holt, yr request shall be put on the face of the books this day,' adding, 'Ime sorry I can't send them at government expense.'

I returned His Excellency utmost thanks, saying that tho His Majestie's soldiers had robbed, burned and destroyed all my property, yet that I hoped the Almighty would raisse a friend to pay their passage. (Gentle reader, as there is no guarding against Fate, the most amiable and humane Lady Latoutce [La Touche] was so gracious as to do it.)

The foregoing conversation caused some of the gentlemen present to seem to have compassion for me. The Revd Thos Brownrigg, said 'Holt, will you lay your hand to your breast and declare yourself – as you was before – a faithful subject? If you do, you shall be captain of a corp of horse and go through the country and take up all the men and arms you can find, as from yr knowledge you'd be of more service to Government than any individual, and you need not leave your own country. Moreover, should you fall during yr exertions, there shall be a handsome provision made for yr wife and children.'

I returned him thanks, saying, 'Yr offer is good, but I have done as much as

---

220 For many years Lord Rossmore had commanded the Royal Irish Dragoons stationed at Newtownmountkennedy.   221 Holt is probably referring to his leadership of the insurgents. A more interesting possibility is that what rankles is his 'wretched station' as a barony sub-constable, when he felt he deserved promotion and, had it not been for his enemy, Hugo, was destined for higher things.   222 How old was Holt at the time? If we take the entry in the baptismal register at Castlemacadam as the most reliable clue, he was thirty-nine, approaching his 'decline of life', which would begin on his fortieth birthday, in 1799.

could be expected and that, to yr knowledge, before the late insurrection. And now, was I to comply with your request, some individual could come forward and swear my life away with more ease then when they attempted it before. Otherwise, in time of taking such proceedings, some person might deservedly take my life – as now, by going forward in order to make a prey of creatures I have so lately endeavoured to influence, that I should be guilty (before the Almighty) of an unpardonable crime. And my interior wouldn't allow me to do it. Therefore I choose to go into a foreign land.'

On which His Excellency expressed that he much approved of my sentiments, adding that he should like a man of no deception, and, further, that I gave very propper reason for not accepting of the sd proposal, & wished me success. Lord Powerscourt sd he wished such an offer was made me the 9th day of May last. Lord Rossmore told His Excellency that he knew me for many years in various employments, and that he knew me to discharge my duty most satisfactory. So they all wished me a Good Morning & disappeared.

Next day, I was visited by Captain Robert Gore of Sea View, and that amiable gentleman sat with me for some hours, shewed me where he received a dreadfull wound from a pike in the Battle of Newtownmountkenedy. He often repeated that he wished earnestly to see me the night of sd battle, as he should confide in me for protection. Sd Mr Gore now resides in the plaice aforementioned, and I now declare that I should use my utmost exertions to save and protect him, as his humanity is unlimited to all known distressed and honest men.

He told me that he would have a collection made to liquidate the expence of my familie's passage (but I saild before the time he was so good to appoint), leaving me a guinea at his departure.

I was next visited by Thos. King, Esqr., near Rathdrum, County of Wicklow, who asked me several questions concerning the day I engaged his cavalry, telling me that the two first shots my company discharged wounded two of his men. I said that I did not know, or I should have spared one hundred of them. (Reader, them two shots were fired from a rifle piece by a French man,[223] but, as he and I was not on good terms, he soon disappeared.)

The last respectable visit I received was from the Revd. Doctor Weeks [Weekes],[224] from Anamo [Annamoe], a gentleman who had a particular affection for me, who seemed much agrieved whe[n] he found I was destined to go abroad, wishing me every happiness in my journey. He seemed much pleas[ed] to hear that my wife and family got permission to go with me. I said to Mr Weeks: What was the use of that

---

223 See note 141.   224 Who might be presumed to be a staunch Loyalist, and close acquaintance of Thomas Hugo. In the following year, Weekes's brother would shoot Andrew Thomas dead, on the outskirts of Castlekevin, which is adjacent to Annamoe. Thomas was reputed to be one of the illegitimate children of Thomas Hugo.

grant to me if it was not for the most amiable Lady Latoutche, who was so generous as to pay their passage? Reader, I must remark that I detested the very idea of possessing myself of wealth procured from plunder, or I should not be necessiated to [have] applyed for sd lady's most liberal kindness.

My wife came, leting me know that those who were in her debt made a general refusal of payment, on which I replyed that was most ungrateful treatment. She remained with me till the last day of December, when O'Bryan came in, saying we should move down to a small room.

Next morning, being the 1st of Jany, 1799, a coach came to the door, accompanied by Wilkinson, who sd I should go in this coach: 'First, I am directed to put a single iron on one of your leggs. Which will you have it on?'[225]

From this sudden, and not so soon expected mandate (as my wife an children were not in a piparatory state for the voyage) as struck us both with that anxiety of mind as I am not able to describe. My wife swooned away. I endeavoured to console her, saying, 'I hope that some of these criminal miscreants shall soon wear a rope about their necks.'

So, taking my leave, I passed into the coach, in which I was accompanied by two troopers, whom I conversed with for some time, when they confessed that the heads of sd insurrection commenced it too soon, as they should have waited the assistance of England and Scotland, as the[y] were confident that their assistance should have been innumerable, adding that, had they know[n] the substance of what they were ordered for to Ireland, 'dam their eye[s]' but the[y] should have first deserted, and that it wouldn't be long till their would be a disturbance in England and Scotland.[226]

When I discovered their disposition, I told them that I should be much gratified to let the coach man stop at [the] next tavern to have a parting glass. I said to them, when in the tavern, that it consoled me much to get out of a country where I saw such mandates of tyrany put in execution as wilful murder, hanging, pickpocketing, flogging, &c.

When we arrived at the Pidgeon [Pigeon] House[227] sd troopers took their leave of me. A boat came from my destined vessle, conducted me to it, where I was received by the captain, name of Christopher Dopson [Dobson], who, on my approach, exclaimed to the creatures on board, 'Sure, you are well enough now you've got your general on board.' There were eighty men under the deck, who with an acclamation of joy, welcomed me. Th[e] captain replyed, 'Take him into Mess

---

225 'Holt, double-bolted, handcuffed, and encompassed with what is called an iron circumference, was lately put on board a transport to be conveyed to Botany Bay. He swore, blasphemed, and inveighed most bitterly against "breach of treaty"'(*Courier*, 16 January 1799).   226 The two British troopers may have known of the mutinies at the Nore and Spithead in 1797.   227 The Pigeon House fort did not derive its name from any ornithological association but from a Mr Pigeon who had, in earlier times, been in charge of the fort, at the place of embarkation in Dublin Bay.

Number [5?],' in which were none such as was there for the crimination of United Irish men.[228]

Reader, I wish to let you know some of the inhumane disposition of our captain. I discovered that he formed an agreement with Government to land us for a stipulated sum, by giving each person, each day, one pound of bread and one pound of meat and, out of this scanty allowance, this barbarous captain made the following Isirue [issue]: he first appointed a person for its distribution, with possitive direction to average it so as to give 7 pound instead of 10. It was no use to seek redress, for any that did was chained to the deck.

Reader, wishing to give you a detail of my passage, my messmates were:

John Lacy, metal founder, Dublin [229]
Joseph Davis, cutler, from do [ditto]
Farrel Cuff [Farrell Cuffe], school master, from Kings County [230]
Jn. o. Kincade [Kincaid], from Armagh
William Henry do
Charles Dane (Dean], of Dublin, an apothecarie's apprentice
Richard Dry [231]
Saml Car [Carr], from Armagh, brother to Parson Car of sd plaice
Thos Brady, from Co Wicklow, who was chief clerk at the Gold Mines [232]

Both William Henry and Charles Deans' constitutions, with several others, not being able to stand the treatment given by our tyrant captain, expired before the[y] reached the Cove of Cork.

Mr Brady addressed me, saying, 'This is a wretced lodging for you.'

I said, 'God has ever been propitious to me, and I hope he shall continue his wonted assistance.'

[228] There may have been some who withheld their 'acclamations': Several newspapers had published that Holt had given 'much information' at Dublin Castle and the news must have circulated among his comrades on board. [229] Lacey would be permitted to bring his wife with him aboard the *Minerva*, when it set sail for New South Wales. There he would have a 'numerous infant family', two houses and 1,080 acres of land. [230] Cuffe, aged twenty-four at the time he sailed with Holt on the *Minerva*, came from Edenderry. After the Irish conspiracy of 1800 in New South Wales he was ordered to receive five hundred lashes. Later he set up a school in Pitt Row, Sydney (renamed Pitt Street after the arrival of Governor Macquarie). In 1828, Cuffe, now married with one son, was farming thirty acres. [231] Dry (1771–1843), a Protestant, was born near Wexford and became a woollen draper. At Dublin, in September 1797, he was convicted on political charges and sentenced to transportation to New South Wales for life. He had not been long there before he was sent to Norfolk Island, which suggests that he was suspected of being involved in plans for an Irish insurrection near Sydney. Eventually, Dry prospered – dramatically: by 1820, through his own industry and perseverance, he owned 12,000 acres in Van Diemens Land; in 1828, he was one of the founders of the Cornwall Bank, and in 1832 of the Tamar Steam Navigation Company. Dry's son, Sir Richard Dry, was premier of Tasmania from 1866 to 1869. [232] The fact that Brady had been an active proselytiser, at the political, or civil, level, for the United Irishmen, and that he was a friend of Holt's, is another circumstantial factor pointing to Holt's probable enlist-

Mr Brady shared his coarse pillow with me, which was composed of a small lock of hay. The plank, on which was our gangway all day formed our bead at night, and each motion of the vessle, the beolge [bilge] water would flash [flush] under our sides. The deck should have formed our covering but the hatch ways were left open tho the fact is, were they shut, we should have expired from suffocation and stench, as there was a large tub placed in the centre of the vessle. This tub was a receptacle to hold the excrements of 80 persons whom, being new sailors, resorted very often to it, this chamber mugg not being discharged but every 24 hours, from the agitative motion of the vessle which kept the contents in a state of continual evaporation which, to weak constitutions, was reely noxious. Frosty winds descending, at other times rain falling! – which brought to my recolection the sufferings of [?under] Lord Cornwallis, on which was a well known song composed, the reflection of which animated my languid spirits, and which song I began to sing, which much surprised, tho helped to rise, the drooping spirits of my fellows sufferers.[233]

Jany 2, 1799. Dopson received orders to sail. He soon weighed anchor when, looking on around, I espied my disconsoalate wife on shore, we both wishing to vent our plaints together, but could do no more than make motions of filial affection.

I had but five shillings in my possession. On the 3rd inst. I got a view of Wicklow mountains, on which I said: 'Was I there again that neither Lord nor Lady should get me under their jurisdiction,' adding that I 'hoped that I should return once more to shew my countrymen how undiservedy I have received this cruel treatment, which I am sorry I made good,[234] for though none is killing by slaughter, many are in a worse state by lugging on an insupportable load of oppression, but, thanks to my Redeemer, that I am now like the cuckoo who shoots to the south and leaves bad days to men.'

So we continued our voyage, which was accompanyed with most inclement weather, which rendered it more tedious. We suffered extremely from thirst, as o[u]r allowance of water was but one pint in 24 hours.

At length, we arived at Passage,[235] near Waterford, where Dobson cast anchor at which time I saw a great struggle with some of the creatures aboard for some paticles of ice which adherd to the ship's sails to serve them in place [of] drink and, further, I saw a man expire whose last words was, 'Water,' realy expiring through excessive thirst. I was determined as soon as I should reach Cork Cove to seek redress.[236]

Our delay here gave the favourable opportunity of writing to my wife which, when done, I formed a letter to Mrs Latoutche, whose humanity doth never cease in relieving the known distressed.[237] The purport of my letter was that, hoping that

---

ment in 1797. **233** Probably 'The Croppy Boy': 'Twas early, early in the spring, / When the birds did whistle and sweetly sing ...' **234** See note 225: 'breach of treaty'. **235** Passage West. **236** See Holt's letter written from Passage West, transcribed on page 163. **237** See note 195. The La Touche family were very wealthy bankers. Mrs La Touche was the wife of the magistrate, Peter La Touche, son of David La Touche, who was a member of parliament and one of the Privy Council.

as she was intrumental as to induce me as to resign my mountanious life which seemed to form a total exclusion from a most affectionate wife, the absence of which was more dear to me than my life, that I found that I most ardently begged and entreated that Her Ladysh[ip] might please to restore her company to me, as I was divested of the smallest help to defray her passage, 'for which I most sincerely pray that the Almighty will return you a suitable reward.'

I received her most bountifull and gracious answer, not only complying with my request but also saying that she would also defray the passage of my children and, as she had a particular affection for my daughter who she had in her care, saying, 'I will take care of her education, heal[t]h and morals,' saying, 'the country you are bound for is not a good place for females,'[238] also that she had directed a banker of Cork to give me what money was sufficent for their passage.

Her Ladyship sent for my wife, leting her know the contents of my letter, and asked her if she would make up her mind to live without me. If so, that she would settle her and children and allow them a handsome livelihood. She answered Her Ladyship, 'What is the world to me if I lose the company of my husband?' Her Ladyship replyed, 'I see ye have equal affection.' She then turned to my son, saying that she would have him well instructed and have him ta[u]ght any trade he fancied. The child, being moved with affection, replyed, 'I choose to go with my father.'

Peter Latoutche Esqr. asked my wife how she intended to get to Cork. She replyed that she had no way, save only my brother's horse and car. He said, 'Perhaps, poor women, you might be killed on the way for what you have not,' giving her five guineas, saying, 'That will pay a coach.' Gentle reader, I am far short of words to explain my sentiments and encomiums which that gentlest and amiable gentlemen and weoman deserved, but hopes this slender remark on there goodness will ever remain in the annals of history.

Reader, I now return or refer you to Ballyhack.[239] By this time the report of the transports ariving there had reached the ears of this neighbourhood. As for the title of 'General Holt' it was quite universal, which induced many of the most respectable inhabitants to come to behold me. My raiment was as of a superior officer of troops.

One day, about the hour of two o'clock, as I was taking my skanty and coarse repast, I perceived several persons on deck, some of them endeavouring to get sight of me – on which I ordered my company to stand so as to obstruct their view. Cn Dobson called me, saying, 'Holt, come up!', but I never seemed to hear him. I [He] repeated again, in a commanding tone, 'Come you, sir, when you are called!'

---

238 Her misgivings were well founded, and are echoed in the letters of Michael Hayes, another United Irishman. Carr, *The Grand Irish Tour* gives the following account of how Mrs La Touche might have provided for Marianne Holt at Bellevue: '... a schoolhouse where twenty-eight girls received a good liberal education.' The writer, Mr Carr, noted approvingly that when the girls married 'honest labourers' Mrs La Touche provided them with a dowry. Marianne married William Shaw.   239 Opposite Passage West.

I replyed that, to gratify him, I should not, as he would keep even the air from me should he think it served me.

He then said, 'There is a gentleman here who wants to see you.'

I answered, 'You have as much power to let him down as to keep me down, therefore I will stay here.'

So, finding my determination, four came down with Dobson.

Says Dobson, 'You wouldn't come up to please me?'

I answered, 'No, but was you going to be hanged, I should be happy to execute the opperation.'

One of sd four was in a millitary officer's habit and, from the number on his buttons, bespoke that I should have some diversion with him, as I had taken some of sd reidgment on Lugnacullagh [Lugnaquillia]. He asked me if I remembered of the 89th Reidgment?

'O yes, I do, very well, for I can't ever forget them.'

He turned to his company, saying, 'Didn't I tell ye so?'; turning to me, [he] say[s], 'We gave you a very hard chace over EEmale [Imail].'

'Yes, air, the chace was rapid, but your party was in front. I must acknowledge your men to be remarkably swift, as I almost cracked my hind [wind] in pursuit of them. Their motion put in mind of swallow shooting, and I hadn't time to level my piece. We only took 3 prisoners and a few wounded. I am sorry His Majestie has such dastards to pay.'

Which excited much laughter from the rest of his company, which was reechoed by my fellow sufferers in the ship. His countenance bespoce much agravation, so he disappeared.

There was a gentleman Transport aboard sd ship, name of John St Leger, who hath been captain of a troop and hath become a United Man.[240] He frequently drank with Dobson, having plenty of money, one night got so tipsy that they disputed. Next morning St Leger was called on deck to be ironed. I was also called. Dobson said that, 'I will put the Captain and General together.' I answred that, 'I shall take care you shan't. You have seen no misconduct in me and therefore I shan't suffer to become linked as they do criminal goats.' He called to the serjant to bring me up, which he refused, saying that hede take care of me below, & that dam him if I should be ill treated as long as I should behave myself propper. Dobson sd hede complain of the serjant. Says the serjaunt, 'By G.d, there will be complaints, and you will have your share of them.'

From my non compliance, St Leger got free from confinement.

During our time on this river, several boats came with provisions to sell but Dobson gave no permission to any to buy, though knowing we were in a state of starvation, from many of the creatures on board being 8 months on the water and who hadn't means of shifting themselves was an inexpressible state of torment, being covered with vermin.

240 St Leger had been a captain in the 24th Light Dragoons.

On the 23rd we arived in the Cove of Cork. Our arival soon transpired through the city. Serjaunt Wiggan went a shore. I wrote, by him, to General Myres [Myers],[241] stating the cruel state we were in, hoping that hede be so good as to send to inspect our deplorable situation. In about an hour after he received the letter, there came 4 officers on board. From the statement of my letter, they ordered all and very person on deck. Their appearance was wors than I could describe. One of them puled out the letter and asked Dobson to produce the weights he made use of weighing the prisoners' allowances; on which he produced honest weights. Then the person whom Dobson employed to weigh as creaner [grainer?] was called for, who happened to be a Thos Byrne, a plasterer, best known by [the name of] 'Boxing Byrne', from Dublin. Says Dobson to Byrne:

'Didn't you weigh the prisoners's provison?'

Byrne answ[ere]d, 'Yes, sir, but not with them weights.' He ran to where the weights really was, saying, 'Gentlemen, here is the weights I was directed to use.'

On proving them, they were found to be same as my letter specified. Dobson endeavoured to make excuses but to [no] effect, one of the officers holding my letter in his hand, which confuted him. Several of the prisoners were asked questions and not an individual but brot home unpardonable crimes against Dobson. One of the officers told him that he was one of the greatest robbers the vessle contained. Dobson said it was a made up thing betwixt them all against him, but replyed one of sd officers:

'He who wrote this letter has not belyed you.'

Then I steped forward, giving a broad side, whis finished sd business at once.

'That is my hand writing. Can you deny anything there stated?'

Sd gentlemen asked me a few questions, saying they should be happy in having some conversation with me at another time. Dobson was ordered to go in the boat. One of them said that he ought to be hung out of the yard arm and further, that should he escape punishment for his present crimes, that he should never earn a shilling under Government again.

So Reader, we should adore our king and praise his laws, and abjure those that is the cause of purpetrating tyranny, which by the above you plainly see.

Reader, it is a particular gratification to me to spare no trouble in giving you a detail of every thing I think worthy of your observation during my painful to[??]er [tour?]. Our ship, *Minerva*, lay long side the *Pollyphemus* [*Polyphemus*], and employed to carry the prisoners to New South Wales. She received orders to receive all the prisoners were in the *Lively* packet, which she did. And then was a new(s) circulated in that damed vessle of Dobson's, that all the prisoners' clothes should be thrown overboard, which induced several of them to part their clothes for a pint of whiskey. I was standing on deck when a Doctor Archer came on board. I asked him was it possible that every one should give away their clothes? He replyed:

---

241 Major-General William Myers was much involved in Intelligence work.

'That's at their own option, as any who has clean clothes may bring them.'

I thanked him, going down letting the prisoners know the fact, which soon put stop to the cheap sale.

There was a Santippe [Xantippe][242] of a serjaunt who had engaged my entire aparel to clothe his children. At his return I saw a lighter coming from our ship, *Minerva*, I instantly went down and shaved an cleaned myself. The convicts' clothing came on board sd lighter. Sd serjaunt picked out two large jackets for me. He went to the ships, requesting that hede ask me if I did, or did not, prefer the green before the blue?[243] 'Yes,' said I, 'for, should I take my oath to the contrary, I shouldn't be believed.' So I took two jackets, two pair trouseres, two shirts, two pair of shoes, two pair of stockings, a hat, a small flox bead [flock bed?], a blanket and rugg, which furnised my share of His Majestie's donation. Each prisoner got the same as aforementioned. Next came the barber to shave my head. I gave him a slap, bidding the damed rascal begone. On which was a complaint for disobedience. I replyed: 'Do you want to shave my head off, as my hair was taken off before as bear as could be done with a scisors?'

The Santippe serjaunt said, 'Sir, will you throw me up them clothes?'

I said, 'Come down for them.'

He said he couldn't quit his post.

I replyed, 'Stay there and be damed, for you shan't get one stitch of them. You are with me like an overgrown sweep, quite out of yr time.'

I then went on the deck and proceeded to the lighter, and went in first cargo to the *Minerva*. The first man I met was the cheif mate, a Mr Harrison. The time being busy, I walked the deck and was quite reconciled to get rid of Dobson. A Mr Howe was second mate, quite a gentlemany man, a Mr Heggerty [indecipherable] and no deception for he was full as bad as he looked, William Douglas quater master, James secon, John Thompson third, the fourth had such a variety of names as would puzzle the alphabet to explain. Salkel [Salkeld] was captain, who got married to a lady in the city of Cork, a Miss Graham, a glass blower's daughter. William Bolton, from County Wicklow, was ship carpenter, a Martin Short, from Naas, his mate – so the *Minerva* was filled out in a most propper manner for the conveyance of her cargo.

Next morning I was addressed by a Wm Cox, Esqr.,[244] who was paymaster to a millitary corp of [New] South Wales, who shook hands with me, saying that he was sorry for my misfortune, next enquired for my family. I related Mr and Mrs

---

[242] Xantippe was the wife of Socrates, and a notorious scold, or shrew.   [243] A rare instance of Holt identifying himself with Nationalist aspirations.   [244] William Cox (1764–1837) was born at Wimbourne in Dorset. In addition to being paymaster he was in charge of all convicts on board the ship. Cox would play a major role in Holt's fortunes in New South Wales. Probably he knew little about farming and was canny enough to recognise that this man, who would become his manager, had much to teach him. Holt was expert in the making of roads and bridges: Cox would be in charge of the party which built the 101 mile road over the Blue Mountains in 1814. Perhaps Holt might deserve some reflected glory for that feat which 'unlocked' the interior of Australia.

Latoutche's goodness to me, showing him Her Ladyship's letter. He expressed much pleasing words on finding my family was coming with me. He then asked me to his cabin, where he gave me refreshment. There I saw Mrs Cox, who is a respectable and amiable weoman, with four beautiful children on board, namely Charles, George, Henry and Edward, and ever after proved most affectionate to me.

In a short time I had many visitors in the ship, asking several questions concerning the late insurection. Captain Cox, Captn Salken and Mr Harrison would always volunteer their presence when these curious spectators would appear. My answers didn't please them much, as they was always contrary to the approbation of the yeoman [245] as they couldn't bear to hear the truth, as men who are not under military jurisdiction will never be good soldiers in time of danger. As for the Rebels, their loyalty was sincere, which was grounded on good reason, as self preservation. There came a large party on board from Cork, one of which spoke so impertinent to me that I was under the necessity of asking my captain for pistols to exchange a shot with him, which made him crave pardon, in presence of my captain. When the throng went away, it excited much laughter in the officers of the ship and, in future, done me much respect.

March 6th, I was walking on the quarter deck in company with Mr Harrison, casting my eyes toward the Cove, when I espied my wife and son distant about half a mile. I told Mr Harrison that I thought I descry my wife and son, on which he took a view with his glass, asking me was her features such and such – which ensured me it was them. He order[ed] the quartermaster to get ready the chair, which soon fetched Mrs Holt and son on board, which was an inconceivable pleasure to me, as no one can describe our mutual joy at meeting at a time when we had hopes of never parting till death. Mr Harrison brot us into the cabin and treated us in a most friendly manner. Captain Salken made an agreement with me for their passage, which was the sum of 120 guineas,[246] on which I gave him an order on a banker of Cork, which he instanly received. Mrs Holt went ashore to get some necessaries she wanted, letting me know when she would return, so her and son went a shore. Then Captain Salken gave orders to the carpenters to take off a small cabbin from the steerage for Mrs Holt and me, for the Reverend Henry Fulton[247] and family as well, as Mrs Fulton was going to accompany her husband to New South Wales. I must inform you that he was sent on the same cause as me but didn't earn his passage so well, as he had not sport for his journey. Mrs Fulton was daughter to

---

245 As a soldier, Holt had a special contempt for the yeomen, probably because they had so little military training.   246 I have seen the receipt in the National Archives. The actual amount was £136. 10s.   247 Henry Fulton (1761–1840), born in England and educated at Trinity College, Dublin, was a Protestant clergyman who had been imprisoned at Limerick for taking the 'Defenders Oath'. In May 1803, Mrs William Kent, niece by marriage to the former New South Wales governor, John Hunter, having visited Fulton and his wife on Norfolk Island, wrote to her mother: 'Mr Fulton was most wrongfully sent from Ireland in the disturbances four years ago on a groundless suspicion of sedition and without any trial.' Fulton was granted a full pardon in 1805 and, in 1806, returned to the mainland of Australia. A resolute anti-Papist, he led the Protestant party in its opposition to Governor Bourke's education policy in New South Wales.

Parson Walker, who resided at or near the Silver Mines, which is near Waterford. Likewise Revd Father Harrel [Harold],[248] from near Reculla,[249] in the County of Dublin, who was priest of that parish, Doctor O'Connor and his brother in law, William Henry Alcock,[250] who was captain of a reidgment of foot soldiers.

I now humbly beg to make the following observations as here you see – the following and aforesd gentlemen, in the same predicament as me: Captains of full pay, whos duty is but to fulfill necessary orders – which is but a little conversation; Ministers, who occupy or get the tenth of the parish for giving an exortation once a week – which is but a little conversation; Prists, who for marrying, baptizing and all his other duties has a stipulated sum which is but a little conversation. When such was disaffected, it must in a great measure serve to doubly excuse poor oppressed creatures who were dragging on insupportable burdens of extra rents, tythes and other innumerable impositions.

But the last bulletin I have received specifies that there is a contagion, or pestelince, reached the bottom less pit, which is of such a malignant nature as caused all the inhabitants to die which, if found true, Impostorours and Extortional Exercises will cease, as every one may think for himself, and go his own road.

I took the liberty of asking sd gentlemen the following questions: First – Did the[y] sustain great loss?

Answer: 'No.'

'Was your house burned?'

'No.'

'What battle was ye in?'

'None.'

'Did ye rob any one?'

'No, we were taken too soon.'

I replyed: 'The D'l's cure to you to be transported for a soldier's crime, that is nothing.'

248 Like Holt, Harold's allegiances may have swung between two poles: in Ireland he had been an opponent of armed insurrection and had tried to persuade his parishioners at Rathcoole, Co. Dublin, to surrender their pikes. Suspected of being a party to the Rebellion of 1798, his house was burnt down and he was arraigned at Kildare, where he was sentenced to transportation for life. On arrival of the *Minerva* in Sydney Harbour, on 11 January, 1800, Father Harold was given a rousing welcome by the Irish convicts. Significantly, Holt held aloof from that welcome. Michael Hayes called him 'a learned man' who 'did not practise all he preached.' This was because two Irishmen, charged with involvement in plans for an Irish insurrection in September 1801, had been arrested on 'information' given by Father Harold; the charges were found to be 'malevolent and groundless.' And yet, because he was believed to have been associated with plans for that same insurrection, Harold was banished to Norfolk Island. Pardoned in New South Wales in 1810, Father Harold went to America, where he stayed for five years before returning to Ireland, where he worked in Fairview parish, Dublin, until his death in 1830. 249 Probably Rathcoole. 250 During the Rebellion Alcock had been a captain in the Wexford Militia. He would prosper in New South Wales: on 18 August 1810 Governor Macquarie appointed him to 'superintend and direct the making, construction and repairing of the streets, highways and bridges within the town of Sydney'.

Mrs Holt and son returned, according to promise. We had to regret then only the absence of our daughter. I often was the cause to excite Mrs Holt to laughter: on calling these gentlemen to Drill or Exercise, I frequently told them that it was necessary that they should do some labour for their passage, as they had not earned it before.

Mrs Fulton, son and daughter came. Then the Minister and I was in possession of every comfort that a good husband could wish for.

Mrs Allcock [Alcock], sister to Dr O'Connor came to pay a 'friendly' visit to her husband and brother, so that I conceived that her happiness would be redoubled, as on the voyage she could, with gratification, constantly see two friends at once. I think she didn't lose her time by coming to the *Minerva*. As you may observe from the following, my observation was just concerning this lady – as she influenced her husband to make over his entire income, by virtue of a Deed of the annual sum of £300. For to purfect sd deed, she procured an alert attorney. When sd deed was purfected, Mrs Allcock and said atty passed into the boat, biding Mr Allcock good by. I shall never forget the cool form of accent Mrs Allcock's good nature directed her to deliver her parting words. I can't but remark that I endeavoured to dissuade Mr Allcock from signing sd deed, as I had a clear foresight that it might be instrumental of being the means of him losing both his poperty and wife, which was really the case, as he never saw her more. I know that the influence of wine, accompanyed by the wiles of an ungrateful weoman, often hath fatal effects on Man. The only thing he had to console him was that he fortunately had her picture, with some of her hair, enshrined in gold, which he hung about his neck, which is all he possessed in lieu of his wife and his own property, as he hath never got any with her. I was acquainted with him for fourteen yrs after his arival in [New] South Wales, during which time she hath never as much as sent him a letter.[251]

I wish to here express my sentiments on this subject, as a good and virtuous wife is a jewel of inesteemable value, but ungratefulness in a wife is banefully unpardonable.

I now shall specify the particular description of persons were on board the ship with me for Disaffection: Captain Allcock, who had full pay with the Annuity of £300 a year. It's a mystery to me what could create in his mind disaffection. Captain John St Leger, under full pay from a good king – so I am at a loss what could induce him to desert his honourable commission. There was Parson Fulton, who had his parrish. I am at a loss to know what should induce him to become a Rebel; and priest Harroll, who had his parish – but I must acknowledge his jurisdiction was not within the limit of compulsion. However I am at a loss to know his inducement. Dr O'Connor who, by selling herbalist's juices, burgundy pitch-plaisters, emetics, bleeding, feeling the vibrations of the heart, renovating the decayed bloom of ladyes from which &c, &c. he could procure a comfortable living.

---

[251] Holt spent thirteen, not fourteen, years in New South Wales, having arrived there on 10 January 1800 and departed on 4 December 1812.

Not wishing the least to exclude any thing against myself, I was Deputy Allinger [Alnager], under Sir John Blacquer [Blacquière], which brot me in from eighty to a hundred pounds, by agencys sixty pound a year likewise, Chief Barony Constable, Tory hunter, thief catcher – taking coiners, pickpockets, murderers &c – which brot me at least fifty pounds a year. Should I be so mean as to take bribes, I might have one hundred and fifty. Likewise, over seer and projecter of roads – taking away hills or elevated places, and filling hollows – with various emoluments arising therefrom I may justly add fifty pounds more. But my most hard endeavous was soon destroyed and consumed by a most baneful individual, described in the foregoing part of my history.

So that here you have a descriptional view of a curious medly of criminals expelled from their native land to the distance of at least 16,500 miles, and but one of them can say that, during the late insurection, hath saw in opposition as much as the explosion of a gun.[252]

I now commence a detail of what passed during our destined voyage. Mr and Mrs Fulton were put in the cabin with me and family. My son was 12 years old, April 4th, 1799, and quite an active lad of his age. Captain Salkel asked me if Ide let him go in the Boatswain's Mess, saying he would be the wholesomer to be with the officers of the ship than to be walking under deck. He had his scheme in that, but I discovered it, saying that I had no objection, but that the boy should be so many hours at school, as sd Farrel Cuff [Farrell Cuffe],[253] from Kings County, was a teacher. However, I consented, and my son, Joshua, was entered on the ship's books and put in the Boatswains's watch. Some days he was permitted to attend school, at others he was not, which was very unpleasant to me for him to be absent from his Learning;[254] but, on the other hand, I was delicate in saying any thing contrary, so I let it pass.

Some time in June, Captain Cox was in company with General Myres and Major Ross ashore, and both of thes[e] gentlemen wished to see me.[255] Captain Cox came to me, informing me of the matter, desiring that I might go and dress myself, which I accordingly did. At this time the[y] were ready: Captn Cox, Lieutenant Mondrell [Maundrell?], with serjaunt Hobs [Hobbs] and I, with two sailors to rowe the boat. We lay under the Batterrey, about a quarter of a mile from shore. We soon reached land. I was conducted to General Myres and, as I walk through the barrack

---

252 *Reductio ad absurdum*: Holt at his most brash and fatuous. The matter of allegiances is of no account: in his eyes, the only reasons any man might have committed himself to that rebellion would have been self-interest and because, as a 'sportsman', he knew how to handle a gun. Absurd though his analysis may be, it probably serves as the most simple clue Holt could have given to some of the warring elements within his own nature.   253 See note 230.   254 In one of the 'Informations' in the National Archives, Holt is described as 'having a poor address' (see p. 95 above). I take that to mean that he did not speak like the gentleman he longed to be. The very existence of the manuscript of Holt's 'History' testifies to his aspirations to become literate and 'break through the class barrier'. Doubtless, he would have passed on those aspirations to his son, Joshua.   255 See the report of 'Information of Joseph Holt, given voluntarily ...' in Appendix 6.5.

yard, I am confident that an assembly of spectators of not less than four hundred, were collected to see me. Had I been an ourangoutang, or kangaroo, they couldn't view me with more seeming surprize. I received the glances of their staring optics with smiles. I was decorated in as decent a manner as I could at this time procure, and as full powdered as any of them, when I came to the apartment where was the General and a Major, who bestowed on me a respectable salute, which I returned with equal complisance.

The bell was rung, on which the butler appeared and ordered to bring me some refreshment [256] which, when taken, the sd gentlemen commenced asking me several questions of various kinds concerning the preriolous dangers that I went through. I answered them in the most deliberate and pleasing manner I could.

The General replyed, 'Should you have gone through such danger for your king as you went through for yr country you should be now a happy man.'

I replied, 'Yes, Sir, that I make no doubt of, but real happiness dwells only in the mind.'

The Major said, 'Sir, your observation is right.'

Replyed General Myers, 'You must know a vast number of the people of yr country?'

I said, 'Most surely, I have seen many of them, Sir.'

The Major continued, saying, 'Sir, I am informed by Captain Cox that yr wife and son are going to bear you company?'

'Yes, Sir.'

Saying, 'What would you think of staying at home and you needn't go? I will send to the ship and bring yr wife and son ashore?'

I said, 'Sir, I believe it too far gone to elope now or think of any such thing.'

Major Ross says, 'Not at all, sir, provided that you do what you are desired..'

I replied, 'Perhaps that's not in my power.'

Says the General, 'I think not. If you had a good corp of cavalry under yr command, you might do more service than ever you done hurt.'

I said, 'If so, the[y] should be more valiant than any I have ever fought against, for most of them are very thin skined and don't stand firing.'

He said, 'Very well, as you know so many, you could be of great service by prosecuting them.'

I said, 'No, Sir, I should rather kill twenty with my sword or pistol than one by the testimony of a book, as it is too low a carector for me,' returning him thanks, but begged leave to ask him one question, which he granted me.

I said, 'Sir, on yr honour, is not yr advice in behalf of Government?'

He answered, 'Yes, sir.'

I then replied, 'I ventured my life many yrs for my king and country, and to support His Majestie's laws, and received bad treatment, so I must refuse all offers.

---

[256] Once more Holt's social pretensions are to be flattered and his tongue loosened with liquor.

Hester Holt 'expecting'

The passage is paid for my wife and son, and I think that I have earned mine better than any United man in the ship. So, in the name of God, I will go and try my fortune in a country where I am not 'known'. [257]

On which, Major Ross spake and said, 'You are a man from yr word and resolution.'

Mr Cox repeated some certain facts that he had been told by one of the arch, who gave me a full carector, on which the General directed Mr Cox to give his compliments to Governor King, [258] and hoped he would do something for me. This rested in the mind of Mr Cox and, in four years after, it met me with a pleasing return, as the foregoing part of my [history] will descibe in its regular couse. As for Mrs Holt, she would rather go than stay for, as she truly said, it was better to go to any country than stay where the greatest rogue's oath in the world would be taken for truth. So both of us mutually agreed to proceed on our journey.

We still lay in the harbour. Mrs Holt had no appearance of being in the family way when I agreed for her passage but, at this period, she seemed near lying in. Captain Salkel [Salkeld] called to me one morning, saying, 'Mrs Holt had no appearance of being with child when I agreed for her passage with you.'

I said, 'Surely she is.'

He replyed, 'You had better go to Cove and take a lodging for her in time.'

I said, 'No, sir, you must do that yourself.'

He said, 'I will not. She, nor you, didn't tell me she was so when you was agreeing with me.'

I said that th[e]re was no occasion to do so, 'I agreed with you for so much money for the passage of my wife and son and, if you stay here much longer, I hope she will have another, so get on the way as soon as you can. Get ready one of the state rooms and let Dr Price have some employment.'

The state room was got ready when Mrs Holt wanted it, and she was attended by Mrs Hobbs. In Cove of Cork was seven children born for, between soldiers and prisoners, there was 34 weomen. Mrs Cox and my wife made 36 weomen, 132 men prisoners, 27 privates, 4 serjaunts, one lieutenant, 3 mates, 4 quarter masters and 20 sailors. [259]

---

257 As we have seen, Holt had already given enough 'Information' to damn him in the eyes of his comrades. What then are we to make of his refusal to enter into active military service for the government? Quite simply, I think we are to believe that he thought that this would have amounted to treachery, while the 'Information' he had given against a 'Rebellion' which had been taken over by bigoted Catholic banditti was not. Interpretations of his motives in giving 'Information' (see note 255) are bound to differ. No doubt some will see that 'Information' as groundless, trumped up by Holt, and merely evidence of his desire to curry favour. My own opinion is that Holt was probably in earnest.   258 A lapse of memory. Governor Hunter was in charge until 28 September 1800, when Governor King took over.   259 The journal of Charles Barrington (1755–1804), 'the Crown Prince of Pickpockets', born in Maynooth, and educated at the Bluecoat School, Dublin, gives 162 male convicts and 26 females as the figures.

On the 17th July, at 6 o'clock in the morning, Mrs Holt had a young son born;[260] and, on the 19th, he was baptized by Parson Fulton and Mr Harrison,

William Henry Allcock [Alcock] & Mrs Hobbs stood sponerrs [sponsors] for him.

And, on the twenty fourth August we weighed anchor and sailed with a fair wind.

---

260 Christened Joseph Harrison Holt, his second Christian name obviously chosen as a gesture of gratitude to the chief mate.

EDITOR'S POSTSCRIPT

Joseph Holt left New South Wales in December 1814, just when his fortunes looked most auspicious and Governor Lachlan Macquarie was ushering in an era of some prosperity and dignity for the colony, thus laying the foundations for an egalitarian society. Macquarie, recognising his agricultural expertise and enterprising character, tried to persuade him to stay and Holt later regretted that he did not. He and his wife Hester probably returned to Ireland for the very human reason that they wanted to be reunited with their daughter, Marianne.

It was curiously naive of Holt that, on his return to Ireland, he should have chosen at first to live in the Liberties, that part of Dublin which was notorious as a redoubt for the Wicklow and Wexford veterans of '98. There he set up a tavern, the Plough (the building, a pub known as 'The Good Times', at the corner of Kevin Street and Redmond's Hill, was demolished as recently as 1986). His career as a publican was troubled, as he tells us in the latter part of his memoirs:

> I found a moral impossibility for me to command my temper and passion to live as publican for this reason: one vagabond set would come in and call me 'a bloody Croppy'. Them I used to kick properly. And if I showed them I had the protection of the law because I suffered under laws of my country for being so, whether guilty or not, another gang of ruffians would come in and call me 'a bloody Orange man'. And I am sure many of them was bribed for doing so, to rise a mutiny in my house by my ill hearted neighbours.
>
> My Gentle Reader, I was so tormented with these rascals I thought better to get shut of trouble at once, so I gave up public business and came to the country.

Perhaps the Dublin gossips were better informed than the General realised, for Holt had, after all, been a qualified informer. That he should have moved from the Liberties to an Anglo-Irish enclave, Kingstown (Dun Laoghaire), was typical of a man whose allegiance for much of his life had swung violently between two contending causes. In Dun Laoghaire he built several houses, which still stand. One of them, No. 72 York Road, is where he lived the latter part of his life, where he probably wrote most of his 'History', and where he died. The adjoining houses he rented to tenants.

But even in Kingstown, as his friendly neighbour, Sir William Betham, remarked, Holt was never accepted into respectable society; not so much perhaps because he was suspect as the former notorious rebel chieftain, as because Holt would always lack the social graces, literacy and accent of speech to match the gentleman figmented in 1838 by the literary skill of Thomas Crofton Croker.

The manuscript of Holt's 'History' obviously held no interest for Irish historians. Holt's failure to qualify as a literate gentleman would have consequences reaching far beyond his life span. For more than a hundred and fifty years, historians too readily accepted the authenticity of the text of Thomas Crofton Croker.

Sir William Betham died in 1853. His manuscripts were sold at auction in London by Sotheby and Wilkinson in 1860, among them being the manuscript of Holt's 'History'. It was purchased by the antiquary and bibliophile, Sir Thomas Phillipps, of Worcestershire, who died in 1872. In 1938, it was auctioned at Sothebys and purchased from the Phillipps estate by the State Library of New South Wales

APPENDICES

1. SOME OPINIONS REGARDING JOSEPH HOLT

1.1 From an obituary in the *Dublin and London Magazine*, July 1826 published shortly after his death

This insurrectionary chieftain has at length gone 'to the house appointed for all living'. He had been residing in New Dunleary, or Kingstown, for nearly the last seven years, and had succeeded in gaining the friendship or goodwill of most of his neighbours; there were a few, to be sure, whom no concession, no care on his part, could thoroughly soften. The men of the old ascendancy school, the deeply dyed 'true-blues', could never forget the General's earlier transgressions. His subsequent good conduct and peaceable demeanour could never, in their eyes, atone for the past. This unmitigated spirit of hostility seriously annoyed poor Holt, for it was his wish to be on friendly terms with all.

I first met him soon after his arrival at Dunleary. He had been engaged in Dublin for a short time in the public business, but the noise and confusion attending such a trade disturbed him. He was getting old, and, as he told me, he was now anxious for rest and retirement. He said he had secured a sufficiency for the remainder of his days, emphatically adding, that though it came from Botany Bay, it had been fairly and honourably earned.

I was eager to hear from him something of his exploits in ninety-eight. He said there were many of those transactions that he did not like to dwell on. He had done many things in the heat of passion that he afterwards bitterly repented of. He was like many other well-meaning men, *forced* to become a rebel, against his better judgment and inclination. Holt was a substantial farmer in the county of Wicklow, he dealt largely in wool; he was Protestant, and, for a time, barony constable, a post seldom filled by men of questionable loyalty. He was a man of good heart, and of liberal principles; he could not join his Orange neighbours in insulting or injuring those who held another creed. He was constantly the humble advocate of his Catholic brethren, and this, in the eyes of the ultras, was a sort of apostacy, it was worse than the sin of popery itself. He, consequently, became what was then called a marked man. He was cursed with an over-loyal squireen for a neighbour. This little tyrant annoyed him in various ways; he denounced Holt as one of the disaffected, and at length, when the rebellion broke out, he proceeded with a troop of yeomanry to his dwelling for the purpose of arresting him. The latter was away at Carnew on business; the women fled as they saw their old enemy approaching, not calculating much on his forbearance, and the loyal band, after searching the place, found a few letters, which they construed into treason. They instantly set fire to the house, and Holt on his return home found but a heap of ashes, where he had so recently left a comfortable farm house and a large haggard of corn.

1.2 Diverse opinions of Holt given to Luke Cullen, selected by the editor from Cullen's writings

He had an unbounded and habitual desire of thrusting himself forward.

Holt was a coward boasting good-for-nothing fellow.

Not a difficult task to poison the minds of the natives of the mountains against him.

Holt could not keep himself quite [quiet].

Notwithstanding there were men far superior to him in the qualifications of a warrior ... but he knew the country and the people better perhaps than any man.

Not very well liked.

I could not clearly see how men who habituated themselves to the cry and din of loyalty could quickly turn around and figure in the opposite extreme ... He called himself a Tory hunter, then considered the expiring spark of priest hunting, and he wished them to consider him entitled to some celebrity in that way.

As a constable with long standing associations with the magistracy and the yeomanry, he was in a position to assess the principal assistance to those of his new affiliation when martial law began to make inroads into the organisation.

He was a kind of Jonah Barrington in his own circle. He was extremely vain and had an inordinate desire for popularity. He was not a favourite with the people of his part of Co. Wicklow. He called himself a Tory hunter and he wished to be considered entitled to some celebrity in that way. Many of the Catholic community looked on him as a qualified informer. In conversation and debate he joined the strongest party, and if they passed any remark on his volatile disposition, he joked and talked them out of it. He talked much, and there was a general watch on him around the time of the commencement of the Insurrection. He was not trusted much. He thrust himself into every company that was available to him, in public houses in particular. His inquisitiveness at times became intolerable to some of his neighbours.

Against this we may range the balanced account (see below) given of Holt more than half a century after the Rebellion by a reliable man who had often served under him, Miles Byrne.

Some opinions regarding Joseph Holt

1.3 The following extracts from the *Memoirs of Miles Byrne* provide an interesting and convincing assessment of Holt's skill and courage as a soldier, and of his personal character

A night expedition was now decided on to go into the country villages at some distance, to bring salt and any dry provisions as we could get back to our camp in Glenmalure, where it was resolved the intrepid Dwyer should remain with the men he commanded to defend the entrance of the glen during our absence. The famous Holt, who had just arrived, was to have command of the night expedition, and at dusk when we had all our men assembled near the smelting-house and ready to march, some county Wicklow men who knew Holt came to tell us that his wife had come to join him, and that she had been making terms for him with the enemy at Rathdrum, in which town Holt was well known to all the authorities, having been employed to put the seals on the flannels at the fairs, having been Bumbailiff, etc.; and as her own family, the Mannings, were notorious Orangemen, they feared it might be dangerous to confide in Holt; that he would lead us perhaps into some ambuscade from whence we might not be able to escape, etc. To all this we listened with great attention, and as we, the county Wexford men, were the majority, we decided to send to Holt who was at Pierce Harney's house, with his wife, at the very head of the glen, to let him know that we were ready to march, resolving at the same time not to follow his plan. When he arrived, we asked him in what direction he intended to march, he replied to the Seven Churches: we objected, saying that neighbourhood was too poor, that it would be better to take another direction into a richer country, to which he at once agreed most cheerfully; no doubt to prove to us that he had not any interested motive for going to the Seven Churches, though it was the county of his wife's family. Or, perhaps, what weighed most with him was a desire to comply with the wishes of the county Wexford men, whom he perceived formed the majority of the detachment then under arms and ready to march. It was at once decided to march on the Rathdrum road as far as Greenane bridge, and from thence to turn into the country parts which had not suffered by the war.

We mustered for this expedition two or three hundred of our men, who were best able to bear up with great fatigue, leaving the weak, sickly and wounded under the care of Dwyer, who acted as governor of Glenmalure, our citadel or stronghold in the Wicklow mountains. We set off in good marching order and in high spirits. Holt and a friend of mine, John Doyle of Aughrim, and myself being mounted. We rode at the head of our little column, with a few men on foot who preceded us, as an 'avant-garde' about fifty yards. As the night was very dark, we recommended our men to observe the greatest silence but the noise made by our own horses could not be avoided and might be heard at some considerable distance. Doyle and I were riding on each side of Holt, who was telling us his plans, and the great things he thought we should perform before returning to Glenmalure. In the first place he observed that he thought all the isolated houses, which might serve as places of refuge to the enemy, particularly if they were covered with slates, ought to be burned. This sentence was scarcely pronounced when we perceived flashes of light like so many stars from the pans of the enemy's fire-locks, within pistol shot of us, and instantly the whizzing of balls through our ranks and over our heads. This discharge came from the English army which had marched from Rathdrum to reconnoitre our position and had only time to reach the bridge of Greenane, when on hearing the noise of our columns advancing, they halted in silence and waited our approach.

I shall never forget Holt's presence of mind and extraordinary exertion on this dangerous occasion. He cried out with the voice of a Stentor, to our pikemen to march *en masse* and cross the bridge, and he gave orders to our gunsmen at the same time, and in the same loud voice, to wade the river, and to get on the enemy's flank, so that not one of them might escape, etc. Many of the Rathdrum yeomen who accompanied the English army in this night expedition, became terrified when they heard Holt's voice, with which they were well acquainted, and this no doubt added to the disorder which already prevailed in their ranks, for they suddenly retreated back to Rathdrum; whilst we on our side had the greatest trouble to rally our men and keep them from disbanding themselves, as they feared they had got into an ambuscade. A pistol shot heard in the rear gave rise to this apprehension, consequently, instead of marching in a mass to the bridge, as Holt had ordered, they quitted the road and got into a marshy field on the left side. After some time, finding the enemy's fire had ceased, the panic began to subside, though we did not know at the time that the enemy had retreated. However, we rallied again on the road, when it was thought more prudent to return to Glenmalure, fearing that we might meet other moving columns of the enemy if we continued our night march. Having only three men who had received slight wounds from the first volley fired, we thought ourselves very fortunate to have escaped so well. The darkness of the night with the noise of our horses in front contributed to this, the enemy taking too high aim, thinking we were all mounted. When we returned to the glen we met Dwyer, who told us we might repose ourselves during the night in perfect safety, that he would take care that the pass should be well guarded.

Holt went to Pierce Harney's house at the head of the glen, where his wife still remained, and strange enough, notwithstanding his recent brilliant conduct, several of those men who knew him well, thought he would go away with his wife, and in consequence, they kept a close watch round the house all night to prevent him. Holt, however, sent his wife away next day, and thereby removed the cause of suspicion. How fortunate it was for him that it was not at his suggestion that we marched on the Rathdrum road; for if it had been his plan, he would have been accused of bringing us into the enemy's ambuscade, whereas he had now all the merit of getting us safely out of it, and justly does he deserve this praise ...

They might now see plainly, and, no doubt, with astonishment, the smallness of our body, which had caused so much terror in all their garrison towns. Though we were so reduced, they did not march to attack us; they seemed for the present to confine their operations to burning the houses in the glen, and driving the unfortunate women with their children to perish in the fields from cold and hunger. As we went up the hills, on the opposite side, we could see the flames from the dwellings of these unhappy creatures, where also so many of our sick and wounded, returning from the disastrous campaign of the Boyne, had stopped to recover. The brave Dwyer was now obliged to abandon this stronghold, which he had so long defended, and to march with us. As he, and most of the men he commanded, were natives of these mountains and glens, we were sure to be safely guided through them. After reposing for some time, finding that we were not followed by the enemy, Holt proposed crossing the mountain and marching to the Glen of Imaal, to ascertain whether or not General Sir J. Moore was still encamped there with his division. When we arrived on the mountain in sight of the glen, we could perceive only one tent, which immediately disappeared on seeing our forces drawing up on the adjacent hill. But General Moore and his army had left the Glen of Imaal some time before, and we could not learn where he had marched to; but our plan now became imperative, to avoid as much as possible any engagement with the enemy, except small detachments which we could easily defeat, and from whom we could procure arms and ammunition, without which we could not even make head against those small detachments.

We resolved not to stop long in any one place, and by our continual marching and counter-marching, to show the enemy by this kind of manoeuvreing how difficult it would be to come in contact with us in those mountains, where we were so well guided by the brave Dwyer and his followers. But, unfortunately, this intrepid chief left us again, on hearing that we intended to march towards the county of Wexford. He could never be brought to consent to march us any distance from his native mountains; whilst Holt, though he might perceive that he was not always consulted about our excursions in quest of provisions, was ever ready to march with us, and even to assume to himself the responsibility of the expedition; and he did all with such good humour that we were delighted, and now cheerfully marched with him from the Glen of Imaal to Aughavanagh, and from thence to Croaghan mountain, to try to get some news of what was going on in the counties of Carlow and Wexford; and when we came in sight of the high road leading from Shillelagh to Arklow, we perceived a number of military waggons escorted by cavalry, on their way to the latter town. Holt instantly ordered our little column to march down rapidly in an oblique direction, and to get out on the road, and to stop and attack the convey. The escort composed of dragoons, seeing this manoeuvre, escaped in great speed, leaving the waggons and their drivers to get out of the fight the best way they could. The drivers or conductors were soon captured, and unluckily some of them were killed in the fray. Holt ordered a great pile to be made of the waggons and the provisions of corn, forage, etc., and fire to be put to this pile on every side, so in a short time the flames from it could be seen at a great distance, as the day was very bright. As we knew that the garrison towns on seeing these flames, or on hearing of the disasters of their convoy, would immediately despatch great forces of foot and horse against us, we hastened to repair to Croaghan mountains to avoid meeting the enemy, as we did not muster very strong; and here we learned for the first time that a relaxation of the cruel, cold-blooded murders was taking place in many of the county of Wexford districts. Lord Cornwallis issued a proclamation there inviting all those who had taken part in the war, 'except the chiefs', to return to their homes, where they should receive his formal protection. Whether this was on account of the landing of the French at Killala, and the marching of the English troops out of the country, or for any other reason, a stop seemed to be put for the present to the murderous career of the monster magistrate, James Boyd, Hawtry White, Hunter Gowan, Archibald Hamilton, Jacob and their cruel Orange associates. Besides, the corn now being ripe thousands ventured to return home, hoping to save it for their famishing families. In consequence of this, our small corps was reduced to a mere band. Still we resolved to keep our position in the Wicklow mountains. For though vast numbers left us to return to their dwellings, others, after having remained concealed some days in their houses, had to escape and come back to us. The protection they obtained was of no use to them, if it was ascertained that they had ever been present when houses were burned or if they had assisted at the battle of Ballyellis, where the Ancient Britons were killed. No protection under these circumstances could save them. Such rigorous requisites and formalities or conditions brought back to our standard many fine fellows who had intended to remain at their homes quietly with their families.

About this time I received a letter from Nick Murphy of Monaseed, who had escaped from the Boyne and got into Dublin, where he was hiding, as well as hundreds of our comrades. Their escape, as well as his, seemed miraculous.

When the news of the landing of the French army was known in the capital, Murphy was commissioned to find out some sure means of conveying intelligence to me of this fortunate event. A poor woman, the daughter of one of our tenants, a Mrs Keogh, volunteered to be the bearer of this letter, which she sewed in the hem of her petticoat. She was returning to her home, after taking farewell of her unfortunate husband, who was condemned to transportation for life, and just put aboard a vessel in the river waiting to sail. When I thanked this worthy creature, and observed what a dangerous mission she had undertaken, she replied 'that it was a great consolation to her in her misfortune to be entrusted with such a commission, and to be the bearer of such good news as that of the French landing, though she was doomed never to see her dear husband more.'

Though Nick Murphy's letter was very short and circumspect, still it was cheering and delightful to us. He said it was expected that there would be a general rising in Dublin of the people, if the French were in sufficient force to make head against the English army. That many persons came forward now, who had remained in the background before, and said they were ready to act. Besides, such was the enthusiasm prevailing all through the city at seeing the troops march away, that the Orange yeomen could not help observing it, and trembled for their own safety. That at all events, our forces in the mountains would be the rallying point, and from all he could learn and see himself, there was now every hope of success from the aid of the French army. He added, likewise, how very anxious our friends in Dublin were that we should be able to keep ourselves in anything like a respectable force in the Wicklow mountains for some time.

Though we had heard of the landing of the French, previous to Murphy's letter, yet it afforded us great satisfaction to see by it that our friends approved of our conduct and our perseverance in keeping our ground. We did persevere and kept our ground the best way we could crossing from one mountain to another, defying the enemy to follow us, and this for weeks, until we heard of the surrender of General Humbert and his small army of eight hundred men, to Lord Cornwallis, who it was said, was at the head of thirty thousand English troops. Under such melancholy circumstances, could it be expected that Holt could have had sufficient influence to persuade any to remain with him who could escape to their homes, and hiding there in the most wretched manner? In fact, he never took any trouble one way or another about them, but said, all those who could not remain at their houses might return to us, where they would meet a kind reception. In the worst times he appeared gay, never desponding. I have marched with him, when on setting out we were not able to muster a hundred men, and not twenty amongst them ever had their fire-arms fit for use: yet Holt would have his plans for some great undertaking as if he were at the head of thousands of the best disciplined troops. In short, he had qualities which quite fitted him for the kind of warfare we were obliged to make in the Wicklow mountains, and often did he boast that we were the only troops under arms in all Ireland, fighting for its independence at the time the French landed at Killala. I think it but justice to say so much of Holt, from the many strange stories that have been told of him.

1.4   From William Putnam McCabe's memoir in R.R. Madden, *Antrim and Down in '98*

The insurgents, in all parts of Ireland, had been defeated, with the exception of a few hundred men, who were under the command of Holt and Dwyer. In Wicklow, and who, being well acquainted with all the fastnesses of the Wicklow mountains, supported themselves, and their followers, by the plunder, which they were able to collect from their foes. McCabe knew Holt to be a brave, but ignorant and hot-headed soldier; and, conscious that resistance, under such a leader, and at such a time, could only bring destruction on himself., and his adherents, he wished, if possible, that Holt could be made to submit upon terms, which would save him and them, from that horrible death, which appeared inevitable for them all. He even wrote to the government, under a feigned name, offering his services, to attain that end. It was intimated that his services would be accepted, and McCabe, accompanied by a Mr Farrell, proceeded to Wicklow. They saw Holt, and prepared the way, for that capitulation to which the government, not less than Holt, were willing parties. This attempt to save the life of Holt, put McCabe himself in great peril. The officers of the government knew, at last, where he was to be found, and a party was sent down to Wicklow, to arrest him.

1.5 Extracts from Isaac Butt's review of Croker's edition of Holt's *Memoirs*, published in the *Dublin University Magazine*, July 1838

... Were it a tale of youthday criminality, succeeded by a sincere repentance and an atoning close of life, the production might be approvable; but we look in vain through its pages for anything of this redeeming nature. It is a detail of crime, boasted of, justified, or rather defended, and fondly chuckled over to the end. It is a disgusting farrago of blood-boultered egotism, the irreligious pulings of affected religion, and the conscientious sensibilities of a wholesale murderer.

Now, Holt appears to have been a man of great personal courage; he was highly regarded by, and in the confidential employ of several of the leading gentry of the district, from any of whom he might have claimed protection against wrong. He was, moreover, strong in conscious innocence; and yet, strange to say, instead of awaiting the approach of the civil and military authorities, we find him flying like 'a guilty thing'. He arms himself, and betakes himself at once to a spot which he seems to have known full well was the haunt of men in rebellion!!! Now, if Holt, even in the meridian of his criminality, steeped to the lips in treason and blood, had friends among the leading nobility and gentry of Wicklow, so powerful as to have effected his pardon, how much more might he not have relied upon such men for protection in the hour of his innocence and wrong? His friends, Messrs. Synge and Tottenham, were as near at hand as the gang to which he attached himself; and that excellent man, Lord Powerscourt, was at no great distance farther; and, in despite of all this, he would have us consider him as forced into rebellion against his king and the laws of his country. This we cannot help looking upon as somewhat '*de trop*'; and we should rather say, with Shakespeare, 'Rebellion lay in his way, and he found it' ... [W]e cannot too strongly combat the monstrous proposition, that a subject is justified in rushing into rebellion against his sovereign and the law, because he has received injustice and injury at the hands of a fellow-subject – and this without having made the slightest attempt to right himself by other and legitimate means. This is precisely Holt's case; and it appears to us that the establishing the mischievous doctrine of the 'wild justice of revenge' forms, to a great extent, the object of his reminiscences. Those who take up the book under the expectation of being introduced, as it were, behind the curtain of the rebellion, and hearing the details of that bloody drama from one of the busiest actors on its stage, will be totally disappointed. From the 16th of May to the 16th of June, the most stirring period of the actual outbreak, all is a blank. He informs us, indeed (page 42), that *his* plan was to keep to the mountains and difficult parts of the country; but that he could have given us the details of at least one battle (Newtown Mountkennedy) is evident, from his allusions elsewhere to the conduct of the Ancient British Dragoons on that occasion. We hear nothing of him till a few days previous to the 30th June, when we had him assuming the rank of colonel among some thousand rebels, who had escaped from Wexford, and made a kind of rally in the fastnesses of Wicklow, before penetrating into Kildare and Meath ... [J]ust at the period of Holt's entering upon his mountain career of outrage, the voice of mercy had been heard throughout the land, and misguided men were invited to avail themselves of proffered pardon - of this Holt could not be ignorant - but instead of taking advantage of it, we find him daily plunging deeper into crime. This, in our humble thinking, accords but badly with Holt's plea of being a forced rebel. Had he been really so - had he possessed a fourth part the religious feeling to which he lays claim, he would have been among the first to avail himself of Lord Cornwallis's offer of mercy and protection. It was not until he had acquired that knowledge which every demagogue is sure of arriving at sooner or later, of the little dependance to be placed in associates in criminality, that he manages his surrender to Lord Powerscourt, through the interest of that excellent lady Mrs La Touche. We pass over the swaggering impudence, the ruffian braggadocio which marks his conduct during this period of his history, and come at once to what he seems particularly to pride himself upon, his unbroken adherence to his oath as a United Irishman; and *this* upon Christian, upon Protestant principles!!! he had, forsooth, no one to absolve *him*. The scriptures speak of a man 'straining at a gnat and swallowing a camel'; what shall we say or think of him whose conscience is so tenderly alive and sensitive upon the subject of an obligation in itself illegal and criminal, taken too in the moment of desperation and at the point of the pike, to whom, neverthless, murder, houseburning, outrage, and robbery are in a manner matters of pastime, to say nothing of the Amazon in the green habit, who appears to have 'ruled the camp' in the absence of Mrs H. Faugh! faugh! the subject is really too sickening to be dwelt on.

2. UNREST IN WICKLOW IN THE MONTHS BEFORE THE REBELLION

Extracts from Sir Richard Musgrave, *Memoirs of the Different Rebellions*, 1801, as quoted by Croker in his edition of the Holt *Memoirs*, pp. 21-24

In the spring and summer of 1797 strong symptoms of disaffection began to appear in it [the county of Wicklow], such as cutting down trees to make pike handles, sounding of horns, meetings of the people on moon-light nights for the purpose of exercising, and firing shots to intimidate and keep within their houses the loyal inhabitants. Some vigilant and intelligent magistrates, seeing that nothing but active and seasonable exertions could save the country from destruction, had the landholders and principal inhabitants convened, to take its alarming state into consideration. Notwithstanding the most indubitable proofs that treason fermented and had made a considerable progress in the country, which was evinced by the facts which I have stated, many noblemen and gentlemen were so incredulous, in consequence of the artful conduct, and gross misrepresentation of the disaffected, and of the readiness of the multitude to take the oath of allegiance, as not to believe that they had treasonable designs, and for that reason, the meetings were frequently adjourned; and instead of adopting vigorous measures, the most friendly and pacific addresses to the people were published, inviting them to respect the laws, and to return to a sense of their duty.

The Committees of the United Irishmen regarded their patience and forbearance, as cowardice and pusillanimity; and the lower class of people became daring and insolent, pulling down the pacific resolutions of the county meetings, and denouncing vengeance against such magistrates and loyal subjects, as expressed a disapprobation of their seditious proceedings, or had taken an active part against them; and at length it became dangerous for persons of that description to traverse the country for fear of being assassinated.

At least they were driven to the necessity of proclaiming the whole county, as the infection had spread very widely. Some parts of it had been proclaimed 10th November 1797. The general meetings of the people in their respective districts I have already mentioned. It had a most terrific appearance in the country round Newtown-Mount-Kennedy. The people in considerable numbers, headed by their captains, and variously armed, paraded there. On being interrogated by the gentlemen of the county, who remonstrated to them on the dangerous consequences of their conduct, they said in excuse, that they assembled in defence of their persons and property, against the Orangemen, who, they said, conspired against them, and were to rise and cut off every person of their persuasion, without exception.

I have already mentioned that such reports were framed for no other purpose, but to kindle an inextinguishable hatred in the Roman Catholics against the Protestants; and the effects of it appeared afterwards in the massacres which took place in the counties of Wicklow, Wexford, Carlow, Meath, Dublin, Kildare, Mayo and Sligo.

Matters remained in that state, till the spring of 1798, when a paper containing the proceedings and resolutions of the county of Wicklow Committee was obtained, and was afterwards proved upon oath before the Secret Committee of the House of Lords, which showed the extent and malignity of the conspiracy.

Government still desirous, if possible, to avoid harsh and coercive measures and to induce the people to return to their duty and their allegiance, by mild and conciliating means, Lieutenant-General Craig, by their orders issued a proclamation, dated the 11th May, 1798 [printed by Musgrave, Appendix, No. xvi. 3], and Major Hardy, a humane gentleman and a judicious officer, who then commanded in that county, used the most zealous endeavours to the same end.

Early in the month of May, as the country was in such an alarming state, that no loyal subjects could with safety remain in their houses, the yeomen of the district were ordered into garrison at Newtown-Mount-Kennedy.[...]

From the beginning of the year 1797, it was perceived by some magistrates of discernment, that the lower classes of the people were very unwilling to pay their debts, or to fulfil any engagements. That they appeared surly when called on to do so; and they were heard, when angry, or drunk, to hint on such occasions, that they would soon have an opportunity of being revenged. They were seen to remain later than usual at fairs and markets, and in public houses, and to confer together in whispers. [...]

For some months previous to the rebellion the priests strongly inculcated the necessity of sobriety and peaceable demeanour, to lull the magistrates and government, and to prevent the rebels from betraying their secrets, which had such an immediate and universal effect, that the whiskey houses were deserted, and those who had been the most notorious drunkards, could not by any persuasion be induced to drink any spirits, and abstained from broils and quarrels, and particularly seditious language in any mixed assemblies.

Such instructions penned with energy and elegance were printed and circulated among the people which rapidly produced an apparent reformation in their manners, to the great surprise of those who were ignorant of the secret motives which occasioned it.

3. THE BATTLE OF BALLYELLIS, 29 JUNE 1798

Extracts from Luke Cullen, *Personal Recollections of Wexford and Wicklow Insurgents of 1798*, 1959, pp 43-45

After the battle of Hacketstown, it appears from Miles Byrne's account that the Insurgents retired towards Croghan Hill where they remained from the night of the 26th till the morning of 29th June.

The 27th and 28th passed with very little skirmishing. Early on the morning of the 29th June, it was resolved to march and attack the town of Carnew. The column halted at Monaseed to take some refreshments, and soon after renewed its march on the high road to Carnew. In less than half an hour after its departure, a large division of cavalry consisting of the notorious Ancient Britons, marched into Monaseed from Gorey, followed by all the Yeomen Cavalry Corps from Arklow, Gorey and Coolgreany, under their respective chiefs. When about two miles from Monaseed, at Ballyellis, one mile from Carnew, the Ancient Britons, being in full gallop, to their great surprise, were suddenly stopped by a barricade of cars thrown across the road. On the left-hand side of the road an old deer park wall ran along for about half a mile

> ... On the right-hand side was an immense ditch with swampy ground. In this advantageous position the battle immediately began. A mass of pikemen closed in on them from the rear and the gunsmen began firing from behind the wall. In less than half an hour their infamous Regiment, which had been the terror of the country, was slain to the last man, as well as the few Yeoman Cavalry who had the courage to take part in the action [Miles Byrne's *Memoirs*, pp 197-199].

I scarcely know what to say with regard to this battle as it has so much got into the people's heads of late that the Rev. Denis Taaffe was the person who planned the battle and to whose skill, prudence and courage the successful issue of the battle is attributed.

Joe Holt would have all the merit to himself. A few years after the occurrence I had an opportunity of hearing even the most minute details from the men that had been in the campaign, friends and near relatives. I heard the details related over and over, and there was scarcely a single act done at Ballyellis that I did not hear told from time to time [...]

When I spoke of Holt to my informant (this is from one Michael Kearns from Baltinglass, who fought there, and was one of Dwyer's outlaws after), he said

> Holt's tongue could never be kept quiet, and although he had an uncommon share of audacity so far as talking went, he particularly checked himself in the presence of Mr Byrne, for he dare not to be impertinent in his presence. However, on that day, when the Britons fell into our toils and our fire opened on them from both sides, and immediately seconded by our pikemen Mr Byrne, on seeing some of the Royal Horse force their way into one of the adjoining fields, ordered some of the aid de camps to bring a party of their rifles round to intercept their retreat. Holt darted forward at the order, and began to command. But the men themselves had actually seen the necessity for this step, and were on their way to the point in question before they received an order. And before Holt was done speaking, they were in front of the Royal Dragoons and obstructed their only chance of escape, and in an instant, cut them down. Holt showed more valour that day than his own countrymen expected from him.
>
> At this time General Ed. Roach with a well-tempered sword was dealing out the most awful destruction on the unfortunate Britons. I never saw anything like it, and in his making a back-hand cut at one of them, he nearly cut the hand off a man named Kenna from Stratford-on-Slaney, who with Michael Dwyer, was at the same post with him. Capt. Michael Dwyer at this moment rushed in to the ruined walls of a cabin after a huge Briton. I endeavoured to get to his assistance, but before I could, the Briton fell and was gasping for death. As I turned round I perceived my friend Kenna bleeding. I had a slight wound myself and was bleeding profusely. I brought my friend to the rear. 'You are wounded severely, Kenna,' said one of our comrades. He said he would fight till he would die by the side of General Roach.

All was again quiet, not even a horse was prancing about, when Harry Neil the trumpeter of one of the Naas corps of Cavalry who had deserted and joined the people, taking trumpet and accoutrements with him, and just as the last blows fell on the unfortunate victims, with right good will, Harry could not restrain a rich turn he had for humour and sounded a retreat for them with all his vigour, and the horses pranced wildly about through the fields in an attempt to fall into line.

As the detachment returned from the slaughter and Joe Holt advanced along with them, Mr Byrne observed to him: 'Well, Holt, none of them got to make that side?'

'No, your honour,' said Joe, 'we never looked to danger but rushed on them and cut them down.'

'You need not have exposed yourselves to combat with them,' said Mr Byrne, 'they would have surrendered.'

'And now suppose,' said he, 'we had neither Mr Byrne nor Mr [Edward] Fitzgerald, had we not Generals Ed. Roach, Perry, Father Kearns and Esmond Kyan, who had seen some service abroad and held a commission in the royal artillery and a score of other men that we could rely on.'

4. CROPPY BIDDY DOLAN

Extracts from the posthumous papers of Luke Cullen

This woman, who acquired much notoriety during the insurrection of 1798, and for some time after that period, was born in Carnew, in the County Wicklow, about the year 1779, and was in her nineteenth year when the rebellion broke out. Her father followed the humble profession of a thatcher, and was generally from home. Her mother paid no attention whatever to the education or morals of her daughter. Let me at once apologize for being obliged to allude to immorality. But in history we can leave nothing to the imagination – truth, however repugnant, must be honestly told. And in this case, that posterity may know even the vilest of the many instruments that were used to aid the blightful Legislative Union of our country.

At ten or eleven years of age this wayward and abandoned girl was sure to be found among rude little boys at their sports, particularly riding the asses of tinkers, when any of them would sojourn in the outlets of Carnew or at a neighbouring forge, where horses were usually brought to be shod; and if she could get up on one of them, or procure any person to lift her up, she was sure to sit astride and gallop the animal up and down the street. She had an extraordinary passion for horse-riding, and at sixteen years of age she could manage the quadruped at his full speed. And in the year 1798 she mostly rode with the rebel cavalry – a buxom *vivandiere* on horseback. Her lack of morals and indecencies are too disgusting to follow, but it will be sufficient to say, that this pampered informer of the county Wicklow, at thirteen years of age, was an avowed and proclaimed harlot, steeped in every crime that her age would admit of; and her precosity to vice, as it was to maturity, was singular. On her own oath, she attended night meetings at seventeen years of age, where a great number of United Irishmen assembled, about two miles from the residence of her father. After the rebellion broke out, she joined the rebel army, and soon obtained a horse, and was foremost in all the deeds of iniquity during the time the people held out in arms. But her intoxications and public debaucheries were then by far the worst of this virago's shameless life. After the remnant of the popular army, which had reached the Wicklow mountains, was dispersed, she continued for some time with Holt. On her return home from the battle-field, she continued to speak at random of everything she saw or heard, and the more wicked the deed the more delight she took in the recital, and with a brutal pleasure exaggerating the atrocity. In a short time she was picked up by the ultra-loyalists, who liked to have her drinking in the public-houses with them, getting her to tell of the deeds she saw in civil war. It was only in the latter end of August she left the outlaw camp; and on the 16th of September she became the ward of Captain Wainright, the agent of Lord Fitzwilliam, the other magistrates of the county concurring in the project to have her for a general informer. She was then sent to Rathdrum, to be put under the training of a little vindictive and crafty attorney, named Tom King, and some old bailiffs.

She was now dressed like a lady, with habit and skirt, hat and feather, and a prancing palfrey was placed at her disposal. In her excursions through the country, where she was often engaged in search of denounced men, or outlawed rebels, she presided at the head of a military party, which, it may be said, she actually commanded, for if they would not do as she wished, she swore that she would return to the garrision and not guide them any further. On one day she rode with a strong party to Ballymaurin, about three miles from Rathdrum, where two brothers, Byrne, were digging their own potatoes. Those men had been out fighting, but had returned home, like great numbers of others, and availed themselves of the Amnesty Act. She had some dislike to them; she pointed them out to her guards, and they were shot without more ado. Historic writers should be cautious in taking details from the papers of those days. The poor fellows that were shot, were called the 'Blacks', by nickname. After some excursions of a similar kind and some swearing of what was called a light nature, such as having men transported, or imprisoned for a considerable time, she was thought duly qualified to come forward to prosecute to the death.[...]

She was young, and under judicious teachers had time enough to learn. Her unblushing audacity was firm and boundless. Drunk or sober, her pert and ready replies to all questions helped to restore her to that portion of favour which only seemed to be lost to her.

All this time she was under the apparent tuition of a bailiff named Tom Philips, from whom I had this incident and much more of her history, but Tom King, the attorney, gave her the principal lessons. Philips was too much of the man, in its physical sense – no man possessed a greater share of personal courage – and such individuals rarely stoop to meanness. It was more on account of his courage than for his instruction that she was placed under his protection; the little attorney at Kingston was, I may say, her sole preceptor. Her public intoxications and debaucheries, her smoking and swearing with the soldiers and others, had now their full swing, and of this scandalous conduct, in his pampered and suborned informer, Tom King was perfectly cognizant, and fully sensible, from her late failure, that no credit could be attached to her informations, yet he kept her on.[...]

16th Sept., 1801, Tom King, of Rathdrum, attorney, by order of Lord Cornwallis (the Lord Lieutenant), £300. And to Bridget Dolan, per Captain Wainright, £22 15s.

This latter seems to be her fixed yearly salary, for it did not appear by her manner of living that she had much more, and this was little enough to support her and a pair of bull-dogs that she kept for her protection. And, notwithstanding that she was always attended by those grim and faithful guardians whenever she walked out, the boys, if they could with any degree of apparent security, would relinquish their sports to have a fling of a stone at her, with the shout, 'Ha, Croppy Biddy!' For this they were often brought before the magistrates; and, so powerful a monitor is conscience on the recollection of guilt, that sooner than stir up the past, the rude lads were generally let off with a magisterial admonition.

She happened to have one child that lived – it was a daughter; but she never had the honour of a husband's protection. As soon as her swearing was over, and in which she seemed to have taken a particular delight, and after being restored to the Orange protection of her friends in Carnew, to live on the wages of perjury and prostitution, and the price of innocent blood, her manner became utterly changed; the florid cheek became quite pale, her natural and impudent levity had flown, and that insensibility to virtue seemed to be now under the severe gnawing of a corroding conscience. She was sour, reserved and morose; when going out, and at every step she seemed to apprehend an assault. She lived for many years with the finger of scorn publicly pointed at her whenever she moved. It was surmised by her neighbours that the Government had withdrawn the salary from her, and that she was left in her declining days to be supported from the poor-box in the Protestant church, or some scanty support from her Orange favourites.[...]

George Kearns, residing at 103, Pill Lane, Dublin, told me that he saw her riding behind Holt with a feather in her hat, and she barefooted and this was the wretch that Holt boasts of as being his 'concubine' and that she was a respectable farmer's daughter, named Byrne.

5. INFORMERS' REPORTS

5.1 Deposition of John Thompson, regarding his experience as a prisoner in the rebel camp, 15–26 June 1798, taken and sworn before William Colthurst, 27 June 1778 (SPO 620/38/243)

County of Wicklow to wit the Information of Joseph Thompson of Roundwood, Wood Ranger to Fras. Synge Esqr. who being legally sworn says that on Monday the 18th of this present month he was taken Prisoner along with his son by the Rebels at a Publick House in Roundwd. There were other Prisoners. Inft. was carried that day to Luggelaw Mountain, where were assembled before night nearly one hundred Rebels, armed with Guns, Blunderbus's & Pikes – They had Plenty of Meat, no drink, but water. They slept that night in the ditches without shelter. Prisoner was kept also in a ditch – The next morng the 19th they marched to the Seven Churches & were joined during their march & the day time by about 300 more Rebels, but from whence they came he can't say, but that they *were Strangers* to *him* – Inft. was tryd by a Court Martial on the 18th Consisting as he believes of about 10 Members, *for being an Orange Man*, however nothing was done to him except being kept a Prisoner. When they had reached the Seven Churches they all halted there that night and on the 20th they were informed that the soldiers were coming to meet them from Powerscourt on which they all marched out with their Prisoners towards Anamoe to give them Battle. The Prisoners were remanded back to the 7 Churches by order of Joseph Holt who was called Colonel but Inft. heard he was no more than a Captain, under a Guard with orders to have dinner ready agst. their return. Soon after Inft. heard a firing & a message was sent to have the Prisoners marched off to the *Whelp Rock* about Seven Miles distance *nearer to Donard than Blackmoor Mountain*. The Firing of Guns Inft. supposes to be the Engagement at Ballinarush – Inft. found at Whelp Rock a Rebel Camp, commanded by one Colonel McMahon [*Mc-Mahon, supposed to be an Attorney in Aungier Street. A little, low, nice, smooth faced man. said to be worth 400 per annum.* Wm.C's note in margin] & Capt. Murphy & consisted as Inft. believes of about 200 Men. Inft. was kept here till Saty morng the 23rd & then was marched with the Whole Camp back to the Seven Churches – Inft. never again saw the *first Party* of Rebels but he *verily believes they are now in the neighbourhood of the 7 Churches & Roundwood concealed* – When Inft. reached the 7 Churches on 23rd, they were joined there by two Large Companies as Inft. believes from the counties of Kildare & Dublin & also from the County Wexford in Numbers together about 4 or 500 men & their Numbers continued hourly to encrease[*sic*], that Inft. thinks they amounted in all to 10,000 Men. The companies that came from Wexford drove an Herd of Black Cattle & Sheep before them. Inft. reckoned 40 Black Cattle and One hundred Sheep, another man told Inft. he reckoned 41 Black Cattle. Inft. heard Firing and was told the Rebels were killing the Cattle. After Breakfast on Sunday about Eight or 9 o'clock they all marched towards *Hackets town* to *Glynnmalur* where they halted about 3 hours. Inft. was told there that the Soldiers had come to the 7 Churches soon after they had left it. Soon after this a Dragoon was seen coming as from Rathdrum, who stopt for some minutes & then returned. The Rebels imagined he was gone back to his Troop & gave orders for 40 or 50 men to lay in Ambush & the Main Body to march on to Hacketstown & Inft. believe if it had not been for the rashness of these Men, the whole of Soldiers wd have been destroyed, for the Main Body marched very slowly, as a lure to the soldiers to follow them & thereby fall in to the snare, and which was prevented by the Rebels firing *too soon* on the Soldiers; these Soldiers retreated and the Rebels continued their march till towards Eveng when they were fired upon by another party of Soldiers, their advance men were driven back, but on the Main Body appearing, these Soldiers also retreated, as Inft. heard towards Dublin. The Rebels incamped [sic] the 24th at night on a hill close to Hacketstown. The next morning the 25th about 9 o'clock they marched to Hacketstown and attacked a Party of Soldiers entrenched in the Town and nearby church and after some Firing put them to flight above the Town. They then took possession of the Town and burnt it, but could not take the Barracks, which were defended by Soldiers, who fired wherever they saw any Rebels. A Dozen he believes were the most that were killed. The rebels then marched back near *Donard*, where they Seperated in different Lots some towards Dublin, Kildare, etc. but the Wexford Man and some of the Wicklow Men remained. At break of day yesterday, 26th, they marched towards the town of Donard, but they were stop'd on acct. of soldiers being in the Town. The Wexford Man marched back as Inft. believes towards the 7 Churches. Inft. was left only with about 20 or 30 men, who soon afterwards seperated [sic] also, on which Inft. made his escape – A Priest or Garret Byrne of Ballymanus commanded the Wexford Party & one Murphy the Kildare – the Wexford Men were the Bloodyest Fellows & and swore they would murder every one that fell into their Hands & once would have stabbed said inft with their pikes, but for the interception of Wm. Lennan a Taylor who happened to know Inft while Inft. was surrounded by these Men expecting his death. Some one cry'd out it was a sin to let Protestant Blood run on the burial Ground of the Catholics the Place being near the Churchyard at 7 Churches. They had a Number of Horses, took provision from every one, said they would destroy Bray, Wicklow, Rathdrum & Newtown. Some talked of visiting Powerscourt and Enniskerry, as it was a fine walk from thence to Dublin & they would be joined by their Dublin Friends. *Inft. upon the whole verily believes upon his Oath that these Rebels are now in, and about the 7 Churches & these parts –*

During the Engagement in Hackets town on the 25th their Powder failing, their officers wanted the Pike Men to advance and charge the Soldiers, they positively refused to do so and this was the cause of their retreat, for had it not been the case, Inft. thinks from their Numbers & their determination they would have forced the Barracks.

On Saty last on their marching to the 7 Churches they met two Men on Horseback with Bags of char Coal, or Heath Coal & he heard them say it was for the Purpose of Making Gun Powder, and on asking about some firing he heard, he was told it was *trying the New Powder*, which they said was Very Good – Inft was informed they had 30 Rounds a Man going into Hacketstown about 500 Guns, Pistols and Blundss.

Joseph thompson
Taken & Sworn before us this 27 of June 1798 (Eight)
Monck
Wm. Colthurst

John Thompson Son to the above being sworn & the above Information being read to him confirms his Father in almost every particular of consequence & further says

That there was one* Fitzgerald a Captain. A Light, thin Man, middle seized [*sic*], very well dressed, seemed to have much command, for he Galloped about Hacketstown during the firing, without seeming to regard the Balls – Heard the Wexford Man say they were to Meet a Priest from thence with a Great flock of Men.

his
John x Thompson
mark

Taken & Sworn before us this 27th June 1798 (Eight) Monck Wm. Colthurst

*There is a man of this discription [*sic*] in Skinner Row Dublin.

5.2 Information given in 1798 concerning Joseph Holt

SPO 620/38/126 *11 June, 6 o'clock* Information of a Martin of Drogheda (also see following extract): 'came here from Rathfarnham and has been around the coast after being through Roundwood & mounts to summon all the men to attack on Dublin tomorrow night. 3 corps are actually forming under Holt, Nugent & Doyle tomorrow night ... plan to assemble at Rathfarnham [...] Holt has a brother at the foot of Mt. Venus.

A prisoner is questioned about his meeting with Holt concerning the projected raid: 'Thos. Harkins states re rising plan to form a camp at the upper end of Glanismore [Glenasmole] at the other side of Rathfarnham & Templeogue to draw the army out of Dublin [...] then they are to rise in Dublin.'

620/38/60 *14 June* Confession of John Martin, a friar of Drogheda. He met Holt behind Rathfarnham, says that Holt is a Captain of the Rebels and he will point out where he lives. Doyle another captain, Nugent another captain.

620/40/36 Wicklow, 11 September, from T.W. (Cr?)itchley   Dear Sir, I have the honour to inform you that large parties of rebels assembled last week in different parts of the country and searched several houses for arms in consequence of the advantages that were reported to have been gained by the French over his Majesty's troops but the news of their defeat which arrived here last Sunday at four oclock has for the present thrown a damper upon their operation. Holt and his party (which have been lately joined by several deserters) still continue to infest the mountains & mark their rout with murder and robbery – you can't conceive the rapidity of their movements & the uncommon secrecy which attends them but I trust from the exertions that are now making they will soon meet the reward of their crimes – as the limits of a letter will not permit me to mention the many evil consequences which daily result from indiscriminately granting Protections.

SPO 620/40/76, *19 September*   On Saturday my friend's journeyman returned from Holt's army - quit it in disgust from want of subordination & (?) robbing being the object. Holt's party reported to be so strong consists of but 400 men attached to him – among which are 20 of the Kings County Militia – all well armed. Holt has quit them on Saturday last as he is gone to Carlow to recruit. He is riding out through the county every day – but sleeps in the town of Carlow every night. A French man of distinction commands Holt's men till his return which is to be on Saturday next. McMahon hitherto joyned to Holt has split from him. They disputed on Friday and quit on Saturday. McMahon is gone to Wexford to raise all he can there ... Holt has no commission, nor ever had, commands robbers only ... Doyle O'Neil and Neil are 3 of Holt's captains. McMahon is very well liked. Holt is not. His party have no subordination. They assemble at Whelp Rock – and at Oaklands or Oakwood - forget which it is called. McMahon and Holt had equal command at Hacketstown.
   [anonymous informer]
              N.B. If Gen. Craig manages this matter well he will get Holt in Carlow
              – as this information comes from Holt's own mouth - on Friday last.

SPO 620/40/126 *Thurs. 18 October*   Holt has now done what I told you would be his plan when the mountains was no longer tenable. He arrived in Dublin on Tuesday night last - wounded. On Tuesday night last he slept in a cellar in Francis St. My man is after him ever since & I must be in the way if he makes him out ... at Hacketstown fight [?] and other of the heads say they will make one desperate attempt this winter – say there is no patrols – guards – or hindrance & that it will be easy for numbers to gather unknown to government – The Castle will be the first object.

SPO 620/40/172 *Fri. morn. 19 October*   Holt slept on Tuesday night in a cellar in Francis St. – on Wednesday night in Neil's cellar at Plunkett Street – was visited there by some of his friends yesterday morning. Neil was drill sergeant of the Liberty rangers – a Captain under Holt - but quit him some time since. The Executive met at Wright's on Monday last in the day. McMahon and Shaw was there. They came to a resolution, that all shd. be over & not to act without the French, or till the English troops are recalled. I bound Oliver Carleton to secrecy, described Holt to him. He has set his man on the search for a man of the description but not to know the name – as that alarm may spoil all.

Sun. morn., 4 November   This is the great night of meeting & deliberation among all the disaffected in Dublin I learned late last night that every thing they proposed doeing is to be determined this night. – different partys in different places – McMahon's party at O'Harra's [?] or [indecipherable] – Shaw's party collect at the Elephant in Eustace Street & adjourn to some secret private room – Holt's party some street off Thomas st. Holt slept last night but one in the Back house of a widow poor woman who lets beds in Dirty Lane [now Bridgefoot street]. To come near them is impossible as none but 2 men of themselves know of the meeting till they are brought to the spot. This is the last night many of them will meet preparatory to going to Bush (?) & then to see.

If it be an object to get them – why not a general sweep among all suspected houses this night – they will never be got by any other plan unless intercepted at sea. Why not Mr Swan one district – Mr Sirr another. Mr Carleton another – you know all the haunts from me repeatedly. It is useless to trouble you further if this be not done. Those that remain will form new & more secret plans – those that escape(d)? go to assist your natural and determined enemys.

6. DOCUMENTS CONCERNING HOLT'S SURRENDER AND INFORMATION GIVEN BY HIM

6.1   Extract from a letter from Under-Secretary E. Cooke, 9 November 1798, to Viscount Castlereagh concerning Holt's offer to surrender

Holt means to surrender. Lord Monck was with Lord Cornwallis on the subject. Lord Cornwallis said he could promise no terms, but if he surrenders after any conversation between Lord Cornwallis and Lord Monck, how can he be executed? I saw Lord Cornwallis today, who mentioned the subject; I suggested the danger of letting him surrender, though no terms were offered him ... I think it appears we shall have further expeditions from France. Hardi was in hopes that Sir John Warren was in the Texel fleet. They say their attacks on the north are to lead us from their main object – Cork.

6.2 Letter from Joseph Holt to William Keegan

Wilm [William] Keegan of Behina [Bahana] to forward to Lord Poursort [Powerscourt] or Lord Monk [Monck]

This is to let the Gentle men know my Intention present and the cause of my being so headstrong The burned my house and substance and in curse I cud not help but turn outto fight for my life I never would only for such useage but im tid [I'm tired] of fighting against the Crown I would manfully faught for it and if my wife was paid about half my loss which is 30 Guineas and the Lord Liftennat signs my pardon I am able & willing to sarve my king and Contry and I know very well how to Do it but as to give myself up and be transported I never will I would suffer to be shot in pieces first for I am not afraid to Die of Either sids [sides] I make no doubt but my plans would be very usefull at any time to my country because I know as much as is necessary in all points pray don't believe that me or any of my men are the peopple that Robs for be god I would put a robber to death in one minute worning let my wife know as soon as possible and if the Contents of this will not be done let us all mind ourselves I wish my Country men Well no more.

6.3 Deposition of Joseph Holt made at Dublin Castle, 16 November 1798 (SPO 620/41/39A)

Lord Powerscourt and Mr Colthurst as magistrates examined Holt in the Castle, not on oath and recd. the following hints, in addition to what he had given before – [The *Comment* is a marginal note by William Colthurst.]

Owen Byrne Of Bone Valley near Luggelaw – Farmer. Holt heard from Long Peter Nowlan's wife on Saty the 10th ult., and whose Daughter is married to Owen's Son Terence, that Owen Stole the Beds from Luggelaw House, and brought [*sic*] them back again at a Guinea each

[*Comment*] This fact I partly know to be true – as I heard it from a Person concerned in the Matter of the Beds. Wm. C.

Owen was at the first attack on Mr Hugo's House, but not at the Burning, because he was looked on *as so great a Rogue to All Parties*, as to have *sold the Pass* and was trusted by no Party –

[*Comment*] This I believe, as Mr Hugo's Steward's watch I found in W. Byrne's Pocket when I took him in the Mountains. Wm. C.

Heard that Owen, his Sons and others Robbed Smythe the Innkeeper at Roundwood's House – Darby Carberry Owen's Son in Law, a noted Rogue for 15 Years past – a Great Gang of Robbers about Roundwood viz

Thomas Harris } Brothers
John Harris }
Valentine Browne, with a crooked Eye

} These 3 keep in Town viz. Dublin, except whilst Robbing

[*Comment*] (I believe it and will look after them when they think matters are blown over)

Wm. Repton to be found at Holly Park near Rathfarnham at the house of one Byrne
Michael Wafer } these keep in Town except whilst Robbing,
– Wafer } & others whose names he knows not

[*Comment*] I brought Smythe's wife to Dublin to prosecute and W. Byrne for this Robbery, hearing she knew the Men and would do so. She positively told me she would swear to Owen his 2 sons and Darby Carberry his son in law being present. She said so to Mr Hugo and others – yet on the tryal of Andrew she denied every word – Owen, John his son, & Darby Karberry are now in the Prevost. We hope to get Mathew the uncle shortly & Terence Byrne, with fresh Evidence. Andw Byrne has been found Guilty – Sentence not known.

Matthew Byrne Owen's Brother is a Great Robber and supposed to have amassed a great Deal of Plunder, to the amount of near £500.

[*Comment*] As to the sum I doubt it.

... which he has concealed – Owen Byrne was one of the most active Men in the Rebellion & used to stay 4 or 5 nights together in Roundwood drinking the money he recd. for Pike Heads – Terence Byrne was in Clohogue last Fryday the 9th ult.
Believes that about 14 or 15 good Fire Arms are concealed about the 7 Churches -
Wm. Brady of Roundwood was a Captain, supposed to be in Dublin
James Kavenagh near the Paddock, now[?] Long Hish, Son of Andrew Kavenagh,

[*Comment*] There is such a man. A watch upon him, not at home at present – Wm C.

Jas. worked mostly in Addown, and worked with Samuel Wallis of Old Court near Blessingtown. Could give *Most Material Evidence* as he was deeply concerned in all the robberies in the Rebellion – he might be taken at Wallis's by a party from Blessington, and is a soft fellow –

Informt suspects that arms are concealed in Stacks of Corn and Hay in Addown, Ballysmutten & Ballylow, villages much frequented by the Rebels.

[*Comment*] Intend making an early Search in these 3 Villages in a few days, at one Instant – At present things have not cool'd since Holt's taking. Strongly think Holt is right as we have during the Rebellion found arms in that Situation.

Charles Nowlan son of Shanogue about a month since had a large Pistol – John Walsh, blind of one eye, had a Fowling Piece – Andrew Byrne a Musquet – John Byrne an handsome Carbine – These all came to him in Addown this day five weeks, also Garret Nowlan had a musquet, they all marched with him to Oakwood.

[*Comment*] There are such people

Young Classon the Farmer near Roundwood was eager in the Rebellion at first – knows nothing of him lately
Rebels not afraid of the Yeomen, very much of the Army – the Militia ought to be looked after –
Thos Smith is shot –
John Walsh of Bonavalley could give as much information as any one, his Father's nickname, *Rockstown*
Wm McQuirk who robbed the Banquetting House at the Waterfall keeps in Ballysmutten. Old McQuirk who recd. the goods (his father) keeps at Glynbride near Oakwood.
Wm. McQuirk fretted much at not finding Inft. Holt the night the Powerscourt & Meath Corps lay in Addown & Shraunamock as he was in search of Holt to give him notice & had Holt rcd. the notice, he would certainly have attacked us, with great Success, as he had then about 180 musquets with him.
Recommends great attention to our Escorts on Ammunition – 3 Hessians The Lietrim & Sligo Deserters brought him most ammunition –There is one Keg of Powder somewhere in Barnesky in the Barony of Arklow near Arklow

[*Comment*] I believe Holt here, from observations of my own in escorting ammunition &c.

Had about two months since about 128 Soldiers from 13 Regts. of Militia &c.

5	Cavan Militia
3	Hessians
22	Kings County
8	do do

[contd.]

28	Antrim do	106	men
16	Lietrim do	2	Durham Fencibles
9	Sligo do	1	Josh. Bigley an Englishman
5	Carlow do	109	
5	Kildare do		
5	Dublin	does not recollect at present the names of the others	
106			

[*Comment*] This exactly agrees with an Acct. that Capt. Philip Armstrong of the Kings County & I made out some time since – Wm. C.

On being asked what had become of these Men & the Deserters in General, he said Many were Killed, Many Hanged & the most of the Remainder exchanged their muskets with the Rebels for Pistols & were robbing their way in Gangs to their own Counties – Sometimes not 2 together

[*Comment*] (Col. Rochford of the Cty. Carlow & others assured me this was the Case – If so & the Cols of Regts. to whom they belong had persons ready to recieve them on their going home much Good would arize [*sic*]. Every Deserter is known where to have come from. it could be easy to secure them.

The Dogherty that was killed at Ballyfad at the time it was said Hacket was kill'd belonged to the Antrim – It was not the Carlow Dogherty

The two Harmans, one Porter, John Haley, Andw Thomas & John Byrne, all living in & about the 7 Churches, told him that Hatton, Burbridge & Freeman were Easy, for they were Dead & brought him One Marks a Prisoner

Patrick Warder, the Hatter near Mooneystown [*sic*] beyond Roundwood would be a Proper Person to tell who killed Freeman and the others – has an House of his own there –

Inft. never had either directly or indirectly any communication with the State Prisoners in the different Goals in Dublin or with those Prisoners hang'd - Had no Commission; only the Men in Common call'd him General - the 4 Instances he mentioned being at when murder was committed in Cold Blood were

1st   Hacket killed one Cooper at Newbridge, was not actually present

2d   The Antrim Deserters shot one Josh. Tate. Inft. was present but wanted to save both these men –

3d   The Kings Cty took a Man at Ballybeg, he had a sword Cane, the Kings Cty shot him – was present.

4th   They were going to shoot a Protestant out of some Prisoners, Inft. sd. he should not be shot & after some altercation 1 Protest and one Papist were shot in Cold Blood.

James Butler at Ballymoneen near the Divil's Glyn, son of Walter Butler has one musquet – One Smullen, whose Father lives in the same place, has another.

Katty Kingshelagh Wife of Val. Browne's, a proper person for setting Robbers, and her Husband is a great Robber also –

Informt. had much difficulty in saving Rusborough House from being burned –

Father Lowe of Derrilossory Parish & our 2 priests very good men –

6.4 Letter from Joseph Holt to Mrs Peter La Touche, written from Passage West, Co. Waterford

To the Right Honourable Mrs Peter Latuice stephen's green Dublin

Dear Lady

may it please you to receive this my last pittison to Ireland. I hope you will through your bountyfull goodness yild me the greatest comfort and pleasure that I can wish for at your request and the-two noble lords that i resined my self to and put myself under theire purtection. I thought I would be let to imagrait for life and that I would be let to bring my Dear Wife and childer with me whos lives are dierer to me than my owne know all that I wish for is that you and the noble lords may interseed to his Excellency for my wife and childer to be let come along with me and if god and your goodness will grant me that favour you will make me happerer than all the [?] of the wourld cud make me o noble lady consider my dear wife and childer luck on them with compasion it is in your power to make them happy or for ever to breake their hartes and mine for myself if you dont get the favour granted I hope I will soon yeld my last and painfull breath for I dont wish to live on this earth one moment if I am parted from my sweet family so I hope you will take pitty on the Innosent sepose you dispise me it would not so much afflitted me if I had got too or three days notices that I might have the pleasure of taken my last farewell of my dear childer and wife O honoured lady if you and the noble lords cant get the grant for them to come with me get my time shortened that I may come for them when the wourld settles and bring them to some place that I will provide o give me some hope of living it is now in your powrs

Noble lords altho I was forst to misfortune it has not changed my hart for I hope I will be usefull to my king and country all i know can wish is that you may mind the very words that I told Mr Masdon for I declare the are the truth and any one sais to the contrary the truth is not in them i am sorry that Alderman James did not get the last piece of riting that I roat in the tower and I had no time to send it to him it would be of use to your contrey and I dropped it in the sea for fear it would be seen my lord I am still bolted there is no differ between the robbers and others only the cant be so much despise I have good hopes of god and my contrey o may I beg and imploar of some of you to send me answr to relieve my distressed hart if you derect to waterfort passage or else where

Noble Lady pardon me if I have roat improper it is hard for me to indite and my person at passage and all my thought at home – I remain your umble sarvant

Joseph Holt
January the 15th 1799
passage near the forth of Duncannon

6.5 **The report of 'Information of Joseph Holt, given voluntarily and by his own desire' during his interrogation at Cork Harbour. The report is dated 27 February 1799, and is taken from the Castlereagh** *Memoirs* **(vol. ii)**

Says, that since the arrival of the convicts from Cork, viz, Dry, Desmond, Cox, Fitzgerald and several others, they have held conversations, all of which tend to state positively that there are 20,000 rebels organized at Cork and its neighbourhood and that they are determined to make a rising on the evening of Easter Sunday next, when they expect the French. A feint is to be made at Killala but the principal attack is to be about Cork. That he has heard through those people, and from the conversation of several there, that the whole country is organising with more activity than ever, especially in Munster, and is assured and believes that great numbers of the Militia soldiers are sworn and ready to join them, and expresses strongly a desire that the Government will be very attentive to the conduct of the militia. He is certain they have given up meetings, but they carry on their plots by writing little notes to one another, and that they encourage the disaffected to enlist in the regiments of Militia. These are, on what they call the big day (Easter Sunday) to assimilate the well disposed, and to secure their arms and ammunition. He is certain that the country will experience great disorder next summer, and recommends again and strongly the strictest watch of the Militia, who, he says, and is certain, are not to be trusted, and that the country is now preparing for rebellion more strongly than ever, and in greater numbers. The Dutch, and particularly the Spaniards, are expected to come to their assistance. With great anxiety he again entreats that Government may exert itself in time and take measures to prevent rebellion, that is certainly determined on, and that of the most universal nature. The common conversations are that there is not a Catholic who would not kill a Protestant as soon as he would a rat. He is satisfied that if there were but five Catholics, they are determined and will pursue this principle and intent as long as they exist. Joseph Holt adds, that he is himself a Protestant.

6.6 **Letter to William Colthurst, written by Joseph Holt from Cork Harbour**

To – Wilm Colutrus Esqr. tinnahinch Bray
County Wicklow
Cove of Cork May 18th 99

Sir
   your well known humanity to me has imboldened me to troble you with these few lines I am happy to hear that Matthew Doyle is taken he is the only man can give you the most information of any one in the County Wicklow or Wexford or Dublin if he likes to do so he all so can tell who shot Coper and who robbed Lord Waterfords house keeper for he himself had 25 guineys and James hues 25 more so he must know who toock the hole of it and I must say he was the only man of his perffession that always strove to save the lives of protestants but what I am afraid he wont give a true infirmation as there is hardly one of his sort ever does there is a man of the name black pady Murrey he lives in brokey near seven Churches I luck on him to be very useful to take he can give good infirmation of arms for he is very handy in repairing locks and knows who has arms in all that country

   Sir I am also happy to hear of the fate of byrne and Nowlan and I hartly wish you may sarve more of them so and I also wish that every country may dispence with theire own for I think there is no use in transporting them out of one country in to another for the say in this ship that the will begin in bottony the same business but I hope as I was deemed a good tory hunter in the County Wicklow I will I hope be very much useful in bottony to hunt both sorts and I wish every protestant in the world new theire intentions as well as I do and if you take notice of my Infirmation you will find it will be of the greatest use I main that I left with Alderman James for it is better for the Lords and gentlemen of Ireland to have waist houses on their Estates than to pursarve the lives of peopple that does intend to murder themselves sir I asure you i am very happy as a prisoner for our Captain is a gentleman of the best morals I ever new and all his offisers to such as disarved indulgence

   I have nothing more to ad but my wife and son and my self are in good helth and ever will pray for the success of Lord Power scourt & Lord Monk and you sir
              I remain your sincare and truly Devoated humble sarvant
                                                          Joseph Holt

6.7   Letter from Holt to Matthew Doyle, 22 November 1798

7. A NOTE BY THE EDITOR ON HOLT'S ENEMY THOMAS HUGO

Thomas Hugo was a blackhearted tyrant whose legendary deeds would match those of the villains who bestride the melodramas of Boucicault. One of his sports, it was said, was to organise 'shearing' parties. Shearing? Taking pot shots at their prey, a Papist priest.

Commander of the local yeomanry; a magistrate; a lecher who did not scruple to defile the marriage beds of his tenants, or to exercise his droits de seigneur by deflowering their daughters; a scoundrel with no compunction about burning down the derelict cabins of some of his tenants so as to 'improve the property' – the legends about Hugo have proliferated in north-eastern Wicklow. He died in 1809. His body lies behind formidable railings in Derralosarry churchyard. Perhaps it needed protection.

Robert Childers, brother of the late president of Ireland, Erskine Childers, and who lived at Glendalough House until his death early in 1997, had tales to tell of the man who had once owned the estate at Drummin, bordering Annamoe, and from whose son his family had purchased it in 1838. Having warned me that he was 'no historian', and was largely relying on hearsay, Mr Childers said he thought that Hugo was a Huguenot and that he was notorious in the Barton-Childers family. 'I'd heard that he was no gentleman,' he said, 'and that he gained his estate – about 15,000 acres spread over various parts of the district – by informing. To my knowledge he had four separate estates. He was reputed to have had many mistresses and to have made free with the daughters of his tenants.'

Mr Childers took me out of doors and pointed to a small square window set high off the ground. It was said that Hugo often sat in the room within. If set at the normal height, he would have been a sitting shot for his many enemies. Mr Childers pointed to a building known as 'the slaughter house'. Then he showed me the site of 'the murdering tree'.

'This I can tell you for a fact,' he said. 'I'd heard that Hugo would bind the men he intended to shoot to a tree which stood on that spot. My uncle, Robert Barton, had several trees out there cut down because the roots were causing seepage from the pond. The trees were taken to the sawmill to be cut up. Shards of metal flew out from the "murdering tree" when it came under the whirring blades. The trunk proved to be riddled with bullets.

'One of the properties sold in my lifetime was the old mill at Laragh,' he went on. When I visited the owner of the building, Mr Carstairs, he told me that he had heard of the dark doings of Hugo but was reluctant to be specific: 'Well, I'd heard that he had various molls in cottages spread about Drumeen.'

Others in the district spoke of Hugo's ways of forcing tenants to yield up their wives to him. Shane Bisgood, at one time manager of the estate at Drumeen, said, 'It was because Owen Byrne, a herdsman on the estate, refused to give up his wife that he had his house burned and was shot dead.'

More tales: Hugo had a mistress called Sal Lindsay, who was reared in the gardener's house. He shot a man called Mooney, whose widow became a beggar. If you travelled up the drive at dusk, the ghost of a grey woman might reach out and clutch you by the sleeve Hugo had many bastard children, among them Mary Healy, Neil Devitt and Andrew Thomas – the latter two afterwards serving in Joseph Holt's army. Andrew Thomas had once got possession of his father's blunderbuss, Roaring Bess, and lay in wait to ambush his father as he drove up the drive. He missed! In 1799 Andrew was shot dead at Castlekevin, decapitated, and the head displayed on a pike outside the Flannel Hall at Rathdrum.

'I never heard a good word about the man,' said that legendary seanchaí and historian, the late Billy Byrne of Glenmalure. On second thoughts, Billy said he could, after all, put in a good word for Hugo: Billy's great-grandfather's brother, Terry Byrne, of Glenwood, was a cow doctor who, as a United Irishmen, had a price on his head. Hugo's cattle were stricken with a mysterious disease. Only Terry, it seemed, might cure them. Provided immunity were granted him, Terry would come and do what he could. Hugo agreed and the cattle were cured. Later, Terry was arrested and sent to Cork harbour where he was put on a ship ready to be transported to Botany Bay. His wife appealed to Hugo, reminding him of his pledge, and Hugo wrote out a pardon on the spot. His wife hurried down to Cork, only to find that the ship had sailed three hours earlier. It had been scheduled to sail two or three days later and it was said that the date of departure had been put forward because word had gone ahead that Hugo might grant a pardon to Terry.

'I believe the family were connected with the Synges,' said Billy.

'I think the family later intermarried with the Stewarts and were connected with Parnell,' said Joan Kavanagh, curator of the Wicklow Heritage Centre.

The late Sheila Holt, of Roundwood, had heard that Hugo was once a humble blacksmith, the only one in the neighbourhood ready to shoe the horses of the English troops. 'For that he was given grants of land and began to make his way up in the world. His real name,' said Mrs Holt, 'was Hugh Gowan (i.e. Hugh, the smith). Later the name was shortened to Hugo.'

'He may have been descended from the Mac Hugos, a sub sept of the Bourkes of County Galway,' said Martin Timmons, of the Roundwood Historical Society. The former professor of history at University College, Galway, the late Tom O'Neill, also thought this possible; more likely, he said, than that Hugo was of Huguenot origin.

The memoirs of Luke Cullen provide more tales of the villain: Hugo, Robert Cotter and 'Big John' Gilbert plotted to strangle Father O'Toole; they invited him to dinner; when the priest was seated at table, Gilbert seized him from behind and attempted to throttle him; the murder was thwarted by the timely entrance of a maidservant.

Are such stories admissible in any serious attempt to evaluate the man? In view of Holt's naming of Hugo as the villain of *his* story, it would be folly, scholastically over-scrupulous, to ignore them. No doubt some are apocryphal but the persistence of the Hugo legend down to our own times surely suggests that some of the tales are founded on fact. Nor would the stories have grown up to fortify the reputation of Joseph Holt as the rebel-in-spite-of-himself painted by Thomas Crofton Croker, for no historian – not Madden, Lecky, Dickson – had ever had occasion to identify Hugo as the arch-villain named by Holt; by suppressing Hogo's name Croker had seen to that.

Of course, it must be allowed that, given Hugo's black reputation, Holt may have seized on this as a plausible justification and magnified a minor difference he had had with Hugo into an enormity which would affect the whole course of his life. If Hugo had actually earned the critical role Holt gives him, one might expect him to recur obsessively and rancorously in Holt's story: in fact, having told the reader that Hugo burned his house, far from dwelling on the subject Hugo thereafter scores only a few mentions in passing. Half way through this text there is an ironical reference to 'my old friend, Hugo'; and, dining with Lord Powerscourt, Holt reverts briefly to Hugo as the arch-villain when he proposes a toast, 'Bad luck to Thomas Hugo,' a toast, he suggests, to which his host does not fail to respond (see p. 111 above).

'Not a gentlemen?' Did Robert Childers mean this as a comment on Hugo's lowly social origins, or was he merely stating the obvious – that the man was a ruffian? I should have asked him.

8. HOLT WITNESSES AN 'EXEMPLARY' FLOGGING IN NEW SOUTH WALES

An extract from the Australian section of Holt's *Memoirs*

In 1800, after plans for a rebellion fomented by Irish convicts, many of them veterans of '98, had been foiled, a public flogging was carried out at Toongabbie, about twenty-five miles west of Sydney. Although Holt was exonerated, he was compelled to attend this example of what he might expect should he ever become involved in a rebellion. Here is Holt's riveting description of that flogging:

I did attend to the minute and we marched up to Toongabbie where all the government men was, and this was the plan – to give them the opportunity to see the punishment inflicted on several. There was one man of the name of Mauris Fitzgarrel [Maurice Fitzgerald] and he was ordered to receive three hundred lashes. The place they flogged them – their arms pull against a large tree and their breasts squeezed against the tree so the man had no power to cringe or stir. Father Harrel [Harold] was ordered to lay his [*illegible*] against the tree by the hand of the man that was flogging. There was two floggers – Richard Rice, and John Johnson, the hangmen from Sydney. Rice was a left handed man and Johnson was right handed, so they stood at each side, and I never saw two thrashers in a barn move their strokes more handier than those two man killers did. The moment they begun I turn my face round towards the other side, and one of the constables came and desired me to to turn and look on. I put my hand in my pocket and pull out my pen knife and swore I rip him from the navel to the chin. They all gather round me and would have ill used me but Mr Smyth came over and asked them who gave them any orders about me, so they were oblige to walk off. I cud compare them to a pack of hounds at the death of a hare, all yelping. I turned once about and, as it happened, I was to leeward of the floggers and I protest, though I was two perches from them, the flesh and skin blew in my face as they shook off the cats.

Fitzgarrel received his three hundred lashes. Doctor Mason – I never will forget him – he used to go to feel his puls, and he smiled and said, 'This man will tire you before he will fail. Go on.' It is against the law to flog a man past fifty lashes without a doctor and, during the time he was getting his punishment, he never gave as much as a word, only one and that was saying, 'Don't strike me on the neck. Flog me fair.' When he was let down, two of the constables went and took hold of him by the arms to help him in the cart, I was standing by. He said to them, 'Let my arms go!', struck both of them with his elbows in the pit of the stomach and knock them both down and then step in the cart. I heard Doctor Mason say, 'That man had strength enough to bear two hundred more.'

Next was tied up was Paddy Galvin, a young boy about twenty years of age, he was ordered to get three hundred lashes. He got one hundred on the back, and you could see his back bone between his shoulder blades. Then the doctor order him to get another hundred on his bottom. He got it, and then his haunches was in such a jelly the doctor order him to be flog on the calves of his legs. He got one hundred there and as much as a whimper he never gave. They asked him if he would tell where the pikes was hid. He said he did not know, and if, he would not tell: 'You may as well hang me now,' he says, 'for you never will get my music from me.'

So they put him in the cart and sent him to hospital.

There was two more got one hundred each and they sung out from first to last. One of their names – Mick Fitzgarrel, shoemaker by trade. Them three men was County Cork men, live near Sir Henry Browne Hayes.

SOURCE REFERENCES

Mitchell Library, Sydney (State Library of New South Wales): Holt manuscript MS A 2024

National Library of Ireland: newspapers as cited in footnotes.

National Archives (incorporating Irish State Papers Office etc.)
620 – 17/18, 20, 30/66; –35/48; – 37/43, 45, 127, 128, 210, 221; – 38/48, 51, 60, 93, 112, 114, 120, 126, 160, 243; – 39/9, 38, 69, 73, 80, 83–93, 219; – 40/36, 76, 139, 172; – 41/12, 39a; – 46/126; – 47/38; – 51/238.

Barrington, Jonah, *Historic Memoirs*, 1835
Byrne, Miles, *Memoirs*, 1863
Castlereagh, Viscount, *Memoirs and correspondence*, 1848
Costello, Con, *Botany Bay*, 1987
Croker, Thomas Crofton, *Memoirs of Joseph Holt, General of the Irish Rebellion in 1798. Edited from his original manuscript, in the possession of Sir William Betham*, two vols, 1838
Cullen, Brother Luke, *Memoirs*, 1948
——*Personal Recollections* and *Memoirs. ms 8339*
——*Personal recollections of Wexford and Wicklow insurgents of 1798*, 1959
Cullen, L.M., *Politics and rebellion: County Wicklow in the 1790s*
——*The emergence of modern Ireland*, 1981
Dickson, Charles, *The life of Michael Dwyer*, 1945
Elliott, Marianne, *Wolfe Tone*, 1989
Fitzpatrick, W.J., *The sham squire*, 1866
Foster, R.F., *Modern Ireland*, 1988
Gordon, Reverend James, *A history of the rebellion in Ireland of the year 1798*, 1803
Joyce, J., *General Thomas Cloney, a Wexford rebel of 1798*, 1988
Lecky, W.E.M., *A history of Ireland in the eighteenth century*, 1902
Madden, Richard, R., *The United Irishmen: Their lives and times*, 1846
——*Down and Antrim in '98*
Maxwell, W.H., *History of the Irish rebellion in 1798*, 1845
Musgrave, Sir Richard, *Memoirs of the different rebellions*, 1801
O'Donnell, Ruan, 'General Joseph Holt and the Rebellion of 1798 in Co. Wicklow', MA thesis, University College, Dublin, 1991,
O'Farrell, Patrick, *The Irish in Australia*, 1987
O'Shaughnessy, Peter, *A rum story (Joseph Holt in New South Wales)*, 1988
Pakenham, Thomas, *The year of liberty*, 1969
Sheedy, Kieran, *Upon the mercy of government*, 1988
Teeling, Charles Hamilton, *The Irish rebellion of 1798 and Sequel*, 1876
Tone, Theobald Wolfe, *Life of... written by himself and continued by his son; with his political writings and fragments of his diary*, 1826

INDEX

Alcock, William Henry, 131, 132, 136
Allen, Miss, 75
Allen, Mr, of Glenmalure, 74, 75, 76
Anacurragh, 80
Ancient British Dragoons, 44, 144, 147, 149
Annamoe, 21, 122
Antrim Militia, 27, 30, 33, 60, 61, 64, 73, 162
Archer, Dr, 128f
Archer, Capt. Thomas, of Mount John, 15
Archbold, Capt. of dragoons, 51
Ardee, 47
Arklow, 34, 35, 43, 60, 61, 66, 73, 143, 161
Armstrong, Capt. John, 30
Armstrong, Capt. Philip, 162
Arnold, John, 32, 42, 78
Ashford, 78
Ashtown, 21
Athdown, 69, 100, 161
Aughavannagh, 46, 61, 96, 143
Aughrim, 41, 78, 80, 82
Avoca, 20
Avonbeg river, 93
Avonmore river, 94
Aylmer, Sir Fenton, 48
Aylmer, William, of Painstown, 48, 56, 105

Bahana, 110, 159
Ballawley Hill, 107
Ballinacor, 20, 31
Ballinacorbeg, 90
Ballinalea, 32
Ballinamuck, 78
Ballinascorney, 31, 35
Ballinastoe, 120
Ballinvalla Hill, 34, 36
Ballyarthur, 73
Ballyboy, 59, 76, 77
Ballyconnell, 79, 86
Ballycrystal, 22, 23
Ballycurragh, 42, 45, 66
Ballycurry, nr Devil's Glen, 32, 33
Ballydaniel, 19, 100

Ballydonnell: see Ballydaniel
Ballyellis, 42, 43, 144, 149
Ballyfad, 162
Ballyfolan pass, 57
Ballyhack, 126
Ballyhara, 80
Ballylow, 57
Ballymahon, 46
Ballymanus, 39, 41, 45, 66, 79, 83
Ballymaurin, 152
Ballymoneen, 19
Ballymore-Eustace, 58
Ballynabrocky, 69, 71, 99, 110
Ballynakill, 117
Ballynastockan, 71
Ballynatona, 104
Ballyrahan House, 23, 24, 42
Ballysmutten, 161
Ballyteige, 78
Ballyvore, 46
Baltiboys, 88
Baravore, 58
Barrington, Charles, 135
Barrington, Sir Jonah, 140
Barry, Richard, prisoner, 36
Barton, Robert, of Glendalough, 166
Barton-Childers family, 166
Beauparc, Co. Meath, 47
Begly, Joseph, prisoner, 98, 103
Bell, Thomas, of Delgany, 21
Bellevue, 126
Benson, Parson, of nr Baltiboys, 89
Beresford, Lady Frances, 120
Beresford, Brig.-Gen. W.C., 55
Betham, Sir William, 16f, 37, 74, 81, 137f
Bisgood, Shane, 127
Black Ditches, 39, 40, 59, 67, 68, 88, 102
Blackmore Hill, 34, 37, 47, 154
Blackwater region of Wexford, 64
Blacquière, Sir John, 20, 119, 133
Blessington, 58, 60, 67, 88, 90, 160
Bluebank Hill, 85
Bohernabreena, 31, 56
Boland, W., from Aughrim, 80, 83
Booterstown, Co. Dublin, 39

Bolton, William, carpenter, 129
Bonaparte, Napoleon, 104
Bond, Oliver, 105, 114
Bond Men of Cronebane, 84, 85
Botany Bay, 118, 123, 139, 167
Bourke, Governor of NSW, 130
Boyd, James, magistrate, 144
Bradnor, Thomas, 22
Brady, from nr Ballymore, 46
Brady, of Ballinalough, 109
Brady, Bryan, 95
Brady, Edward, 27
Brady, Edward, of Ballinacorbeg, 31
Brady, Thomas, 26, 32
Brady, Thomas, clerk, 124, 125
Brady, William, of Ballynatona, 104
Brady, Capt. William, of Roundwood, 160
Bray, 155
Brest, 101
Browne, Valentine, robber, 110, 163
Brownrigg, Thomas, 120, 121
Broadleas, 46
Bryan, Capt., 116
Buckingham, marquis of, 48
Bulger, of Ballycrystal, 22
Bunclody: see Newtownbarry
Buncrana, 105
Burbridge, 162
Butler, James, of Devil's Glen, 163
Butt, Isaac, 17, 146
Butter Mountain, 57, 106
Byrne, Andrew, 161
Byrne, Ann, 58, 70, 74
Byrne, Billy, of Glenmalure, 167
Byrne, Brian, sealer, 20
Byrne, Bryan, of Roundwood, 119
Byrne, General Garret, 26, 34, 38, 39, 40, 42, 49, 50, 54, 56, 105, 145, 151, 155
Byrne, Garret, the elder, of Ballymanus, 23
Byrne, Jackey, of Anghavanna, 96, 97f
Byrne, James, of Imail, 72
Byrne, John, of nr Seven Churches, 161, 162

172

Index

Byrne, Laughlin, of Ashtown, 21
Byrne, Martin, alnager, 20, 119, 120
Byrne, Matthew, of Luggala, 160
Byrne, Miles, 23, 45, 64, 73, 74, 104, 140, 141, 149, 150
Byrne, Miles, of Ballynabarney, 30
Byrne, Owen, from nr Luggala, 159, 160
Byrne, Ted, of Glenwood, 167
Byrne, Terence, of Luggala, 159, 160
Byrne, Thomas, plasterer, 128
Byrne, William (Billy), 30

Carlow, 157
Carlow militia, 162
Camden, Lord, lord lieutenant, 26, 27, 38, 109
Canning, Lord, 112, 113
Carberry, Darby, rogue, 160
Carbury hill, 49
Carleton, Oliver, 158
Carnew, 22, 30, 44, 45, 139, 149, 153
Carr, Samuel, from Armagh, 124
Carrig, east Wicklow, 37
Carrigroe, 49
Cary's Field, 56
Castlecarbury, 49, 57
Castle Inn, Dublin, 114, 115
Castlekevin, 122, 167
Castlemacadam, 19, 121
Castlereagh, Lord, 101, 109
Castlepollard, 55
Castletown, 63
Cavan militia, 161
Celbridge, 63
Chamney, of Ballyrahan, 24
Chapman, prisoner, 78
Childers, Robert, 166, 168
Clarke, Mary Anne, mistress to duke of York, 69
Classon, a farmer nr Roundwood, 161
Cloghogue, 28, 35f
Clonard, 48–50, 57
Clone, 59, 60, 61, 80
Coates, Charles, of Clone, 44, 80, 81
Cotter, Robert, 167
Colthurst, William, 35, 38, 156, 159, 164f
Connell, prisoner, 61
Connolly, Bart, 54
Connor, James, of Hacklestown, 69
Conway, who kills Holl's brother, 97

Cook, Edward, Under-Secretary, 35, 58, 101, 109, 158
Coolgreany, 61, 149
Coolattin, 66
Coolattin Yeomanry, 24
Corbet Hill, New Ross, 34
Cornwall Bank, 124
Cornwallis, Lord, lord lieutenant, 38, 56, 60, 67, 116, 125, 144, 145, 147, 153, 158
Corragen, Capt., 70, 74
Cox, Capt., Wm, 129, 130, 133ff
Cox, convict, 164
Craig, Lt-Gen., 61, 63, 87. 148, 157
Crawford, Sir James, 104
Critchley, Abraham, of Derrybawn, county treasurer, 29, 31
Critchley, John, of Laragh, 31
Critchley, T.W., informer, 157
Croghan nr Arklow, 61
Croghan Hill, 39, 67, 149
Croker, Thomas Crofton, 16f, 19, 25, 37, 70, 74, 76, 88, 146, 147, 168
Cronebane, 73, 74, 84, 85
Croughan mountain, 144
Crumlin, W. Dublin, 55
Cuffe, Farrell, schoolmaster, 124
Cullen, Bro. Luke, 16, 20, 26, 29, 39, 42, 44, 51, 63, 67, 75, 82, 91, 140, 151, 168
Cullentragh, 93

Dalton, Capt., 50
Davis, John, cutler, 124
Dean, Charles, apprentice, 124
Defenderism, 87, 120, 130
Delany, John, of Roundwood, 99
Delgany, 55
Derralossary, 163, 166
Derrybawn, 93
Derry river nr Tinahely, 80
Desmond, convict, 164
Devil's Glen, 31, 32, 163
Devinan, 23
Devitt, James, of Ballincor, 90
Devitt, Neil, 31, 167
Dickson, Charles, 19, 168
Dieman, Commissary, 34
Dixon, Fr, 41
Dixon, Madge, 41
Djouce, 110
Dobbs, 23
Dobson, Christopher, 123–9 passim
Dogherty, Patrick, of Carlow, 70, 86, 90
Dolan, Croppy Biddy, 57, 66, 67, 70, 151ff,
Dollardstown, 47
Donard, 49, 60, 154, 155
Donegal, 105
Donnelan, Fr, of Black Ditches, 39
Donohoe, James, 103
Douglas, William, quartermaster, 129
Dowling, informant of Cullen, 39
Downes, Henry, 88, 90, 91
Doyle, John, of Aughrim, 141
Doyle, Col. Matthew, 16, 26, 32, 65, 73, 87, 91, 92, 93, 97, 98, 156, 157, 165f
Doyne, Daniel, 54
Drummin, 26, 28, 93, 167
Dry, Richard, 124, 164
Dry, Sir Richard, 124
Dublin militia, 162
Duckett, William, 67, 104
Dudgeon, Mr, 65
Dumbartons, 33
Dunboyne, 47
Dundas, General, 63
Dun Laoghaire, 95, 137, 138
Dunlavin cavalry, 119
Dundrum, 105, 115
Durham Fencibles, 162
Dwyer, Michael, 45, 59, 63, 91, 141, 143, 145, 150

Eardly, Francis, 21
Edenderry, 117, 124
Edge, David, prisoner, 36
Edge, William, prisoner, 36
Edwards, of White Rock, 31
Eighty-ninth Regiment, 60
Elliott, Marianne, 28
Elephant Inn, Eustace St, Dublin, 158
Emmet, Robert, 105
Enniskerry, 113, 155
Eustace, Garret, 71
Ewes, Jonathan, of nr Baltiboys, 88, 91

Fabian's Chronicles, 25
Fancy Mountain, 36
Fananierin, 76, 77
Farringtons, of Talbotstown, 119
Fermanagh militia, 30
Finnamore, Mr, landowner, 46
Fitzgerald, Anthony, 38, 42
Fitzgerald, Capt., 156, 164
Fitzgerald, Edward, 45, 105
Fitzgerald, Lord Edward, 63, 151

Fitzgerald, Capt. of 32nd Reg. of Foot, 20
Fitzgerald, Maurice, shoemaker, 169
Fitzwilliam, earl of, 24, 152
Fleming, Thomas, magistrate, 19
Fulton, Revd Henry, 130, 133, 136

Galvin, Paddy, 169
Garristown, 47
Gowan, Henry, 23, 24
Gowan, John Hunter, of Mount Nebo, 23, 78–80, 144
Gilbert, 'Big John', 168
Glandisoun, 34, 36
Glenasmole, 106
Glenbride, 59, 61, 101, 102
Glendalough, 58
Glendalough House, 166
Glenmacnass, 42, 94, 103
Glenmalure, 46, 54, 57, 58, 59, 73, 77, 90, 93, 141, 155
Golden Ball, 113
Goodpay (Peter Kavanagh), 73f
Gore, Capt. Robert, of Sea View, 122
Gorey, 49, 149
Gough, from nr Clone, 44
Gough, Col., 50
Grogan, Cornelius, executed, 43
Greenane, nr Rathdrum, 73, 74, 75, 91, 141, 142
Greendrake, Gregory, tourist, 56
Grogan, Knox, 43
Guinness, Counsellor, 29

Hacket, Capt., 82
Hacketstown, 34, 37, 60, 149, 155, 157
Hamilton, Archibald, 144
Harburton, Lord, 49
Hardy, Major Joseph, 20, 26, 27, 28, 31, 148, 158
Harkins, Thomas, prisoner, 156
Harman brothers, 162
Harney, Pierce, 57, 58, 73, 141, 148
Harold, Fr, 131, 169
Harris, Thomas and John, robbers, 160
Harrison, chief mate, 129, 130
Hatton, 162
Hamburg, 104
Hayes, Sir Henry Browne, 169
Hayes, Michael, 126, 131
Healy, Mary, 167
Hellfire Club, 56
Hendrick, William, constable, 24, 25

Henry, William, from Armagh, 124
Hessians, 67, 101
Higginbotham, 21
Hobbs, Sergeant, 133
Hobbs, Mrs, midwife, 135f
Hoche, 105, 106
Hodges, John, 28
Hoey, Oliver, of Knockalt, 67, 78, 95
Hoey, William, 74
Hoey, Mr, murdered, 119
Holligan, Barney, of Kings Co. Militia, 89
Hollogan, *see* Corragen
Hollybrook, nr Bray, 31
Holly Park, Rathfarnham, 55, 110
Hollywood Glen, 40, 90
Holt, Hester, wife of Joseph, 20, 31, 73f, 80, 91–6, 100f, 106, 110, 113, 115, 117, 120, 130, 132, 135f, 137, 147
Holt, John, father of Joseph, 19
Holt, Jonathan, brother of Joseph, 19, 96
Holt, Joseph Harrison, son of Joseph, 136
Holt, Joshua, son of Joseph, 19, 95, 133
Holt, Marianne, daughter of Joseph, 19, 95, 99, 126
Holt, Mary, sister of Joseph, 19
Holt, Sheila, 167
Holt, William, brother of Joseph, 19, 83, 87, 97
Hornidge, Cuddy, 46
Howe, second mate, 129
Howlet, Tom, 79
Hoyle, Oliver: *see* Hoey, Oliver
Hughes, Capt., 61
Hughes, widow, 22
Hugo, Elizabeth, 30
Hugo, Thomas, of Drummin, 26–9, 30, 31, 33, 78, 111, 116, 122, 159, 160, 166ff
Hugo, Capt. Thomas, 31, 71
Humbert, General, 60, 53, 66, 78
Hume, MP, 95, 97
Hunter, John, governor of NSW, 130, 135
Hutchinson, Sir Francis, 33
Hynes, Justice, 40

Imail, Glen of, 59, 60, 67, 71, 77, 96, 97, 98, 104, 127, 143
Imaal: *see* Imail

Jacob, Justice, of Ballycrystal, 23, 144

James, alderman, 163, 165
James, William, informer, 58
Johnson, John, flogger, 169
Johnson, Richard, farmer from Kippure, 56
Jones, Sergeant William, and wife, 83, 85
Joseph, François, French soldier, 63, 65, 67, 71, 72, 86, 88

Kavanagh, Mrs, 78
Kavanagh, James, innkeeper of Roundwood, 27, 36
Kavanagh, James, of Athdown, 160
Kavanagh, Joan, 167
Kavanagh, Patrick, of Tallyho, 42
Kavanagh, Peter, ex Antrim militia, 73
Kavanagh, Thomas and wife, of Ashford bridge, 33
Kearney, Simon and Mrs, of Ballydonnell, 57, 100f
Kearns, leader, 54
Kearns, Andrew and wife, of Knockrea, 51, 52
Kearns, Fr Moses, 48, 49, 105, 151
Kearns, George, 153
Kearns, Michael, of Baltinglass, 150
Keegan, William, of Bahana, 159
Keenan, Pat, 28
Keenan, Thomas, 25
Kelly, James, deserter from Ancient Britons, 45
Kenna, from Stratford-on-Slaney, 150
Kennedy, James, of Navan, 53f
Kent, Mrs William, 130, 132
Keogh, miller from Whilestown, 91
Kiladuff, 61
Kilcock, 47
Kilcullen, 64
Kildare militia, 162
Kilkenny, 104, 105
Killacloran, 80
Killala, Co. Mayo, 59, 60, 104, 144, 145, 164
Kilmanoge, 61
Kincaid, John, from Armagh, 124
King, governor of NSW, 135
King, Thomas, magistrate, of Rathdrum, 26, 27, 31, 84, 86, 122, 152, 153
Kings County militia, 64, 73, 82, 89, 92, 96, 157, 161, 162
Kingsley, Katty, 163
King's river, 88

Index

Kingstown: *see* Dun Laoghlaire

Kilcarn, Navan, 54
Kirakee, 30
Kippure, 56, 99, 110
Kirwan, Mrs, 57, 59, 69
Knockalt, 59, 66, 67, 78, 88, 99, 119
Knockadroose, 59, 78, 96, 98
Knockananna, 82
Knockfinn, 93
Knockrea, 53
Kyan, Esmond, 39, 54, 105, 151

Lackan, 37
Lacy, John, metal founder, 124
Lake, General, 27, 109
Lannin, William, 41
Laragh, 93, 167
La Touche, David, 125
La Touche, Mrs Peter, 30, 75, 101, 102, 108, 123, 125, 129, 147, 163f
La Touche, Peter, 57, 125, 126, 129
Lecky, W.E.H., 168
Lee, Mr, headmaster at Carnew (1997), 44
Lees, John, 95
Leeson, Lord, 71
Leitrim Light Coy, 64, 68, 73, 162
Lennan, William, tailor, 155
Lennon, William, 36
Lewins, Thomas, 84
Limes, Christopher, of Knockraheen, 21
Lindsay, Sal, 167
Lively, 129
Lockstown, 39
Long (alias of Holt), 107
Long, Mrs, née Manning (Hester Holt's mother), of Roundwood, 20, 95
Longford, 60
Longwood, nr Clonard, 50, 54, 57
Lough Dan, 94
Low, John, 19
Lowe, Fr, of Derralossory, 163
Luggala, 34, 57, 61, 97, 99, 164, 159
Lugnaquillia, 127

McCabe, William Putnam, 145f
McClatchy, James, sub-sheriff, 31
Mcdonald, Capt. Roderick, of Glengarry Highlanders, 69
McDonnell, Matthew, 103
McEvoy, John, 73, 75, 79

McGrath, widow, of Athdown, 57, 69, 70
McLaren, Archibald, 33
McMahon, Col., attorney, 35f, 57, 154, 157, 158
McNevin, 105
Macoon, Maurice, 103
Macquarie, Governor Lachlan, 124, 137
McQuirke, William, 161
Macreddin Hill, 79
Madden, R.R., 145, 168
Malahide, 88
Manning, George, of Ballyleige, 78
Mannings, J. Holt's in-laws, 95
Marks, prisoner, 78
Marsden, Castle official, 114, 163
Martin, Friar John, of Drogheda, 35, 156
Mason, Dr, 169
Meath, earl of, 108
Merrigan, Patrick, 29
Miley, Miles, publican, 90, 93
Military Road, 58
Milltown, Co. Dublin, 113
Minerva, 124, 128, 129, 131, 132
Monaseed, 42, 149
Moneystown, 21, 162
Monkstown, Co. Dublin, 19
Monck, Lord, 109, 120, 156, 158, 159, 165
Montpelier House, 56
Mooney, John, 'Antrim John', 61, 75
Moore, General John, 60, 85, 91, 143
Moore, John, 97
Moore, Thomas Inglis, 15
Moreton, Henry, JP, 24
Moreton, James, of Ballyrahan, 24
Morgan, John, 25
Mount Venus, 156
'Moving Magazine' 37, 59, 68, 76, 78, 92
Mucklagh Hill, 85
Mullawnasmear, 22
Mullally, Patrick, of nr Athdown, 99, 101, 102, 111
Mullenraymond, 31
Mullinaveigue, 26, 30, 33, 94, 96
Murphy, Capt., 154, 155
Murphy, 65
Murphy, Nicholas, of Monaseed, 67, 144f
Murray, Stephen, of Gorey, 54
Musgrave, Sir Richard, 27, 28, 32, 76, 147
Myers, Major-General William, 128, 133f

Nailor, Daniel, miller, 27, 31
Napier, Lady Sarah, 63, 98
Navan, 53
Needham, Susy, 55
Nelson, Horatio, 105
Neil, Capt., 157, 158f
Neil, Henry, trumpeter, 151
Neill, Thomas, of nr Ballycrystal, 22
Neilson, 105
Newbridge, 78, 162
New Ross, 34
New South Wales, State Library of, 138
Newtownmountkennedy, 22, 23, 28, 33, 46, 48, 51, 121, 122, 147–9, 155
Nore mutiny, 104, 123
Norfolk Island, 66, 124, 130, 131
Nowland, Charles, 161
Nowland, Garret, 161
Nowland, Long Peter, of Luggala, 159
Nugent, leader, 65, 156
Nun's Cross, 20

Oaklands, 157
Oakwood, 78, 88, 95, 99, 157, 161
O'Bryan, James, informer, 114ff, 120
O'Connor, Dr, 131, 132
O'Conor, Denis, 102
O'Connor, Arthur, 105, 114
O'Donnell, Ruan, 35, 50, 89
Oldbridge, 93, 94
O'Neill, John, 52
O'Neill, John, 'John Antrim', 79, 82, 96, 97
O'Neill, John, from Redmills, 118, 120
O'Neill, rebel capt., 39, 40
O'Neill, Capt., 157
O'Neill, Professor T.P., 168
O'Rourke, rebel leader, 65
O'Toole, Phelim, of Annamoe, 37
O'Toole, Susy, 37

Parsons, Laurence, 44
Parsons, Thomas, 44
Passage West, 125, 163
Patten, Lt., of Armagh Regiment, 44
Perry, Capt. Anthony, 38, 39, 40, 42, 49, 105, 151
Philips, Tom, bailiff, 152
Phillipps, Sir Thomas, 138
Pigeon House, Dublin,, 95, 123
Pilsworth, Ponsonby, 39, 41, 118

Piperstown, 56
Plough Inn, Dublin, 137
Pluck, Lt., 69
Polyphemus, 128
Ponsonby, Ann, 114
Powerscourt, Lord, 27, 36, 101, 102, 106ff, 119, 120, 122, 147, 154, 155, 159, 165, 168
Price, Andrew, of Roundwood, 20, 21, 28, 31, 33, 34, 36, 37, 95, 96
Prosperous, 48

Radcliffe, Mr, of Ballymahon, 46
Rathcoole, 131
Rathdrum, 26, 32, 41, 58, 73, 75, 84, 141, 142, 155, 167
Rathfarnham, 35, 69, 156
Read, Walter, executed, 37
Redcross, 19
Redwells, 19, 118
Reilly, widow, of Knockalt, 99
Repton, William, robber, 110
Rice, Francis, constable, 24, 25
Richard, Richard, flogger, 169
Richmond, duke of, 63
Roche, General Edward, 45, 47, 105, 150, 151
Robertstown, 49
Robuste, 105
Rochford, Col., of Carlow militia, 162
Roddenagh, 41, 64, 79, 80, 83
Rogers, Patrick, robber, 21, 23ff, 40
Ross, Major, 133ff
Rossmore, Lord, 120, 121, 122
Roundwood, 20, 21, 24, 26, 28, 30, 90, 92, 99, 154, 159
Rourke, Felix, 48
Royal Artillery, 117
Royal Irish Dragoons, 121
Russborough House, 71, 163
Ryan, young prisoner, 81
Ryndville Hill, 50

St Leger, John, 127, 132
Salkeld, Capt., 129, 130, 132, 135
Sally, Felim, 37
Sally Gap, 35
Saul, Edward, 32
Scurlock's Leap, 57, 104
Seven Churches, 36, 47, 53, 78, 94, 141, 154, 155, 160
Shaw, William, son-in-law of J. Holt, 19, 126, 157, 158
Sheilstown, 62, 66
Shillelagh, 143
Short, Martin, carpenter, 129
Skerrett, General, 61, 62
Sinnott, Martin, coiner, 25
Sirr, Major, 41, 89, 114, 116, 118, 158
Sleamaine, 99
Slieveboy, 45, 46
Sligo militia, 162
Smullen, of Devil's Glen, 163
Smyth, innkeeper at Roundwood, 159
Snell, Samuel, 78
Sorrell Hill, 37
Spithead mutiny, 104, 123
Stackallan, Co. Meath, 47
Shelmaliers, 76
Strangford, Lord, 17
Summerhill, 47
Sutton, Lt. John, 73
Swan, Hunter, 158
Sweeney, Mr, of Bray, 19
Sydney, NSW, 44, 168
Synge, Francis, 36, 146, 154, 167

Taaffe, Revd Denis, 150
Talbotstown, 119
Tallyho, 42
Tara, Co. Meath, 47
Taylor, historian, 32
Teeling, 32, 48
Templelogue, 156
Thomas, Andrew, 122, 162, 167
Thomson, Joseph, prisoner, 36
Thompson, John, woodranger, 154ff
Three Lough Mountain, 57, 107
Tigh Linn, 20
Tighe, Sarah, 114
Timahoe, 48
Timmons, Martin, 167
Tinahely, 24, 42, 60, 61, 80, 81
Tinahely Yeomanry, 24
Tinnahinch, 38
Tone, Theobald Wolfe, 18, 65, 67, 105, 106
Toole, Luke, of Annamoe, 21
Tottenham, Mrs Ann, of Woodstock, 30, 33
Tottenham, Mr, 146
Tounrel, Ralph, of Tinahely, 24
Twenty-fourth Light Dragoons, 127
Tyrell, Lt. of Yeomanry, 49

Valleymount, 39
Van Diemens Land, 124
Vartry river, 29, 31
Vereker, Col., 50
Vinegar Hill, 38, 40, 66

Wafer, Michael, 160
Wainright, Capt., 152, 153
Walker, Parson, 130
Wallis, Samuel, of Old Court, 160
Walsh, Jon, of Bonavalley, 161
Warder, Patrick, hatter, 162
Warren, Sir John Borlage, 105, 158
Waterford, marquis of, 90, 165
Weekes, Revd Dr, 122f
Weekes, William, of Annamoe, 31
Whelan, Professor Kevin, 15
Whelp Rock, 35ff, 46, 56, 57, 59, 60, 66, 69, 117, 154, 157
White, Edward, of Ballybrocky, 69, 70
White, Hawtry, 144
White Rock, 31
Wicklow Gap, 42, 45
Wicklow town, 155
Wiggan, Sergeant, 128
Whaley's Abbey, 69, 84
Whaley, Buck, 68, 69, 93
Whaley, 'Burn Chapel', 69
Wright, 107

York, duke of, 68